A Revolutionary Woman

A Revolutionary Woman

Elizabeth Freeman and the Abolition of Slavery in the North

Donna Tesiero

McFarland & Company, Inc., Publishers
Jefferson, North Carolina

LIBRARY OF CONGRESS CATALOGING-IN-PUBLICATION DATA

Names: Tesiero, Donna, 1954– author.
Title: A revolutionary woman : Elizabeth Freeman and the abolition of slavery in the North / Donna Tesiero.
Other titles: Elizabeth Freeman and the abolition of slavery in the North
Description: Jefferson, North Carolina : McFarland & Company, Inc., Publishers, 2024 | Includes bibliographical references and index.
Identifiers: LCCN 2023057579 | ISBN 9781476694535 (print) ∞
  ISBN 9781476653754 (ebook)
Subjects: LCSH: Freeman, Elizabeth, 1744?–1829. | Enslaved women—Massachusetts—Biography. | Enslaved persons—Massachusetts—Biography. | African American women—Massachusetts—Biography. | Slavery—Massachusetts—History—18th century. | Freeman, Elizabeth, 1744?–1829—Trials, litigation, etc. | Massachusetts—Biography.
Classification: LCC E444.F87 T47 2024 | DDC 974.400496/0730092 [B]—dc23/eng/20231220
LC record available at https://lccn.loc.gov/2023057579

BRITISH LIBRARY CATALOGUING DATA ARE AVAILABLE

ISBN (print) 978-1-4766-9453-5
ISBN (ebook) 978-1-4766-5375-4

© 2024 Donna Tesiero. All rights reserved

No part of this book may be reproduced or transmitted in any form or by any means, electronic or mechanical, including photocopying or recording, or by any information storage and retrieval system, without permission in writing from the publisher.

Front cover image: Elizabeth Freeman, watercolor on ivory by Susan Anne Livingston Ridley Sedgwick, 1811, (Massachusetts Historical Society); background © Elninho/Shutterstock

Printed in the United States of America

McFarland & Company, Inc., Publishers
  Box 611, Jefferson, North Carolina 28640
    www.mcfarlandpub.com

For my children, their spouses, and my grandchildren,
and in memory of my parents, Donald and Janet Tesiero

Acknowledgments

Many people helped bring this book to fruition. I am grateful to my wonderful editor, Elizabeth Foxwell, who believed in the book, and the rest of the staff at McFarland who have assisted me throughout the publication process.

I'd like to express my appreciation for the assistance rendered throughout the book's research phase by the staffs of the Massachusetts Historical Society, the Stockbridge Library Museum & Archives, the Berkshire Historical Society, and the Boston Public Library, as well as the docents at the Ashley House in Sheffield, Massachusetts, and the Mission House in Stockbridge, Massachusetts, both properties of The Trustees of Reservations.

I am also grateful to Stephen Kendrick, who read an early draft of the book, and to Jamie Katz, who offered me important insights about the world of publishing. My thanks to my parents, who encouraged my love of history as a child, and to my teachers at Cornell, who honed my critical thinking and research skills and deepened my fascination with American history and women's history. Finally, a loving thank you to my children, Maria, Donnie, Lisa, and Tom, who have given me their love and enthusiastic support throughout the research and writing of this book.

Table of Contents

Acknowledgments — vi
Preface — 1
Introduction — 5

1. Beginnings — 7
2. "Which was the slave and which was the real mistress?" — 22
3. Revolutions Near and Far — 33
4. A New Life and America's Second Rebellion — 48
5. Raising a Family and Building a Government — 61
6. "The main pillar of our household" — 72
7. A Brilliant Career, a Blind Eye — 86
8. A Place of Her Own and a Long Goodbye — 104
9. Big Decisions — 119
10. A Mother to Them All — 134
11. Sunset — 145

Epilogue — 157
Chapter Notes — 161
Bibliography — 181
Index — 185

Preface

As I set out to learn more about the remarkable woman who helped bring about the abolition of slavery in Massachusetts, provided skilled midwifery and nursing services to scores of residents in her western Massachusetts community for decades, and made it possible for one of the most influential Federalist political figures of the 1790s to be largely absent from home while she administered his household and cared for his many children and invalid wife, I faced the sad fact that as an enslaved person, Elizabeth Freeman had never been taught to read or write.

As a result, it was necessary to turn to the voices of the people she so lovingly raised, primarily Henry, Catharine Maria, and Charles Sedgwick, to learn many of her life's details and to gain an understanding of her personality, character, and ethics. This is, of course, not the same as hearing directly from the person herself, but because the Sedgwick children regarded her as their foster mother, their efforts to preserve her memory do supply important knowledge and provide a lens through which to view her life and accomplishments.

During my research, I had the opportunity to explore the voluminous archives available at the Massachusetts Historical Society (MHS). The Sedgwick Family Papers provided original letters that painted a vivid picture of the joys and challenges Elizabeth Freeman faced during her long career as the Sedgwick family governess, nurse, and household administrator, as did the Catharine Maria Sedgwick Papers available on microfilm at MHS, with a duplicate set available at the Boston Public Library. In addition to holdings at MHS, *Letters of Charles Sedgwick to His Family and Friends*, *The Power of Her Sympathy: The Autobiography and Journal of Catharine Maria Sedgwick*, and *Early Letters of Mark Hopkins and Others from His Brothers and Their*

Preface

Mother provided more information and additional perspectives of the Sedgwick family, as well as Elizabeth Freeman's next-door neighbors, the Hopkins family.

But, of course, no matter how much the Sedgwick children loved Elizabeth Freeman—and they clearly did—they inevitably viewed her life through the prism of their own race and class. I found several books particularly important in helping me provide a much more complete picture of what it was like to be an enslaved person, and later a freedwoman, in eighteenth-century and early nineteenth-century western Massachusetts. Emilie Piper and David Levinson's *One Minute a Free Woman: Elizabeth Freeman and the Struggle for Freedom*, Bernard A. Drew's *If They Close the Door on You, Go in the Window*, and *The Autobiography of W.E.B. DuBois* each provided invaluable information about the vibrant African American communities in Sheffield and Stockbridge, which were the anchor of Elizabeth Freeman's life.

Visits to the scenes of Elizabeth Freeman's life also added color to her story. The Ashley House in Sheffield, where she was enslaved for a quarter of a century, still exists as a museum under the stewardship of The Trustees of Reservations, as does the Mission House in Stockbridge, which was the home of Pamela Sedgwick's mother. Though Elizabeth Freeman's farmhouse no longer exists, it is possible to walk to the site of her farm on Cherry Hill Road and get a sense of the natural beauty and peacefulness of the refuge she purchased for herself and her family with the hard-earned wages of her post-slavery labor.

Finally, a word about terminology. In most of my references to Elizabeth Freeman's ethnic and racial identity, I refer to her as "African American." I do so because I believe this is probably how she thought of herself—a person of African ethnicity who had lived her life in America. One or both of Elizabeth's parents may have spent part of their early lives in Africa; certainly some of the enslaved persons she lived and worked with in Claverack and Sheffield had done so. Africa was a real place to her, from which her family originated. She lived a long life in America, much of it as a free woman, which, together with her husband's service in the American Revolution, would have contributed to her embracing the second half of the description as rightfully hers as well.

Preface

Also, there are a few places in the book where the term "master" or "mistress" is used when referring to John or Hannah Ashley's relationship to Elizabeth Freeman prior to the landmark legal case that emancipated her. Twenty-first-century minds recognize that John and Hannah Ashley were her enslavers, but because Elizabeth used the terms "master" and "mistress" when describing her life in the Ashley household to members of the Sedgwick family, I have used those terms when it makes historical sense in the retelling of her story.

Introduction

Most Americans think of slavery as a southern institution, but on the eve of the American Revolution, every northern colony permitted slavery. In New York, at the time of Elizabeth Freeman's birth in the mid–1740s, more than 9,000 "Negroes" were living in the colony, most of them enslaved people. By the time Elizabeth's first master, Pieter Hogeboom, transferred her services to his daughter and son-in-law, Hannah and John Ashley, in the mid–1750s, more than 13,000 "Negroes" were in the colony of New York. These numbers continued to increase, reaching a high mark of about 20,000 enslaved people in the early 1770s. The last enslaved people living in the state of New York would not be freed until 1827.[1]

This could have been Elizabeth Freeman's fate. Hers turned out otherwise because of different labor conditions and less egregious laws in Massachusetts, the colony where she would be a slave for a quarter of a century, and because of her own determination to free herself and her young daughter. This is her story.

1

Beginnings

As the American Revolution came to a close, a Patriot war widow considered her options. Elizabeth Freeman and her young daughter were slaves of a prominent family in Berkshire County, Massachusetts. At the beginning of the war, her husband had enlisted with the Americans, probably in the hope of gaining his freedom and then eventually purchasing his wife and daughter from their master. Elizabeth had clung to that hope as she bid him goodbye, but he had never returned home. Now, as the white citizens of Berkshire County exulted in their new freedoms, Elizabeth wondered if the high-sounding principles of the Declaration of Independence and the new Massachusetts state constitution applied to her. Her determination to find out would have consequences for thousands of other Massachusetts slaves.

In about 1744, on a large farm in Claverack, New York, not far from the banks of the Hudson River, a female slave child was born. As with most slaves, there was no formal recognition of her arrival—no birth or baptismal record. Many decades later, the people whom she regarded as her foster children would make their best estimate of her birth year. When she died at the end of 1829 and they buried her in their family plot, the marker they placed there set her age at eighty-five years old.[1]

After the American Revolution, as a free woman, the slave child who was known as Bet would take the name Elizabeth Freeman and would be employed for more than twenty-five years in the home of Theodore and Pamela Sedgwick, acting as governess to their children and the manager of their household. It would be a gargantuan task because Pamela Sedgwick suffered from long bouts of mental and physical illness for much of her adult life. For great stretches of time, Elizabeth was the primary caretaker of both Pamela and Pamela's nine needy children.[2]

Elizabeth never learned to read or write. She was about thirty-seven years old before she gained her freedom, but she had stories to tell of her past, and the people to whom she told those stories, Theodore and Pamela's children, were among the most literate people in early nineteenth-century America.

Catharine Maria Sedgwick, the family's youngest daughter, was America's most famous female novelist in the decades leading up to Harriet Beecher Stowe's *Uncle Tom's Cabin*. All four of the surviving Sedgwick sons, Theodore II, Henry, Robert, and Charles, became lawyers. Henry was also a noted editor and writer. Charles, the youngest, would act as Elizabeth's executor and trustee of her estate. Theodore II's wife, Susan Ridley Sedgwick, was a talented artist. Though there is a brief record of the landmark legal case in which Elizabeth gained her freedom and much has been written about that case, it is through the eyes, ears, and pens of the Sedgwick family that we know many of the significant events of Elizabeth's life, and it is also how we know what she looked like.[3]

According to Henry Sedgwick, Elizabeth was first owned by Pieter Hogeboom and "was purchased at an early age by Col. Ashley."[4] By 1744, Pieter Hogeboom, then sixty-eight, was the widowed father of ten grown children. The son of a Dutch immigrant, Pieter was born in Albany, then known as Fort Orange, in 1676. By 1720, Pieter was leasing a large farm about forty miles south of Albany from the Van Rensselaers, the patroon family who owned much of the upper Hudson Valley. Under the patroon system, a large tenant farmer such as Hogeboom paid annual rent in farm products and labor. His leasehold could be passed down to his children, but if it was sold, a payment of 25 percent of the sale price was due to the patroon.[5]

The patroon system discouraged European immigration into the Hudson Valley. Unlike the Mohawk Valley to the north and west, which had many small freeholds and few large estates employing slave labor, the Hudson Valley was packed with large tenant farms that relied primarily on the labor of enslaved people.[6]

During the period from 1732 to 1754, slaves composed 35 percent of the total immigrants coming into the port of New York. Many of these slaves were purchased by owners living in New York City or New Jersey, but many others were bound for the wheat farms of the Hudson Valley.

1. Beginnings

In 1756, about 15 percent of Albany County's population was made up of Black slaves. Rural Claverack, in the southern part of the county (which after the Revolution was split off to become Columbia County), probably had population figures similar to neighboring Ulster County, where enslaved people constituted almost 19 percent of the population.[7]

Catharine Sedgwick describes Elizabeth Freeman as "a remarkable woman of unmixed African race."[8] Pieter Hogeboom probably bought Elizabeth's parents separately at one of the nearby slave markets that existed in Poughkeepsie, Newburgh, Kingston, and Albany.[9] Though probably born in Africa, both of Elizabeth's parents had likely spent some time as slaves in the West Indies. Canny northern slave purchasers preferred "seasoned" slaves who had endured the harsher conditions in Jamaica or Barbados and who understood that the penalty for misbehavior could be a return there.[10]

Elizabeth's father labored in Hogeboom's fields, planting and harvesting wheat and corn crops and herding livestock, while her mother performed domestic service in the home and garden that included cooking, preserving, cleaning, washing, weaving, spinning, soapmaking, and candlemaking.[11]

Elizabeth's parents would have picked up some English during their time in the West Indies, and if they were of different ethnic groups, it may be how they communicated with each other. Though the English had taken control of the province of New York from the Dutch almost a century before, the Dutch remained the dominant ethnic group in the Hudson Valley. Hogeboom spoke Dutch to his family and friends, but because English had become the language of commerce over the years, he spoke English for many business transactions.[12] He probably issued his commands in English to new slaves, but as time wore on, they certainly picked up some Dutch as well.

Elizabeth spent part of her childhood in Claverack and knew her parents. The will that Charles Sedgwick drafted for her in 1829 bequeaths to her daughter, Betsey, a gown "recd. of my father" and "a short gown that was my mothers."[13]

* * *

Colonel John Ashley, the man who Henry Sedgwick says "purchased" Elizabeth "at an early age," was the husband of Pieter Hogeboom's youngest child, Annetje, born in 1712. Annetje's name was anglicized to "Hannah" from the time of her marriage in September 1735.[14]

John Ashley, born in 1709 and a graduate of Yale, was one of the original settlers of Sheffield, Massachusetts, a town in the southwestern region of the state just north of the Connecticut border in the Housatonic River Valley. As a young man, John helped survey the region at the behest of his father, who was a member of the committee designated by the Massachusetts Bay Colony government to organize settlement there.[15]

Occupied by several dozen Algonkian-speaking Mohicans who had migrated there from the northwest during a time of famine more than a generation before, this relatively empty bloc of territory, which in 1761 would become Berkshire County, was of interest to the expanding Anglo American population of Massachusetts. At least in the beginning, the group of Mohicans living there was not averse to company in this vast wilderness. In 1724, their sachem, Konkapot, and twenty other adult members of the tribe, known as the Housatonic Indians, and later the Stockbridge Indians, deeded to the Massachusetts Bay Colony a tract of land beginning four miles east of the Housatonic River and extending west to the New York border, for which they were paid £460, three barrels of cider, and thirty quarts of rum. They reserved for themselves a strip of land five-eighths of a mile wide, in which were located their two villages. Within a few years, this strip of land was swapped for what would become the village of Stockbridge, located about fourteen miles north of Sheffield.[16]

John Ashley's father and the other members of the settlement committee selected 120 settler families. The settlers paid thirty shillings for each one hundred acres purchased. They were obligated to erect a dwelling and cultivate at least twelve acres of land within three years. They were also required to be members of the established Congregational Church. The settlers' purchase money went to fund the payment to the Housatonic Indians and the erection of Congregational meeting houses.[17]

John's father never moved to Sheffield, preferring the more civilized comforts of his residence in Westfield, Massachusetts, thirty miles to the east. John went in his place, and from the time of Sheffield's founding in 1733, he was regarded as one of its leading

1. Beginnings

citizens—a gentleman and a man of business. When Sheffield's Congregational meeting house was raised in the summer of 1735, although he was a young man of twenty-six, he was not expected to perform manual labor. Instead, it was his duty to "Dool out Drink to the labourers ... and Likewise to Sell Drinks to Strangers or Townspeople and also to receive the money."[18]

Though Sheffield was in Massachusetts, it was much easier for its settlers to ship agricultural products to New York City than to Boston. Rather than haul their farm products 150 miles east overland on bad or nonexistent roads, Sheffield men brought their crops and livestock thirty miles west to Claverack Landing (now the city of Hudson, New York), where goods could be loaded onto boats and floated down the Hudson River to New York City. Pieter Hogeboom's farm on Claverack Creek was only about four miles from the port. It was probably on a trip bringing his produce to Claverack Landing that young John Ashley met Hannah Hogeboom.[19]

John Ashley and Hannah were married in the Dutch Reformed Church in nearby Kingston, New York, on September 3, 1735. Almost immediately, Ashley brought his new bride back to Sheffield, for he had many enterprises taking shape there that could not be neglected. He built for himself and his wife a handsome wooden two-story home located on the western bank of the Housatonic River about three miles south of the Sheffield meeting house. With a kitchen, a dining room, and servant quarters on the first floor, an elegant pine-paneled study for John, and large, sunny family bedrooms on the second floor, it was the finest house in Sheffield.[20] John and Hannah would live the rest of their long lives there, and Elizabeth would toil there for them for twenty-five years.

The Ashleys quickly produced a family. John Ashley, Jr., was born in 1736, followed by three daughters, Jane, Mary, and Hannah, in 1738, 1740, and 1744.[21]

John Ashley owned several male slaves who performed most of the agricultural labor on his large farm.[22] We don't know what kind of domestic help Hannah had in the early years of her marriage. She certainly had someone. Domestic labor was hard, and no man of John Ashley's standing in the community could fail to provide his wife with a servant or two, especially when she had been accustomed to them in

The home of John and Hannah Ashley, where Elizabeth Freeman was enslaved for a quarter century (The Ashley House, Sheffield, MA, photograph by the author, courtesy of The Trustees of Reservations).

her father's house. This does not mean that Hannah did not work. Like most frontier wives, she would have worked from dawn to dusk every day but the Sabbath, but a servant would have performed the heaviest and dirtiest labor while she supervised. The servant's role was sometimes filled by the excess daughter of a poor neighbor, but this was unreliable because such girls got married and left their employment. A European indentured servant was also sometimes used. These girls' commitments were longer, usually seven to ten years, but they, too, were free to leave at the end of that time. It may have been such an event, or the death of a female slave, that set Hannah casting about for a replacement in the mid–1750s.

Hannah's father, Pieter Hogeboom, died in early 1758. His will provided that all his "negroes and negresses, big and little, young and old, and all my horses and cattle" were to be divided equally among his ten children.[23] This means that by the age of fourteen, Elizabeth, "Bet," and a younger sister called Lizzie were separated from their parents and sent to the Ashleys. But Elizabeth would tell the Sedgwicks that she "had been purchased at an early age by Col. Ashley." It may be that prior to Pieter Hogeboom's death, Hannah needed domestic labor due to the end of an indenture, the marriage of a European American servant, or the death of a slave. At the same time, Hannah's elderly father may have thought he had too much household help. Children of slaves were often sold at a young age if a house was already well staffed. Under such circumstances, slave children were deemed an unnecessary expense. Knowing that Hannah needed help, that he had too many slaves for his own needs, and that Hannah was to inherit slaves upon his death, Pieter Hogeboom may have worked out a deal with John Ashley whereby Ashley rented Elizabeth and her sister from his father-in-law with the understanding that they would become Hannah's inheritance when Pieter died.

No one would have thought it important to tell either the affected children or their parents the details of such an arrangement. They would simply have been told that Colonel Ashley had bought the girls and to say their goodbyes. As a bright teenaged girl, if she had been on the Claverack farm at the time of her master's death, she would certainly have known that he had died, and as a result, she was going to his daughter because his household was broken up and his slaves were divided among the Hogeboom siblings. The fact that Elizabeth told the Sedgwicks that Colonel Ashley purchased her indicates that the separation from her parents came earlier, perhaps around 1756, when she was about twelve (old enough to receive a gown as a parting gift from her father) and her sister was two or three years younger.[24]

The abrupt parting must have been traumatic for Elizabeth, her parents, and her sister. It was, of course, some comfort that the girls would be together. Elizabeth was older and both mentally and physically stronger. Many years later, Catharine Sedgwick would describe Elizabeth's sister as "sickly" and "timid." Their parents undoubtedly told Elizabeth to watch over little Lizzie. In the harsh environment they were about to enter, Elizabeth would do so "as the lioness does over her cubs."[25]

If the transfer of possession occurred in the summer or fall, Elizabeth and her sister would have made the thirty-mile journey in a two-wheeled cart; if in the winter, they would have traveled by sleigh. People avoided travel in the spring because the muddy roads were virtually impassable. As she made the sad trip to Sheffield, Elizabeth may have pushed her grief and terror away by telling herself that because her new mistress was kin of her old master, she might sometimes be able to pass messages to her parents and might even be able to visit them when her mistress visited Claverack. If Hannah's siblings had not sold off her parents after Pieter Hogeboom's death, male slaves transporting produce from Sheffield to Claverack may indeed have been able to transmit an occasional message from Elizabeth to her parents. Whether she ever visited Claverack again would have depended on Hannah Ashley's convenience or her kindness. We know she would prove to be a harsh mistress, so a kind gesture can probably be ruled out. As to convenience, after her father's death, visits by Hannah to Claverack were probably less frequent, and she would have had more use for Elizabeth and Lizzie maintaining her home in her absence than attending her at a sibling's home where other enslaved people were present to serve her. It is quite possible that whatever her hopes were as she left them, young Elizabeth never saw her parents again.

* * *

At the time Elizabeth came to Sheffield, the town had been settled for about twenty years, and John Ashley's imprint on it was very clear. Across the road from his home, Ashley operated a general store where the citizens of Sheffield could purchase tea, coffee, sugar, molasses, tobacco, rum, silk, broadcloth, taffeta, buttons, and buckles. Most of these goods were brought in by cart from Albany or Hartford because the Housatonic was only partially navigable.[26]

About a mile from his home, at a waterfall on a tributary of the Housatonic, then known as the Ironworks River and later renamed the Konkapot River, Ashley operated a sawmill, a gristmill, and an iron foundry. In addition to these businesses, Ashley owned a large farm, which by the time of his death had grown to 3,000 acres. Some of this land was worked by Black slaves and European American laborers, and some of it was leased to European American tenant farmers.[27]

1. Beginnings

As Elizabeth gazed out at the wheat fields that surrounded the Ashley home, it would not have seemed a very different place to her from the farm on which she had grown up in Claverack, thirty miles to the west. A quarter century would pass before she would comprehend that her forced removal from Claverack, New York, to Sheffield, Massachusetts, would make all the difference in her life.

Though producing similar agricultural products, western Massachusetts and New York's Hudson Valley were culturally very different places. While the patroon system of landownership in the Hudson Valley depressed European immigration and encouraged slave labor, Massachusetts's settlement plan for its western counties encouraged small freeholds, with labor supplied mainly by family members or by European immigrants and European American laborers who expected someday to be able to purchase land. Fourteen percent of New York's population was made up of Black slaves, but in Massachusetts, only 2 percent of the population was made up of Black enslaved persons, and most of those enslaved people labored in the eastern maritime counties.[28]

The fear of slave rebellions due to their large numbers in New York made for harsh laws governing its slave population. Dutch religious attitudes toward Black enslaved people compounded the law's tendency toward harshness. The Dutch Reformed Church, dominant in the Hudson Valley, taught that God had ordained African slavery. Treatment of slaves on Dutch farms was often severe compared to their treatment in New England, and the slave market in Albany was reputed to be the cruelest in the north.[29]

In contrast, Puritan Congregational teaching held that slavery was a matter of misfortune rather than inferiority and looked to the Mosaic laws of bondage for guidance as to how slaves were to be treated. As a result, enslaved people in Massachusetts possessed a number of legal rights they lacked in New York, including the right to own property, to serve as witnesses, and to sue in the courts. Elizabeth would eventually take advantage of this last right to prosecute the lawsuit that would result in her freedom.[30]

But that happy day was a long time in the future. For the present, she was a unit of labor to the Ashleys, and she was immediately put to work upon her arrival. Even enslaved children aged five or six were expected to perform simple tasks such as shucking corn and peas. By seven or eight, they were expected to perform any domestic task that did not involve strength or judgment. Weeding the flax fields that produced the family's linen supply was a job frequently assigned to children because their small feet were less likely to damage the tender stalks. By the age of twelve, a tall, strong girl, as we know Elizabeth was, would have been performing most of the heavy labor expected of adult female slaves.[31] This would have included hauling water from an outdoor pump to the kitchen to fill a large brass or copper cooking pot that was always kept boiling. Though male slaves cut wood for the home's fireplaces, Elizabeth would also have been responsible for carrying wood inside and keeping the fire in the kitchen and upstairs fireplaces burning.[32]

There would also have been the daily duties of cooking and serving, sweeping and polishing, and the onerous task of doing the wash, usually performed once or twice a month.[33] Added to these tasks would be a raft of seasonal duties. Fall was a particularly busy time. Men slaughtered the animals. Women made sausages and headcheese and smoked other cuts of meat in the smokehouse, and they used animal fat for candlemaking and soapmaking. The fall was also the time for dealing with the fruits of the harvest. Six to seven barrels of apples needed to be pared in order to make a family's winter cider supply. Other fruits and vegetables were pickled, candied, or preserved for use during New England's long winters.[34]

Elizabeth probably milked the Ashleys' cows year round, and she would have been involved in butter and cheese making.[35] Though the Ashley family's finest clothes were made from imported material, linen and wool cloth for everyday clothing was produced by the Ashley women and their slaves. Flax from Ashley fields was converted to linen, and wool from Ashley sheep to wool clothing by a complicated process of spinning and weaving. Though professional weavers sometimes did the weaving, the Ashley women and their slaves would have spun all the thread and yarn for the weaver's use. The women would also have been responsible for knitting all the family's and slaves' stockings and mittens.[36]

* * *

The family that Elizabeth served was growing up. If she did indeed arrive in 1756, John Ashley, Jr., age twenty, was away at Yale for most of the year. It was Hannah Ashley and her three daughters, Jane, age eighteen, Mary, sixteen, and Hannah Jr., twelve, and, to a lesser extent, John Ashley, Sr., who were a daily presence in her life.[37]

As Elizabeth later described her years of servitude to the Sedgwicks, it was Hannah Ashley who was the bane of her existence. Exacting and reluctant to forgive, she was a harsh taskmaster to Elizabeth and her sister. Elizabeth regarded John Ashley as fair and decent. Occasionally, she was able to appeal to him when Hannah's dictates were too unreasonable.[38] But the reality was that John Ashley was frequently away. Not only were his days spent overseeing his businesses and his farm, but by the time Elizabeth came to his household, Ashley was representing Sheffield at the General Court in Boston and he was commander of the local militia. In 1757, as the French and Indian War raged, he spent weeks from home as he led a force of Sheffield men to Fort Edward in upper New York and waited there while senior officers debated relieving the nearby ill-fated Fort William Henry.[39]

Elizabeth and her sister slept in a small room off the kitchen on the first floor of the Ashleys' home. The Ashleys' male slaves slept in an outbuilding adjacent to the house. Elizabeth and Lizzie's days started before sunrise with a simple breakfast of bread and milk, probably shared with the male slaves. Then they went quickly about their tasks.[40] They were not at liberty until the family's supper was served and cleared in the evening. On summer nights, the sisters were probably allowed to sit on the back steps and watch the sun set and the first stars appear in the inky sky. On winter evenings, they probably sat knitting together by the kitchen fire.

Their only day off was Sunday. Congregationalists believed it was a sin to labor on the Lord's Day, and this applied also to slaves. In 1743, John Ashley and another man received permission from a church committee "to build a pew on the hind seats on ye womens side provided they do not raise the floor of the meeting house."[41] This back pew was probably occupied by whatever female servant the Ashleys then had and by the Ashleys' young daughters. John sat on the men's side and Hannah sat on the women's side at the front of the meetinghouse with Sheffield's other leading citizens.[42]

By the mid–1750s, the Ashleys' three daughters were old enough to sit with their mother at the front of the women's section or perhaps in the gallery with young men who were chastely courting them.[43] Now that there was no need for childcare services, did John and Hannah still require their female slaves to accompany them to Sunday meeting? Probably they did. In addition to any moral scruples about saving the girls' souls, they had adequate domestic staff, so neither of them would have been anxious to have Elizabeth or Lizzie reproduce. It would have meant a noisy baby in a house that was not particularly large, and later, an extra and unnecessary mouth to feed. Better to keep the girls where they couldn't get into trouble on Sundays, and if they picked up some religion along the way, well and good.

For Elizabeth, this meant a long day at church each Sunday. There was both a morning and an afternoon sermon, each two or three hours in length, and prayers that lasted an additional hour or two, all conducted in an unheated building. The lengthy service did give her time to think, undisturbed by the demands of her mistress. It also gave her time to socialize with other slaves during the noon break. In summer, she would have been able to share a simple picnic lunch with her friends. In winter, she and the other slaves would have gathered at the back end of the noon-house, a long building near the meeting house with a fireplace at one end and horse stalls at the other end.[44]

* * *

As Elizabeth got used to life in western Massachusetts, a girl and a boy who would play important roles in her life were growing up nearby. The girl was Pamela Dwight Sedgwick, born in 1753 in Stockbridge. Like John Ashley, Pamela's mother, Abigail Williams, was one of the original European American settlers of the region. Abigail's parents, Ephraim Williams and Abigail Jones, migrated from eastern Massachusetts in the late 1730s, bringing with them Ephraim's two children by his first marriage and their seven children, the eldest of whom was Pamela's mother, who was born in 1722.[45]

In August 1739, Abigail Williams married the Rev. John Sergeant, missionary to the Stockbridge Indians. It was a love match; John wrote to a friend of his bride: "The more tenderly I love her the more thankful I am to Heaven, who has form'd her as if on purpose for me." Abigail and John Sergeant had three children together: Electa, Erastus, and John Jr.[46]

1. Beginnings

Whatever criticisms we may now have of European efforts to convert Indigenous peoples to Christianity, John Sergeant was a sincere friend to the Stockbridge Indians, learning their language and seeking to serve as a buffer to the harsher effects of European settlement. He and Abigail operated a school for the Indians together until his death of a fever in the summer of 1749.[47]

About eighteen months later, with the strong encouragement of her father, Abigail married Joseph Dwight. Pamela was born in 1753, and a son, Henry, followed in 1757. Older than John Sergeant and recently widowed himself, Dwight had already served as a representative in the Massachusetts General Court and had achieved the rank of brigadier general in the militia in the 1745 siege and capture of Louisbourg during King George's War.[48]

The government in Boston appointed Dwight as a trustee of the Indian school. A very different man from John Sergeant, he saw the

The home of Pamela Sedgwick's mother, Abigail Williams, and her first husband, Rev. John Sergeant, missionary to the Stockbridge Indians (The Mission House, Stockbridge, MA, photograph by the author, courtesy of The Trustees of Reservations).

Indian school as a revenue opportunity rather than as an institution for the benefit of the Indians. He was soon embroiled in a dispute with the Rev. Jonathan Edwards, who had replaced Sergeant as Stockbridge's minister in 1751. The legislature sided with Edwards against Dwight and gave him control of the mission funds.[49]

Not long after, the Schaghticoke Indians launched a raid on Stockbridge in revenge for the murder of a member of their tribe by a white man. Pamela, a toddler at the time, was dropped in a raspberry bush alongside the road by a fleeing family slave but was rescued by another servant and returned to her terrified mother.[50] Both this raid and Dwight's loss of face in the dispute with Jonathan Edwards played a role in the family's relocation to a large house in Great Barrington (then known as Housatonic) a few miles south of Stockbridge and a few miles north of Sheffield.

Despite his defeat by Edwards in the Indian school dispute, Joseph Dwight remained one of the most prominent men in the area. In 1761, when the region was split off from Hampshire County and became Berkshire County, Joseph Dwight, John Ashley, and two others were appointed judges of the Court of Common Pleas.[51]

As two of the leading families in the area, the Dwights and the Ashleys knew each other well. They were guests in each other's homes, and the Dwights were probably invited to the weddings of the Ashley daughters, Jane to Captain Ruloff Dutcher in February 1763, Mary to Captain John Fellows in March 1763, and Hannah Jr. to Martin Vosburgh in January 1764.[52] As she got older, Pamela would have accompanied her parents to some of these social occasions. The first time Elizabeth Freeman and Pamela Dwight met was probably when Elizabeth waited on Miss Dwight as a guest in the Ashley home.

Meanwhile, Pamela's future husband, Theodore Sedgwick, was growing up in Cornwall, Connecticut, twenty-two miles south of Sheffield. Theodore, the youngest of four children, was born in 1746 in Hartford, but his family moved to a modest farm in Cornwall when Theodore was two. Tragedy struck the family in 1757 when Theodore's father suddenly died. Though only fifteen, Theodore's elder brother John heroically stepped into the role of provider, working the family farm and operating a small tavern. His efforts enabled Theodore to enter Yale in the winter of 1761–62 with the goal of becoming a minister. As Theodore freed himself from the drudgery of farm labor to join New England's educational elite, Elizabeth, who would play such an important role in his future professional success, was still two decades away from her emancipation.[53]

2

"Which was the slave and which was the real mistress?"

THE MARRIAGES OF THE Ashley girls in quick succession in 1763 and 1764 should have made Elizabeth's life better by reducing the number of people she needed to serve. In reality, these events, coupled with an Ashley family tragedy, made her life worse. Hannah had always been difficult and demanding, but now her girls were leaving her, and two of them, Jane and Hannah Jr., were moving away from Sheffield: Jane to Canaan, Connecticut, and Hannah Jr. to Claverack.[1] When news came back from Claverack that Hannah Jr., "light-hearted and spirited," Hannah's baby and namesake, had died only nineteen days after her wedding at age twenty, something in Hannah snapped.[2] Now the very existence of Elizabeth (who was about Hannah Jr.'s age) and her sister Lizzie was an affront to Hannah. Why were they alive when her beloved child was dead?

At some point, Hannah's misery and rage morphed into serious physical abuse. Catharine Sedgwick related the story she had heard many times from Elizabeth: "On one occasion, when Madame A— was making the patrol of her kitchen, she discovered a wheaten cake, made by Lizzy the sister, for herself, from the scrapings of the great oaken bowl in which the family batch had been kneaded. Enraged at the 'thief,' as she branded her, she seized a large iron shovel red hot from clearing the oven, and raised it over the terrified girl. Bet interposed her brawny arm, and took the blow. It cut quite across the arm to the bone."[3]

Despite the weeks of pain she endured from the wound, Elizabeth understood that Hannah had gone too far and that there was a way to punish her. Catharine Sedgwick quoted her as saying, "Madam

2. "Which was the slave and which was the real mistress?"

never again laid her hand on Lizzy. I had a bad arm all winter, but Madam had the worst of it. I never covered the wound, and when people said to me, before Madam—'Why Betty! What ails your arm?' I only answered—'ask Missus!'"[4] Catharine Sedgwick concludes the tale, "Which was the slave and which was the real mistress?"[5]

Unfortunately, Elizabeth did continue to be Hannah Ashley's slave,[6] but the balance of power had shifted in an important way. Not only did Elizabeth succeed in humiliating Hannah before the Ashleys' friends (Abigail and Pamela Dwight may have been among those who saw the ugly wound), but also his wife's cruelty shocked John Ashley, and Elizabeth's bravery in protecting her sister gave him respect for her. This respect enabled Elizabeth to stand up to Hannah when another defenseless young girl, this time a European American one, needed her help.

This incident was another of the stories Elizabeth told the Sedgwicks years later. Catharine Sedgwick remembered: "She retained so vivid an impression of its circumstances, that when she related them in her old age, the blood of her hearers would curdle in their veins."[7]

People sometimes came to Judge Ashley's home to make legal complaints. As Catharine Sedgwick relates, "'It was in May,' she would say, 'just at the time of the apple blossoms; I was wetting the bleaching linen, when a smallish girl came in to the gate, and up the lane, and straight to me without raising her eyes, "where is your master? I must speak to him."'"[8] When Elizabeth told the girl Judge Ashley would not be home until nightfall, the girl told her she had to wait for him.

Elizabeth told the Sedgwicks, "'I saw it was no common case. Gals in trouble were often coming to master. But,' she continued, 'I never saw one like this. The blood seemed to have stopped in her veins; her face and her neck were all in blotches of red and white. She had bitten her lip through; her voice was hoarse and husky, and her eyelids seemed to settle down as if she could never raise them again.'" Elizabeth took the girl to the small room off the kitchen where she slept and closed the door, but Hannah Ashley had seen the girl arriving. This was a problem. As Elizabeth told the Sedgwicks, "She never overlooked anybody's wrongdoing but her own, and she had a partic'lar hatred of gals that had met a misfortin; she could not abide them."[9]

Elizabeth's sympathy for the downtrodden impelled her to rise to the occasion. "I heard her coming and I threw open the bedroom door; for seeing I could no way hide the poor child—she was not over fifteen—I determined to stand by her." As Elizabeth expected, Hannah wanted to humiliate the girl: "There was no foul thing she didn't call the child; and when she had got to the end of her bad words, she ordered her to walk out of the house. Then the gal raised her eyes for the first time; she had not seemed to hear a word before. She did not speak—she did not sigh—nor sob—nor groan—but a sharp sound seemed to come right out of her heart; it was heartbreaking to hear it."[10]

This was too much for Elizabeth. "'Sit still, child,' I said." Hannah told Elizabeth the house was hers and again ordered the girl to leave. "'Sit still, child,' says I again. 'She shall go,' says madam. 'No missus, she shan't,' says I. 'If the gal has a complaint to make, she has a right to see the judge; that's lawful, and stands to reason beside.' Madam knew when I set my foot down, I kept it down; so after blazing out, she walked away."[11]

Elizabeth knew she had to proceed carefully. So far, she was in the right. But she must give Hannah nothing that she could hurl against her when John Ashley came home: "'When dinner-time came,' she continued, 'I offered the child a part of mine; I had no right to take madam's food and give it to her, and I didn't; but poor little creature, she could no more eat than if she were a dead corpse; she tried when I begged her, but she could not.'"[12]

When John Ashley got home, he did indeed listen to the girl's complaint. She was an incest victim who had remained in the situation in an attempt to protect her mother and little brother.

Catharine Sedgwick recalled, "When Mum-Bet got to the point of her story ... the tears started from her eyes, and she quietly wiped them away with the back of her hand. She was not given to tears. They were not her demonstration."[13]

Ashley allowed the girl, Tamor Graham, to stay at the house, and Elizabeth stood by her when the father was arrested and the girl had to formally accuse him. Elizabeth told the Sedgwicks, "He was an awful-looking man," and when she led Tamor in, "I've seen awful sights in my day, but nothing near to that."[14]

The girl's ordeal was not over. Friends of the father abducted Tamor while he was being held for trial. Ashley called up a posse of

2. "Which was the slave and which was the real mistress?"

militia. They found her being held prisoner in a hut deep in the woods, and the father was eventually convicted and executed for his crimes. All of this, because Elizabeth stood up to Hannah Ashley. As Catharine Sedgwick proudly remarked, "One should have known this remarkable woman, the native majesty of her deportment, the intelligence of her indomitable, irresistible will."[15]

Catharine Sedgwick's words were written decades after Elizabeth's death, when in hindsight she knew that Elizabeth had eventually gained her freedom and lived a satisfying life. But, as Elizabeth sweated her youth away toiling for the Ashleys, there were surely many days when she felt neither indomitable nor majestic. As she herself told Catharine, "Any time, any time while I was a slave, if one minute's freedom had been offered to me, and I had been told I must die at the end of that minute, I would have taken it—just to stand one minute on God's airth a free woman—I would."[16]

* * *

Though John Ashley's respect for Elizabeth did not extend to an impulse to free her, it did result in Elizabeth being able to practice a profession. It was common in New England for slaves to be rented out when their own masters did not need them to perform either skilled or unskilled labor. Often, master and slave split the rental money.[17] Over the years, Elizabeth developed nursing and midwifery skills. She still had to perform her duties in the Ashley household, but John Ashley allowed her to go out into the community to attend patients, and he probably allowed her to keep a portion of her fees. On at least one occasion prior to her employment in the Sedgwick household, she nursed a nephew of Theodore Sedgwick through a bout of typhoid fever. These forays into the community allowed her to build relationships with people other than the Ashleys and to gain an increased understanding of how the larger world worked. These experiences, together with the understanding she was gaining of legal rights and due process by being the slave of a judge and a legislator, would eventually help her cast off the yoke of slavery.[18]

As Elizabeth endured her service in the Ashley household, Theodore Sedgwick was coming into young manhood. As someone of modest social standing but strong opinions, Theodore had a rocky time at Yale. He made it to the end of his senior year, but then disaster struck.

A Revolutionary Woman

The academic year 1764–65 was a difficult one for Yale and its aging president, Thomas Clap. The construction of a chapel had exhausted the college's funds, and a tuition increase was required to pay Yale's three faculty tutors their modest salaries. For someone like Theodore, who had to ask for more money from his elder brother John, who was already struggling to keep him in school, it was a real blow. Theodore may have complained.[19]

Given what is known about Theodore's later religious beliefs, he may also have been in open sympathy with two of Yale's three faculty tutors who disputed the orthodox Congregational doctrine of imputed righteousness, which held that there was no spark of goodness in human beings and the only reason God granted forgiveness to humans was that he imputed Christ's goodness to them. The highly orthodox Clap dismissed the two tutors, and he was probably looking to root out heresy among the student body as well.[20] What Catharine Sedgwick would later describe as "boyish gayeties" very near graduation gave Clap his excuse. Theodore was expelled.[21] To the credit of his classmates and Yale's next president, Naphthali Daggett, there was a persistent feeling that Theodore had been treated unfairly. In 1772, Clap's decision was reversed, and Theodore was granted his degree and enrolled as a member of the class of 1765.[22]

At the time, however, it must have been very painful to go home and tell his brother there was no Yale degree. Within a few months, he decided to study law with his second cousin, Mark Hopkins, a lawyer in Great Barrington, and the husband of Electa Sergeant, Pamela Dwight's elder half sister.[23] Though Theodore was certainly introduced to Pamela at this time because he was living with Mark and Electa, Pamela was only twelve. It would be another eight years before they became a factor in each other's lives.

Theodore was admitted to the bar in 1766 but struggled to establish his practice in Great Barrington.[24] He decided to move to neighboring Sheffield, a larger town, and there his practice took off. A young man with scholarly inclinations, Theodore had already achieved substantial knowledge of English law.[25] He appeared often before Judge John Ashley, and Ashley was impressed with him. Like Pamela Dwight, Theodore probably first met Elizabeth Freeman when she served him as a guest in her master's home.

2. "Which was the slave and which was the real mistress?"

Big changes were taking place in Pamela's life, too. The same year she met Theodore, her father died. Her mother, Abigail, remained in the big house in Great Barrington for two or three more years and then returned to Stockbridge to live with her eldest son, Dr. Erastus Sergeant, who lived in a house on the hill overlooking Plain Street and the Housatonic River.[26]

Abigail was financially comfortable, and she was determined that Pamela should have a proper education in the social graces. During her teens, Pamela spent a significant amount of time in Salem and Boston staying with friends of her parents.[27]

Highly intelligent and very much influenced by orthodox Congregationalism, Pamela was also experiencing the first stirrings of her lifelong struggle with depression, at one point signing a letter to her mother, "Your weak your worthless child."[28] Fortunately, Abigail adored her daughter, and this was some antidote to Pamela's self-denigrating tendencies.[29]

As Pamela experienced social life in Boston, Theodore was firmly establishing himself in Sheffield and doing so well that he could take a wife. He fell in love with Eliza Mason, daughter of Jeremiah Mason of Franklin, Connecticut, and they were married either late in 1769 or in 1770. They lived together in a house with a garden adjacent to the village green. They also owned a small farm and wood lot. Not yet opposed to slavery, Theodore owned a male field slave and a male household slave named Caesar. Eliza had a cook named Ann Olds, who was probably a European indentured servant.[30]

Soon Eliza was expecting a baby. Though she was eight months pregnant, the honeymoon continued. Theodore would later tell his daughter Catharine that Eliza loved to comb his hair and tie it in a queue for him. This was how she caught smallpox, he believed. Unwittingly, in early April 1771, he brought the dreaded disease into their home. The first pox developed on his scalp, and Eliza apparently touched it before he noticed it. Horrified when he realized he was a danger to his wife and unborn child, he moved out of their home to a "pock-house." Soon he learned that his precautions were too late. Though he got through the disease well and with no significant scarring, Eliza and the unborn child were dead within a week. She was twenty-five.[31]

Inconsolable, Theodore lay sleepless one night shortly after Eliza's death. He related the event to his daughter Catharine many years later: he was tossing about thinking, "If I could but see her as she was, in her everyday dress—see her once more, I should be comforted."[32] According to Catharine, he saw "the room filled with a light—not like the light of a lamp ... not like the light of the sun, but a heavenly radiance, and his wife ... her face lit with love and happiness stood leaning over the bar at the foot of his bed, looking on him." The vision only disappeared when he reached out and tried to touch her.[33]

The experience profoundly affected Theodore, reinforcing his intuition that the fire and brimstone doctrines of orthodox Congregationalism could not be correct. Throughout the rest of his life, he would have periodic dreams of Eliza, further fortifying his belief that her soul survived in a happy place and that he would see her again.[34]

* * *

But of course, none of this solved the earthly problem of a lonely young man with decades of life remaining. Theodore threw himself back into his law practice and into politics. Like most of his classmates at Yale, Theodore had been strongly opposed to the Stamp Act. As a young lawyer, he was certainly also disgusted by the Townshend Act duties intended to replace the Stamp Act.[35] John Ashley was far less concerned.

At the time that Parliament passed the Townshend Act, Ashley was a member of the Massachusetts House of Representatives. The House sent a letter drafted by Sam Adams and James Otis, Jr., to the other colonial assemblies urging them to unite in opposition to the Townshend Act. The British government promptly demanded a rescission of the letter. The House defiantly voted ninety-two to seventeen against rescinding the letter, but John Ashley was among the seventeen who voted in favor of rescission. Gov. Francis Bernard prorogued the House, and Britain sent troops to Boston to enforce the statute.[36]

Berkshire County tended not to be very interested in the travails of the colony's eastern counties where the enforcement of the Townshend Act hit hardest, and this is probably why Ashley felt comfortable voting to rescind. To Ashley's surprise, however, many of his constituents were displeased with his vote, and the Town Meeting at Great Barrington approved a resolution that his vote was "repugnant to the

2. "Which was the slave and which was the real mistress?"

inhabitants of Great Barrington." Though he was reelected the next year, it was a wake-up call for Ashley.[37] He began to pay more attention to the opinions of bright young men like Theodore Sedgwick and Ashley's own son-in-law, John Fellows, who were beginning to wonder if the colonies' ties with Britain could be maintained.

When Britain persisted in paying Massachusetts judges out of customs revenues and began trying certain crimes in Britain, John Ashley agreed to join a committee of eleven men, including John Fellows and Theodore Sedgwick, now a Sheffield selectman, to draft a protest that, after approval of the Sheffield Town Meeting, became known as the Sheffield Declaration. The committee met in early January 1773, probably in Judge Ashley's commodious study. It may have been then that Elizabeth Freeman, stationed on the stairway with a candle and her knitting so she could respond to her master's calls for refreshments and firewood, first heard the concepts that she would eventually believe applied to her too.[38] In addition to specific complaints about violations of the colony's charter relating to judges' salaries and customs duties, the Sheffield Declaration (also known as the Sheffield Resolves) asserted overriding principles of human rights, including the following: "Resolved that Mankind in a state of Nature are equal, free and independent of each Other, and have a right to the undisturbed Enjoyment of there [sic] lives, there Liberty and Property."[39]

A thriving law practice and revolutionary politics were not enough, however, to fill the hole in Theodore's heart. It had now been two years since Eliza's death. In a time when widowers remarried quickly, Theodore was still alone. It was probably his cousin and close friend, Mark Hopkins, who began creating opportunities for Theodore to encounter Mark's pretty and intelligent sister-in-law, Pamela Dwight, now twenty years old.

In the spring of 1773, Theodore and Pamela both began to feel a spark, but there were issues. Theodore kept talking about the grief he felt for his dead wife, and Pamela kept talking about Congregationalism.

Pamela had grown up in Great Barrington, where, from 1742 until 1769, Mark Hopkins's elder brother, Samuel Hopkins, had served as minister.[40] During that time, Samuel had rightly earned the reputation of being among the most stringent Congregational theologians on issues such as election, salvation by grace alone, and the depravity of the human spirit.[41] Despite his move to Newport in 1769, he remained a close friend of Pamela's mother, who reported to her daughter in 1770, "Mr. Hopkins & Spouse from Newport have made us a good visit."[42]

Importantly, the Reverend Hopkins was on his way to becoming an abolitionist. Upon moving to Newport, where he saw slave markets firsthand, he began to understand the evil of slavery. In 1776, he would write a cogent denunciation of slavery, which he dedicated to the Continental Congress.[43] His pamphlet was influential throughout the North and probably affected Pamela's and even Theodore's thinking about abolition.

But in 1773, Hopkins's primary effect on Pamela was that she was deeply concerned the man she was falling in love with could not enter the Kingdom of Heaven because he disagreed with the Reverend Hopkins's conservative brand of Congregationalism. She feared that his soul was at stake if he failed to join her church in Stockbridge, pastored by Stephen West, a Hopkins disciple. She urgently pressed these concerns upon Theodore: "My ardent Desires for your everlasting happiness which with truth I can say is as Dear to me as my own soul."[44]

This debate went on for months. In the end, Pamela decided she loved Theodore

Pamela Sedgwick, in the early years of her marriage (*Mrs. Theodore Sedgwick [Pamela Dwight]. From an original picture in the possession of her daughter, Miss Catherine M. Sedgwick, Lenox, Mass.*, the Miriam and Ira D. Wallach Division of Arts, Prints and Photographs: Print Collection, the New York Public Library Digital Collections, https://digitalcollections.nypl.org/items/a90f77fd-b342-b80a-e040-e00a180635e6).

2. "Which was the slave and which was the real mistress?"

too much to give him up, and Abigail, perhaps remembering that her beloved John Sergeant had been less categorical in his theology than Hopkins, loved her daughter too much to withhold her consent. They were married in the spring of 1774, three years after the death of Eliza. The couple set up housekeeping in Sheffield.[45]

Theodore never joined Pamela's church, though he became a close friend of Stephen West. West was married to Abigail Dwight's younger sister, Elizabeth, Pamela's beloved Aunt West. Theodore respected the family relationship and liked West personally.[46]

As to Theodore's grief for Eliza, Pamela never asked him to forswear it. The daughter of a widow herself, she probably knew he couldn't. When their first child, a daughter, was born in 1775, Pamela nobly insisted that the child be named Eliza Mason Sedgwick. It was one of the reasons Theodore always referred to Pamela as the "best of women."[47]

* * *

As the colonies and Great Britain slid down the slippery slope toward war and Pamela and Theodore began their life together, something wonderful finally happened to Elizabeth. She, too, fell in love. We do not know his name or exactly when it happened, but at some point in the last few years before the American Revolution, Elizabeth came together with the man who would be the father of her only child.

There were only eighty-eight African Americans in Berkshire County in 1764. By 1776, that number had grown to 216, but they constituted only 1.1 percent of the total county population of 18,768.[48] It was a small group of people, and they all knew each other. Though Elizabeth's domestic duties tied her to the Ashley household for long hours six days a week, there were still opportunities to meet a man. The Ashley general store was just across the road from the Ashley home. Elizabeth made small purchases there with her nursing money, and she was frequently out in the Ashley yard, doing the wash, tending the garden, and feeding the chickens. Her nursing and midwifery skills allowed her to visit other people's homes, where she encountered their servants and slaves, sometimes sharing a meal with them. Church was another opportunity, if she still attended, or maybe by her late twenties she had gotten John Ashley's permission to spend her Sundays as she saw fit. Enslaved people also attended community events, such as maple sugarings and the annual Training Day, when everyone turned out to watch the militia drill on the town green.[49]

The most significant social time each year for Massachusetts slaves was the period from the last Wednesday in May through the following Sunday. Congregationalist Massachusetts did not celebrate Christmas until the nineteenth century. In the eighteenth century, it was customary to give slaves these four days in May as time off. Slave festivals were held during the period, including banquets and games and sometimes the mock election of a Black governor who served as an arbitrator of disputes between his fellow slaves for the coming year.[50]

Catharine Sedgwick recalled Elizabeth speaking kindly of John Ashley and of her right to appeal to him on some occasions.[51] It is likely that Hannah Ashley would have been hostile to a man obviously courting Elizabeth, though male slaves in New England were sometimes allowed to call on their sweethearts after working hours.[52] John Ashley may have eventually granted Elizabeth this concession.

There was probably never a legal wedding ceremony. After her death, Henry Sedgwick described her as "a widow" whose husband died not long after their marriage "in the continental service in the revolutionary war, leaving her with one child."[53]

3

Revolutions Near and Far

Some students of Elizabeth Freeman maintain that Henry Sedgwick described her as the widow of a soldier in his 1831 pro-abolition lecture at the Stockbridge Lyceum as a fiction necessary to honor the woman he regarded as his second mother. They suggest that it is possible or likely that Brom, a slave of John Ashley's son, who was her co-plaintiff in the freedom suit, was the father of Betsey Freeman Humphrey, Elizabeth's daughter.[1]

That Brom was Betsey's father is actually quite unlikely, though after the successful freedom suit, Brom, too, worked in Theodore and Pamela Sedgwick's household, leaving sometime in the mid– to late 1790s when he got into trouble for sexual assault.[2] With the exception of the first few years of her life when she was a slave with her mother in the Ashley household, Betsey Humphrey grew up in the Sedgwick household, probably spent some period of time in the Stockbridge public school, and in 1831 was still residing in Stockbridge. If Brom was her father, even if Brom and Elizabeth eventually broke up, it is virtually impossible that the Sedgwick children and the community at large would fail to know who Betsey's father was. To assert a different story about her paternity in a public lecture attended by the citizenry of Stockbridge would probably have elicited snickers from the less polite and certainly would have distracted from Henry's message. It is unlikely he would attempt such a bald-faced lie before a hometown audience.

Moreover, in the writ of replevin drafted by Theodore Sedgwick in the freedom suit, Elizabeth is described as a "spinster."[3] If Brom and Bet were a couple with a child, he would have described them as such. He was arguing the freedom suit to a jury. The taxpayers of Massachusetts towns were deeply concerned at the time that freed slaves would

A Revolutionary Woman

become a burden to the public. Massachusetts, like most other states, had a law requiring owners who voluntarily freed slaves to post a bond that towns could use for the support of elderly or sick former slaves.[4] Members of the jury would have been particularly concerned about whether a single mother would be able to support herself and her child over the long term. It would have made them much more comfortable to think that Elizabeth had a man to support her. Even if there had not been a wedding ceremony, if Theodore had stated that they were living as husband and wife or had referred to Elizabeth as the mother of Brom's child, he could have made his point. Instead, he described her as a spinster, thereby seeming to negate any relationship between the two.

The freedom suit was Elizabeth's idea. When she came to Theodore to ask him to pursue it, he would certainly have been concerned that his sole plaintiff was a woman. Almost all the previous freedom suits brought in Massachusetts had male plaintiffs.[5] Also, he intended to make a broad constitutional argument, and women's constitutional rights were much less clear at the time than were men's. Theodore probably told Elizabeth that her chances of success would be greater if she could find a male co-plaintiff.

John Ashley Jr.'s home was a few hundred yards from his parents' house. Elizabeth knew Brom well and knew that he too yearned to be free. One of John Ashley, Sr.'s field hands, Zach Mullen, had also recently instituted a freedom suit, and there were rumors of other such suits throughout the state.[6] In such a climate, Brom was probably not hard to convince.

Why then did Theodore fail to describe Elizabeth as a widow in the lawsuit, if that was what she was? Since there had been no church ceremony (though the couple may have made vows between themselves or publicly at the May slave festival), he probably felt that he could not describe her as such in a legal pleading. Massachusetts did sometimes recognize common-law marriages between slaves, but the union had been too short to qualify.[7]

Outside the realm of legal pleadings, it was certainly reasonable for Elizabeth to think of herself as a widow and to describe herself as such to her own daughter and to the Sedgwick children. And there is no reason to disbelieve Henry Sedgwick's claim that her husband died as a soldier in the Revolutionary War.

3. Revolutions Near and Far

African American men served in the Massachusetts militia during the French and Indian War, and several thousand African Americans from across the colonies served as Patriot soldiers during the Revolution.[8] At least twenty-two of those men were from Berkshire County.[9]

Though there was some concern about arming African Americans in the early days of the Revolution, the need for manpower soon proved decisive. In January 1776, the Continental Congress decreed that though slaves would not be allowed to reenlist, free Black men already in the continental ranks were allowed to do so.[10]

In the same month, Massachusetts passed a law excluding Negroes, Indians, and mulattoes from the Massachusetts militia and from units being supplied to the Continental Army, but men already in the militia were allowed to stay, and some towns ignored the proviso entirely.[11] At Ticonderoga, Captain Persifer Frazer of the Fourth Pennsylvania Battalion reported to his wife that New England regiments contained "the strangest mixture of Negroes, Indians and whites."[12]

As the war ground on, Massachusetts reversed itself in 1777 and allowed African Americans to enlist in units being used to fill the state's quota for the Continental Line.[13] It was at this time that eighteen-year-old Agrippa Hull, a free Black youth from Stockbridge who would later join Elizabeth as a colleague in the Sedgwick household, enlisted in the Continental Army.[14]

A substitute system developed in Massachusetts in which a slave owner would free a slave in exchange for the slave agreeing to serve in the place of the owner or the owner's son. As antislavery opinion grew in Massachusetts during the war, this was a particularly attractive option for a slave owner. Rather than take the risk of being legally compelled to free the slave in a few years, the owner could voluntarily free him during the war and gain a substantial benefit.[15]

Though the substitute system became more entrenched as the war continued, even at the beginning of the conflict, slaves were being freed to fight. The Belknap family of Framingham freed their slave Peter so he could join the Framingham militia company. He was one of the minutemen who ambushed the Redcoats as they made their bloody retreat from Concord. One of the Americans wounded at Lexington was an African American slave, Prince Estabrook, who faced the Redcoats on Lexington Green with Captain Parker. His master, Benjamin Estabrook, freed him following his service in the war.[16]

* * *

As the storm clouds of war gathered in 1774, did Elizabeth understand that her new-found happiness was profoundly at risk because of the dispute between the colonies and Great Britain? She certainly knew that trouble was on the horizon just from overhearing the conversations of men who regularly visited her master. When news of the Coercive Acts reached Berkshire County in May 1774, the outrage of its citizenry was palpable. The rescinding of the Massachusetts charter affected not just the eastern counties but the entire province. The action was seen as unconstitutional and tyrannical. The young men of Berkshire County, such as Theodore Sedgwick and John Fellows, were now convinced independence was inevitable.[17]

John Ashley, at age sixty-five, had always thought of himself as a loyal subject of the King, even serving as a militia commander in the French and Indian War. But in western Massachusetts, where Ashley had lived his entire life, run his enterprises, and raised his family, the influence of the Crown, though significant, was less than it was in the eastern maritime provinces, even for one of Berkshire County's leading citizens. Ashley's initial impulse had been to compromise, to conciliate, but now that the die was cast, he knew where he stood.

On July 6, 1774, Elizabeth watched Ashley mount his horse and ride north toward Stockbridge. There, sixty delegates from the Berkshire towns were assembling at the Red Lion Inn to take action against Great Britain. Well-liked and respected as one of Berkshire County's founders, Ashley was elected chairman of the convention. Twenty-eight-year-old Sheffield selectman and new bridegroom, Theodore Sedgwick, was elected clerk. The convention voted to recommend to the towns of Berkshire County that beginning October 1, no products imported from Great Britain were to be purchased or consumed, and that cattle should be sent to the outskirts of Boston for the relief of the inhabitants of that beleaguered city.[18]

The convention's decisions affected the business at John Ashley's general store where no British tea, fine British fabrics, or other luxury items would be sold. It also made more work for the women of

3. Revolutions Near and Far

Berkshire County, especially its female slaves and servants such as Elizabeth, who must now produce more homespun clothing for an unknown length of time.

As the summer continued, the mood of the county grew even more defiant. On August 18, 1774, a crowd of 1,500 men, many of them armed, gathered at the courthouse in Great Barrington and refused to let the Court of Common Pleas sit because the judges now held their commissions from the military governor, Thomas Gage. Judge Ashley did not argue with them.[19]

The Battle of Lexington and Concord took place on Wednesday, April 19, 1775. By Friday at about noon, express riders had brought the news to Berkshire County. Before sunrise the next morning, the Berkshire County militia under the command of Colonel John Patterson of Lenox, with John Fellows as second in command, set off for Cambridge, where militia units from around the province and beyond were massing.[20]

Depending on where Elizabeth's husband lived and worked, if he went with this first group of Berkshire County minutemen, there would have been little time to say goodbye. Frightened and sad though she must have been to see him go, he probably told her this was the chance they had been waiting for. He may have been promised his freedom in exchange for his enlistment, and the pay he received would be a fund for purchasing the freedom of Elizabeth and their baby.

Upon arrival at Cambridge, the Berkshire regiment was divided into two units, with Patterson in command of the northern division and Fellows in command of the southern division, which included the men from Sheffield and the other southern Berkshire towns.[21] If Elizabeth's husband was among the Berkshire men, it is likely he was with Fellows. As General Heath reported to John Adams in October 1775, "There are in the Massachusetts Regiments some Negroes."[22]

Fellows's unit was stationed at Roxbury until the British evacuated Boston in March 1776. Fellows and his men were then ordered to New York. Enlistments were for eight months, but the conditions of Elizabeth's husband's manumission may have been that he serve a longer period or for the duration of the war. Also, many common soldiers reenlisted voluntarily for the pay. If he survived the camp fevers, which were so prevalent at Roxbury, he had an incentive to reenlist so he could earn the pay that would free Elizabeth and their baby.[23]

Once in New York and promoted to brigadier general, Fellows and his men participated in the battle of Long Island at the end of August and retreated from New York with the rest of Washington's troops in October 1776. Later that month, they participated in the Battle of White Plains. Fellows would eventually command 1,400 men at the battle of Bemis Heights at Saratoga.[24]

* * *

Theodore Sedgwick also volunteered for service in the Revolutionary War. He served as military secretary to General John Thomas during the Canada campaign in the spring of 1776 with the rank of major. Now immune to smallpox himself, he was one of the officers who had to recommend the retreat from Quebec where General Thomas and hundreds of other American troops died of the disease. The American forces were too sick to fight.[25]

Unlike Elizabeth and her husband, who did not have the blessing of literacy, Theodore and Pamela, though separated by the war, were able to keep in contact and express their longing for each other: "I am dearest Creature, yours & yours alone ... at the distance of hundreds of Miles the dear the pleasing Recollection of those pleasing Moments when I have enjoyed such delightful & extatic Joys still fill my Mind."[26]

By late summer 1776, after the conclusion of the Canada campaign, Theodore was appointed a brigade adjutant at White Plains. Theodore had already seen many terrible things in Canada, but at White Plains he would experience personal tragedy. Mark Hopkins, Theodore's beloved legal mentor and cousin, and Pamela's brother-in-law, was there serving as one of John Fellows' officers. Hopkins either collapsed from camp fever or was wounded in battle there. It was Theodore who commandeered a stretcher detail and had him carried to a field hospital where he died shortly thereafter.[27]

As an officer's wife, Theodore Sedgwick and John Fellows informed Electa Sergeant Hopkins of her husband's death within days of its occurrence. We do not know how or when Elizabeth came to know of her husband's death. Henry Sedgwick says he died in the "continental service." This may mean that he did not enlist until later in the war, like Agrippa

Hull and others who were specifically recruited to fill Massachusetts's quota for the Continental Army. But Agrippa Hull was only eighteen in 1777 when he enlisted.[28] Elizabeth's husband was much older at the beginning of the war, probably in his late twenties or early thirties. It is more likely that he enlisted at the beginning of the war, if the prospect of freedom was offered to him, and that Henry Sedgwick's description was intended to be a general reference to service in the Revolutionary War, or that having heard Agrippa Hull's war stories many times, Sedgwick simply assumed that both men had enlisted in the Continental Army rather than one of them in the Berkshire County militia.

No matter when he first left home, it could have been months or years after his death before Elizabeth knew he was gone. If he died in his original Berkshire County unit, a returning comrade may have informed her. If he reenlisted in some other unit when his original enlistment expired and died thereafter, she may never have been informed. He may simply never have come home. Whether she had the mercy of sure knowledge or whether she slowly gave up on his ever returning as the war neared its end, she knew that her dream of happiness was over. The man she loved was not coming back, and she and her little girl would remain the slaves of Hannah Ashley.

* * *

Theodore Sedgwick went on to serve as a volunteer aide to General Benjamin Lincoln at the Battle of Saratoga in the fall of 1777. He then returned to Sheffield, where he served as a purchasing agent for the northern department of the Continental Army. He was regarded as competent and scrupulous in the role.[29]

When he reunited with Pamela, they soon became the parents of a second daughter, Frances, born in 1778. A year earlier, in 1777, Pamela had lost a baby soon after birth.[30] After the delivery of Frances, perhaps triggered by fear that this baby, too, would die, Pamela suffered a severe bout of postpartum depression that lasted for several months. Her concerned brother, Henry Dwight, stationed at Fort Dayton near German Flatts in the Mohawk River Valley, wrote solicitously to Theodore: "Pray how does my dear Sister ... does she continue in the miserable & unhappy way that I left her; sincerely hope not, but that she may be restd. To Health, and a happy State of mind."[31]

Raids by Loyalist Six Nations warriors led by Joseph Brant in the Mohawk Valley during 1778 were having their effect on Pamela's brother and his comrades at Fort Dayton. The garrison was running out of provisions; he wrote that they had "not any flour and but little beef" and "we have lately recd News that Butler was collecting the Indians at Niagara in order Immediately to strike upon some part of this River." This was a terrifying prospect, for if more Six Nations warriors arrived before the arrival of the provisions, "the consequence may be fatal to us."[32]

Dwight summed up the bitterness of the troops at Fort Dayton as the struggle for central New York between European American settlers and the Six Nations raged: "The Garrison is form'd by the Inhabitants that were burnt off last Fall." There were rumors (which were true) of a substantial force from the Continental Army coming to rescue them: "I sincerely wish for one sufficient to Massacre those Infernal Savages to such a degree that they mayn't be a pair of them left, to continue the Breed upon the Earth."[33]

* * *

The American Patriots' struggle for freedom from the British Crown and their justification of the rebellion based on their natural rights to life, liberty, and property did not go unnoticed by the African American people they held in bondage. Even some among the Patriots themselves began to see the hypocrisy of clamoring for their own rights while denying them to others.

From the time of the Stamp Act protests, there was an upsurge in freedom suits by individual slaves and in petitions by the African American community for the abolition of slavery in Massachusetts.[34] James Otis, a noted attorney and a leading member of the Massachusetts legislature, asserted as early as 1765 that "the colonists, black and white, born here, are free born British subjects, and entitled to all the essential civil rights of such."[35] Nathaniel Appleton, a Congregational minister, published a pamphlet entitled *Considerations on Slavery* in Boston in 1767. Appleton asked his readers, "Can you review our late struggles for liberty and think of the slave trade at the same time and not blush?"[36]

In 1766 and 1767, the Boston Town Meeting instructed its representatives to the General Court to support the total abolition of slavery. In 1767, the Worcester Town Meeting did the same. As a result of these instructions, in 1767, the lower house of the Massachusetts General Court debated a bill that would have outlawed the slave trade and abolished slavery. The bill died when it lacked sufficient support to go to a third reading.[37]

Though abolition of slavery lacked a majority in the Massachusetts legislature, the idea of banning the slave trade grew in popularity, both on moral grounds and as a way of protesting the trade policies of the British government. In 1771, both the lower and upper houses of the General Court passed a bill to prevent importation of slaves from Africa. Thomas Hutchison vetoed the legislation on the ground that it conflicted with his instructions from the king's ministers.[38]

In both 1773 and 1774, a group of Boston African Americans presented petitions to the General Court requesting the abolition of slavery. The General Court responded in early 1774 by passing another bill prohibiting the slave trade. The royal governor again refused to sign the bill. The General Court passed the same bill in June 1774 after Thomas Gage had become military governor of the province. The Boston African Americans resubmitted their petition to Gage in the same month. The petition reminded General Gage that "your petitioners ... have in common with other men a natural right to be free, and without molestation to enjoy such property, as they may acquire by their own industry."[39] Gage's only response was to reject the anti-slave trade bill passed by the General Court.[40]

We do not know the exact moment the question of slavery pricked Theodore and Pamela Sedgwick's consciences. In addition to Samuel Hopkins, other prominent Patriots were publishing pro-abolition pamphlets, including Doctor Benjamin Rush in 1773 and Thomas Paine in 1775.[41]

Despite whatever growing qualms he may have had, before accompanying General Fellows to Saratoga, Theodore purchased from him on July 1, 1777, a woman named Ton and a girl (probably Ton's daughter).[42] Faced with the necessity of leaving Pamela alone with their eldest child, Eliza, then a toddler, to return to his military duties, Theodore took the easiest means of providing her with domestic help. At some point, however, after his return home in November 1777 and before Elizabeth Freeman asked Theodore to represent her in her freedom suit, Theodore and Pamela Sedgwick freed their slaves.

What finally pushed them to do so? Whenever Theodore traveled, Pamela always asked him to bring home reading material, especially theological tracts. Did Samuel Hopkins's abolition pamphlet finally reach her hands in remote Stockbridge? Was Theodore appalled when the proposed Massachusetts Constitution of 1778, eventually rejected by the voters, attempted to formally recognize slavery in a document intended to enshrine the most sacred rights of man?[43]

Perhaps it was Theodore's entry into state politics in 1780, when he was elected to the Massachusetts House of Representatives under the new Massachusetts Constitution of 1780, that proved decisive.[44] The 1780 constitution stated in its first article, "All men are born free and equal, and have certain natural, essential, and unalienable rights; among which may be reckoned the right of enjoying and defending their lives and liberty."[45] Some people thought this language prohibited slavery in Massachusetts. Representative Sedgwick was certainly asked his opinion.[46]

Probably all these factors played a role in Theodore and Pamela's decision to free their slaves. In the small town of Sheffield and the even smaller African American community there, Elizabeth would have found out very quickly that they had done so.

* * *

By the spring of 1781, Elizabeth was likely dealing with the reality of her widowhood and pondering her daughter's future and her own. John Ashley, at age seventy-two, and Hannah Ashley, three years younger, were elderly by the standards of the day. Though both were reasonably healthy, the reality was that they could die at any time. Elizabeth knew what would happen then. Hadn't she once been Pieter Hogeboom's slave? Upon their deaths, the Ashleys' property, including their slaves, would be divided among the Ashleys' three living children. Elizabeth's daughter, Betsey, now about six years old, could be sent off to Connecticut to serve Jane Ashley Dutcher, while Elizabeth was given to John Ashley, Jr., or Mary Ashley Fellows, who both lived in Sheffield, just as she had been sent away from Claverack as a young girl. Even worse, the Ashley children, now in their early to mid-forties,

3. Revolutions Near and Far

all had well-established households with their own domestic staff. They might decide to sell their parents' slaves and divide the proceeds. If such a sale occurred, there was a very significant chance that mother and daughter would be separated.

And even if all this were to happen ten years in the future, young Betsey was reaching an age when her mother could no longer protect her from the harsh reality of what it meant to be a slave. Catharine Sedgwick would later describe Little Bet, as the Sedgwicks called her, as "rather impish."[47] How Elizabeth loved her little girl's high spirits and struggled to preserve them in a household where Hannah Ashley's hostility permeated the atmosphere. When Betsey was a baby, Elizabeth told herself that the baby's father would see that their daughter grew up free. But that dream was dead. It was all up to her.

What was the best course of action to pursue? Young male slaves sometimes successfully ran away. Women with small children almost never did.[48]

It was common knowledge in Sheffield's African American community that both the Declaration of Independence and the Massachusetts Constitution of 1780 asserted that all men were born free and equal and had the right to life and liberty. Both documents had been read aloud in public places, and some European American people were telling slaves that after the passage of the Massachusetts Constitution of 1780, their masters had no further right to hold them.[49]

According to Catharine Sedgwick, shortly before deciding to seek Theodore Sedgwick's help, Elizabeth heard a public reading of the Declaration of Independence. Given the timing of Elizabeth's freedom suit, it may actually have been the new Massachusetts Constitution.[50]

In the early spring of 1781, one of John Ashley's field slaves, Zach Mullen, decided to leave the Ashley farm and accept employment as a laborer nearby. Ashley sent men to bring him back. Shortly thereafter, Mullen filed a suit against John Ashley, charging him with assault and abduction.[51]

Elizabeth cooked meals for John Ashley's field hands. She probably knew what Zach Mullen planned to do. Whether it was she who encouraged him or whether it was his action that encouraged her is unknown. What we do know is that not long after Mullen walked off

43

the Ashley farm, Elizabeth approached Theodore Sedgwick about helping her gain her freedom.

By now, Theodore had probably freed his own slaves, and he had likely stated in public that he thought the new Massachusetts Constitution outlawed slavery. Nevertheless, Theodore was a close friend of John Ashley and was probably not looking for ways to offend him. Ever since Theodore had moved to Sheffield in 1767 as a young lawyer trying to develop a law practice, John Ashley had encouraged him. Ashley admired Theodore's intellectual abilities and respected Theodore's legal and political skills. They had talked each other through the legal underpinnings of the Revolution, serving together on the Committee that drafted the Sheffield Declaration and leading the convention that had approved the boycott of British goods after passage of the Coercive Acts. Ashley had worried about Theodore because he, like John Ashley, Jr., and John Fellows, went to serve the Patriot cause during the war. Ashley also respected Theodore for his courage in insisting that local Loyalists be given due process with respect to the new confiscation and banishment laws, despite attempts at intimidation by more radical Patriots.[52]

The friendship between the Ashley family and Theodore was strong enough that, in August 1780, John Ashley, Jr., lent Theodore $6,400. In 1781, Theodore still owed Ashley Jr. a balance of $4,610.[53]

So why did Theodore agree to help Elizabeth sue John Ashley? Theodore had also known Elizabeth for many years, not just as John Ashley's servant. The Sedgwick family had been the beneficiaries of her nursing skills. When Theodore's nephew caught typhoid fever in 1775, Elizabeth nursed him back to health.[54] Elizabeth had probably also assisted Pamela Sedgwick as a midwife when she gave birth to her four eldest children in 1775, 1777, 1778, and 1780. Under such circumstances, it must have been hard to turn her away when she came to his office on Sheffield Green asking for help.

As Catharine Sedgwick related the story many years later, "'Sir,' said she, 'I heard that paper read yesterday, that says, "all men are created equal, and that every man has a right to freedom." I am not a dumb critter; won't the law give me my freedom?'"[55] How could Theodore tell her it would not, when he believed she had a very good case?

Rather than immediately filing suit, it is probable that Theodore

3. Revolutions Near and Far

first had a talk with John Ashley. If Judge Ashley hadn't already heard about it, Theodore probably informed him of a case recently decided by the Court of Common Pleas in Worcester County. At about the same time that Zach Mullen had walked off John Ashley's farm and sought employment elsewhere, a slave named Quok Walker had done the same thing with respect to his master, Nathaniel Jennison, in Barre, Massachusetts. Like Ashley, Jennison had forcibly removed Quok Walker from his new employer's land, using the handle of a horse whip to subdue him.[56] In a jury trial on June 12, 1781, the Worcester court decided "that the said Quork [sic] is a freeman, & not the proper negro slave of the Defendant." Jennison was ordered to pay Walker £50 in damages.[57]

Judge Ashley probably pointed out to Theodore that the facts of the Walker case were distinguishable. Walker claimed that both Mrs. Jennison and her first husband had promised to free Walker prior to Mrs. Jennison's marriage to Nathaniel Jennison. Massachusetts had a line of cases that held that a promise to free a slave was enforceable. Elizabeth, on the other hand, had never been promised her freedom. Theodore probably countered that the basis for the court's decision was unclear, and though a promise to manumit had been asserted, the court may have decided Walker was free based on the new Massachusetts Constitution.

Ashley disagreed with Theodore. Like many others, he didn't believe that the general language about equality and liberty in Article I of the Massachusetts Constitution freed the slaves. In 1777, the Massachusetts House of Representatives refused to pass antislavery legislation for fear of offending slaveholding states critical to a Patriot victory in the war. True, the 1778 constitution, which specifically recognized slavery, had gone down to defeat by the voters, but neither house of the legislature had a majority for abolition. Pro-abolition forces were grasping at straws to assert that there had been any intent to outlaw slavery in the 1780 constitution presented to the voters. At most, there had been an unspoken compromise to leave the matter unresolved in the document.[58]

As a judge, Ashley believed it was essential to show respect for the rule of law. If any real question about the meaning of the Massachusetts Constitution existed on this point, it had to be resolved through adjudication.

Ashley was also astute enough to understand that opinions about slavery were in flux. Not only did the moral principles asserted by the Patriots before and during the Revolution cause many people to feel it was hypocritical to enforce slavery, but many poor European American farmers resented having to compete with slave labor during the hard economic times that resulted from the war.[59]

Ashley had once before significantly misjudged the political pulse of Berkshire County when, in 1768, he was among the seventeen legislators who voted to rescind the letter to the other colonies advocating a boycott in protest of the Townshend duties. Perhaps Theodore was correct that there was not a jury in the county that would vote to hold a slave in bondage who asserted his freedom. He would not destroy a long friendship over it, especially with someone like Theodore, who, at thirty-five, was establishing himself as one of the leading men of the county and one who was gaining a statewide reputation.

Ashley apparently told Theodore he intended to vigorously contest the case, but there would be no hard feelings over the result. The two men continued to be friends, with Theodore witnessing the execution of a second codicil to Ashley's will in 1799.[60]

Ashley did indeed vigorously contest the case, retaining two well-known attorneys, David Noble, later a judge on the Court of Common Pleas, and John Canfield, a distinguished Connecticut lawyer, to represent him. Likewise, Theodore was determined to win. To be sure he missed nothing, he asked Tapping Reeve to act as co-counsel. Reeve was the founder of the Litchfield Law School, one of the first law schools in America, and was responsible for training some of America's most distinguished lawyers of the postrevolutionary era.[61]

The hearing was held on August 21, 1781. Elizabeth was probably present in the courtroom. Not wishing to incur unnecessary court costs, Ashley had arranged for a continuance of Zach Mullen's case. If Elizabeth and Brom were free based on the new constitution, so was Zach Mullen.[62] There was no mention of the shovel incident at the hearing, possibly because Sedgwick did not want to embarrass Hannah Ashley or possibly because it had occurred so long ago that the statute of limitations had lapsed. Zach Mullen, on the other hand, was suing for assault.

The jury found that "the said Brom and Bett are not and were not

3. Revolutions Near and Far

at the time of the purchase of the original writ the legal Negro servants of ... John Ashley during life and Assess thirty shillings damages." The Court issued a judgment confirming the verdict in Brom and Bett's favor and ordered Ashley to pay the damages and court costs.[63]

Ashley initially filed an appeal, but in September, the Supreme Judicial Court confirmed the lower court's judgment in the Quok Walker case when Jennison's lawyer failed to appear. The Supreme Judicial Court also reversed a lower court decision that Walker's new employers, the Caldwell brothers, had wrongfully enticed Walker away from Jennison. Based on these two decisions, in October, Ashley dropped his appeal and confessed judgment, thereby accepting the Court of Common Pleas' ruling that Brom and Bett were not slaves. The Brom and Bett case and the Quok Walker case (including a third case decided by the Supreme Judicial Court in 1783 in which Jennison's conviction for assault of Walker was upheld) are viewed as having ended slavery in Massachusetts.[64]

At about thirty-seven, Elizabeth's long travail was finally over. Ironically, had she remained in Claverack as the slave of one of the other Hogeboom siblings, she would have spent the remainder of her life as a slave, and her daughter would have been enslaved well into her fifties. New York, with its much larger slave population, did not free its slaves until 1827.[65]

Ashley approached Elizabeth about remaining in his household as a paid servant, but she refused the proposal. Theodore Sedgwick had offered her a position as governess of his children. Not only was this an opportunity to work for the man who had helped her gain her freedom, but also the chance to exchange Hannah Ashley for the gentle Pamela Sedgwick was an opportunity impossible to reject.

4

A New Life and America's Second Rebellion

PAMELA CERTAINLY NEEDED her help. In the summer of Elizabeth's freedom suit, Pamela sent an apology for not writing sooner to her best friend in Boston, Elizabeth Mayhew, citing "the necessary attention to my famely and three Babes, one an Infant always in my arms."[1] That baby was Theodore II, who, in 1780, joined older sisters Eliza and Frances. Elizabeth's daughter, about the same age as six-year-old Eliza Sedgwick, would grow up amidst the laughter of other children rather than the hostile silences punctuated with angry tirades at Hannah Ashley's house. When Elizabeth brought her daughter the four miles from the Ashley farm to the Sedgwick's house on Sheffield Green in the late summer of 1781, it must have seemed a world apart from her old life.

To acknowledge and celebrate the change, she took a last name and a more formal first name. Many slaves were known only by one name. Elizabeth had been simply known as Bet all her life. Free people had a given name and a family name. Many African American Revolutionary War veterans took the last name Freeman either upon enlistment or after their service.[2] Elizabeth may have taken the name to honor her dead husband, or she may have taken it as recognition of her own successful struggle to liberate herself and her daughter. Perhaps she took the name for both reasons, but henceforth, when she paid her taxes, bought real estate, or executed a will, she would be known to the world as Elizabeth Freeman.

* * *

Elizabeth threw herself into her work as the Sedgwick children's governess. Pamela gave birth to another daughter in the fall of 1782.

4. A New Life and America's Second Rebellion

Elizabeth certainly assisted at the birth and then did her best to meet the needs of the three elder children, while Pamela, who did not use wet nurses, occupied herself with the nursing infant.[3]

It was often a primarily female household. Theodore had not stood for reelection to the Massachusetts House of Representatives in 1781, but he did so in 1782 and 1783 and was reelected both times. In 1784 and 1785, he was elected to the state senate. This meant that he spent several months of the year in Boston.[4]

Pamela's deep love for her children and her sense of duty to them earned Elizabeth's affection and respect. As Pamela suffered increasingly with bouts of mental illness and a decline in physical health throughout the 1790s and beyond, Elizabeth would not forget who the person inside the tortured mind and the wracked body really was. Somehow, during Pamela's illnesses, Elizabeth was able to leap into the role of mother to Pamela's confused and needy children and administrator of her household, but during Pamela's periods of remission, she stepped back and let Pamela resume her role as mother and mistress of the household to the extent she was able.

This did not mean there were no class distinctions between her and Pamela. Both for reasons of privacy and because of Pamela's sense of what was appropriate, the Sedgwick family dined formally in their first-floor dining room, and their servants took meals at the big table in the kitchen on the basement level.[5]

Though European American servants sometimes found this system offensive, Elizabeth apparently did not. Perhaps she felt that these mealtimes were when she was truly off duty, a time when she could devote her attention to her own child and listen to the joys and sorrows of her colleagues on the Sedgwicks' staff. She was perhaps glad for a little separation between her and the Sedgwicks. As Catharine Sedgwick observed, "Mumbet ... though absolutely perfect in service, was never servile. Her judgment and will were never subordinated by mere authority."[6] Though she was too intelligent not to recognize the effects that race and class had on her life, Elizabeth was proud of what she had achieved for herself and her daughter and of her many professional skills as a nurse, midwife, governess, and household administrator. She understood the profound effect she had on the children she cared for and that she had their continuing love and admiration.

Commenting on Elizabeth's role in her life many years later, Catharine Sedgwick said, "In my childhood I clung to her with instinctive love and faith, and the more I know and observe of human nature, the higher does she rise above others, whatever may have been their instruction or accomplishment. In her the image of her Maker was cast so hard and pure that circumstances could not alter its outline or cloud its lustre."[7]

In the spring of 1784, Pamela gave birth to a son. This child, like the daughter born in 1782, died in less than a year.[8] The death of two children in such a short period prompted a major decision by Theodore and Pamela.

The mill pond a short distance from Sheffield Green was becoming increasingly polluted as detritus from a saw and grist mill was indiscriminately dumped into it. The pond was beginning to emit a putrid smell and was a haven for mosquitoes in warm weather. Believing the family's health to be at stake, Theodore and Pamela decided sometime in 1785 to move to Stockbridge, still in Theodore's Berkshire County constituency but fourteen miles to the north of Sheffield. Catharine Sedgwick was later told that the "unhealthiness of Sheffield caused by a pond of stagnant water" was the reason for the move, but it is probably also true that given Theodore's frequent absences, Pamela was happy to return to the town where her mother and all four of her siblings resided.[9]

Elizabeth now had to decide whether she would leave Sheffield with the Sedgwicks or find another position. It was apparently not a difficult choice. Unlike Zach Mullen, who eventually returned to the Ashleys as a paid laborer, she was clear she would never return to that household.[10] As to finding work with a different family in Sheffield, she and the Sedgwicks respected each other, she was attached to the children, and it was an opportunity to move her own child to a healthier location.

Theodore purchased land from three Housatonic Indians. European settlement was pushing the Housatonics out of Stockbridge, and by the 1780s, most of them had accepted the offer of the pro–Patriot Oneidas to settle in their territory in the Mohawk River Valley in upstate New York. They would join the Oneidas when that tribe, also pushed out by European settlement a generation later, migrated to present-day Wisconsin in the early nineteenth century.[11]

4. A New Life and America's Second Rebellion

The site Theodore purchased was large enough for both a house and a small farm. Not wanting to wait until their new home was constructed, in early 1786, the Sedgwicks leased a house in Stockbridge from Timothy Edwards, son of the famous Congregational minister, Jonathan Edwards, on what is now Main Street but was then called Plain Street.[12]

When construction was finished, they moved across the street to a home that Theodore and Pamela would occupy for the rest of their lives. A stately home, it was worthy of a man who, along with John Hancock, the General Court in 1786 chose to be part of a five-man delegation to the Confederation Congress.[13] Elizabeth and her daughter occupied a room on the third floor.[14]

While Theodore was in New York City serving in the Confederation Congress, he left Pamela and Elizabeth to deal with another sick baby, this one named Henry Dwight for Pamela's brother. Elizabeth made it her mission to see that this child survived, and he did. He and

Rear view of the home of Theodore and Pamela Sedgwick on Plain Street, now Main Street, in Stockbridge (*The Sedgwick house, Stockbridge, Massachusetts*, the Miriam and Ira D. Wallach Division of Art, Prints and Photographs: Print Collection, the New York Public Library Digital Collections, https://digitalcollections.nypl.org/items/a90eb168-668a-2d34-e040-e00a1806399f).

Elizabeth would share a special bond, and before he died, Henry would assure that the world would know Elizabeth's story.

*　*　*

When Theodore returned from the Confederation Congress in the latter part of August 1786, he found that Berkshire County, like several other counties in the state, was on the verge of insurrection.[15] For the past several years, subsistence farmers had struggled with declining land values and a shortage of hard currency. Many found themselves with mortgages larger than the value of their land, and they suffered loss of the land, cattle seizures, and imprisonment for debt when the mortgages came due.[16]

Others kept afloat by selling bonds that had been issued to them by the state of Massachusetts as partial payment for their wages as soldiers and officers during the Revolutionary War to Boston merchants and financiers for one-third to one-quarter of their face value. In 1786, these veterans were facing the reality that as taxpayers, they had not only been paying 6 percent interest to the new holders, but now they would also pay them the full face value of the bonds. The people who purchased the bonds from the veterans had assumed the risk of a state government default during the precarious years at the end of the war, but now that it was clear the bonds would be paid, many veterans felt they had been cheated.[17]

Some veterans of modest means managed to hold on to their bonds. Agrippa Hull, who had joined the Sedgwick family's staff as a butler and valet when he returned from the war in 1783, managed to redeem a bond that came due that year, but the problem was sufficiently widespread that the outrage of affected veterans was palpable.[18]

As a lawyer, Theodore was often in court representing creditors. As a legislator, he took the view that it was an essential part of the postwar economic recovery for Massachusetts to pay its portion of the war debt both to individuals and to foreign nations through the levying of excise and impost taxes.[19] This meant he was clearly one of the "Ruffled Shirts" who the subsistence farmers of the county were coming to resent.[20]

During the last week of August 1786, Theodore served as a delegate from Stockbridge to a county convention, which was to decide

4. A New Life and America's Second Rebellion

whether the county courts would remain open and whether county representatives to the state legislature would vote for taxes necessary to reduce the war debt. With his usual articulateness and command of facts, Theodore successfully argued to keep the courts open and in favor of the war taxes. He was certain that economic recovery would come only if these measures were taken.[21]

He left the convention deeply concerned. Though the majority agreed with him, he estimated that about 20 percent of the population of the county was so strongly opposed to war taxes and enforcement of debt obligations in the courts that insurrection was possible.[22]

The fall of 1786 and winter of 1787 would prove to be a time of testing for both Theodore and Elizabeth as the aftermath of the American Revolution played itself out in western Massachusetts. In the second week of September, about 800 farmers and veterans marched to the Great Barrington courthouse and refused to allow the Berkshire County Court of Common Pleas to hold its session. While in town, they also broke into the jail and released the prisoners, mostly men being held for debt.[23]

In October, another mob came to Great Barrington, this time to ensure that the General Sessions Court and the Supreme Court did not sit. This time, Theodore was present, and he angrily confronted the mob, telling them before he rode off that their actions and demands marked them as creatures of Great Britain, because the economic collapse of America would surely result in the end of independence.[24]

The anger of the crowd was so great as Theodore departed that he realized he might be murdered if he took his expected route north to Stockbridge. Instead, he rode south to Sheffield and remained there until the mob in Great Barrington dispersed.[25]

A few weeks later in November, Theodore had another close call when "some violent desperadoes" pursued and accosted him. Questioning their courage for challenging him when he was outnumbered, he shamed them into letting him go.[26]

As government authority in Berkshire County broke down that fall, the anti-government men began attempting home invasions against government supporters. On one occasion, several of them came to the Sedgwicks' kitchen door, demanding entry. Elizabeth, who was tending a large kettle of boiling beer, told them she would scald them with it if they came closer. They had come to the servants' entry hoping for no opposition. When they encountered Elizabeth's resolution, they departed.[27]

On another occasion when Theodore was not at home, several intruders went to the Sedgwicks' barn and demanded that the stable groom saddle Sedgwick's best horse, Jenny Gray, and turn her over to them. Elizabeth watched with disgust from the house as one of the thieves tried to mount the horse and was twice thrown to the ground by its bucking and rearing. When this happened a third time, Elizabeth came into the yard, opened the pasture gate, walked over to the horse, and grabbed it by the bridle, leading it to the open gate where she slapped its flank, sending the horse galloping into the pasture.[28]

Few women would have taken the chance of defying four men in an attempt to save her employers' property, but her love of the Sedgwick family and her sense of what was right were determinative. Perhaps it was her years of dealing with Hannah Ashley that taught her how to gauge moral weakness and deal with it effectively. Her estimation was correct. Though they eventually captured the horse, the intruders left her alone.

The situation, however, was becoming increasingly serious. Much of the county militia, mainly composed during the postwar period of aggrieved veterans, had gone over to the insurgents.[29]

Theodore realized that the majority of the men in the county who were opposed to the insurgents must be mobilized, or the county would descend into outlawry and terror. He was determined to stay and fight, but he wanted Pamela and the children to leave. Pamela hesitated. Baby Henry, now a little over a year old, was in poor health. What would be one of the coldest winters in memory was setting in, and she believed he would die if subjected to extreme weather as the family fled.

Elizabeth volunteered to take care of Henry and look after Theodore in the Sedgwick home, while Pamela, now expecting another baby, took the older children to safety. It was apparently agreed that Elizabeth's daughter, Betsey, now about twelve, would accompany Pamela. Relieved of that worry, Elizabeth bade them goodbye and went about her duties.[30]

Theodore turned his attention to raising a volunteer force to counter the insurgents. It was not a moment too soon. In neighboring

4. A New Life and America's Second Rebellion

Hampshire County, a "Committee of Seventeen" former Revolutionary War junior officers who planned to act as captains of the insurgents formed six regiments for the purpose of seizing control of the county government. On Christmas Day, 1786, Daniel Shays, one of these seventeen captains, led a force of 300 armed men into Springfield and closed the courts the following day. Everyone understood that his next move would probably be an attempt to seize the nearby federal arsenal.[31]

It was also known that, in the hamlet of West Stockbridge, only a few miles from Stockbridge proper, an insurgent force of about 200 men was gathering on the farm of Paul Hubbard, a well-off farmer with radical sympathies, and that these men were roaming the vicinity commandeering supplies. Already, their efforts had resulted in eight sleighs bearing relief supplies for Shays' men heading eastward.[32]

By the end of December, Theodore and several other leading citizens of Berkshire County had raised a force of 500 pro-government volunteers based in Stockbridge. As Elizabeth walked about the village, she would have felt that she was in an armed camp that January. Passwords were used, and armed men were everywhere, even in church.[33]

Unlike the preceding fall, she probably felt safe. Not only did government volunteers occupy Stockbridge, but Theodore had probably told her that a state militia force led by General Benjamin Lincoln was advancing on Springfield.[34]

By the third week in January, Theodore and the other officers of the Stockbridge volunteers decided it was time to strike at the insurgents gathered at Hubbard's farm. On January 20, they left Stockbridge, approaching the farm by three different routes.[35]

Theodore was in command of the vanguard of the center group. When he and his men unexpectedly encountered the insurgents' lookouts, he had with him only thirty-seven infantry and seven cavalry. The insurgent sentries fired an alarm, and within minutes, Theodore and his small force were facing all 200 insurgents.[36]

Hubbard commanded his men to fire, but perhaps understanding that killing these men was a hanging offense, the insurgents hesitated. Seizing the moment, Theodore boldly rode up to their front line. In a firm, authoritative voice, he ordered them to lay down their arms, warning them of the consequences if they did not. The insurgent line wavered, and many in the ranks began to turn and run. By then, pro-government reinforcements were arriving, and they gave chase, soon capturing Hubbard and eighty-three others. Brought back to Stockbridge and held as prisoners, they soon agreed to accept the governor's offer of pardon in exchange for taking an oath of allegiance to the government.[37]

A few days later, on January 25, Daniel Shays and his men marched toward the federal arsenal at Springfield. Shays expected other insurgent groups to rendezvous there, but the other insurgent units did not appear, and Shays decided to attack alone. Approximately 1,100 state government militiamen armed with muskets and a few cannons were at the arsenal waiting for him. The militia commander, General Shepard, ordered that two warning volleys be fired over the insurgents' heads, but when they continued to advance, Shepard aimed the third volley into the center of Shays' men, killing four of them. Witnessing this demonstration of resolve, Shays' men broke and ran. Many of his men slipped off into the woods and went home. Others regrouped at Ludlow, a few miles away. Soon Benjamin Lincoln reinforced Shepard at Springfield with almost 3,000 men. After scattering the remaining insurgent units around Springfield, Lincoln chased the remnants of Shays' band to Petersham. Shays escaped into the wilds of Vermont, but upon receiving an offer of pardon for enlisted men, the rest of his force surrendered.[38]

With the rebellion in Worcester and Hampshire counties tamped down, Lincoln and a large force proceeded to Pittsfield, fifteen miles north of Stockbridge, arriving on February 10. When Lincoln arrived, dozens of men who had escaped the encounter at Hubbard's farm, as well as other local Shays' sympathizers, turned themselves in and took the oath of allegiance.[39]

At this point, Theodore and many other government supporters heaved a sigh of relief. From a maximum strength of about 2,000 armed insurgents, only a few remained at large. It was known that one rebel band of about ninety men led by Perez Hamlin had fled across the New York border in the vicinity of New Lebanon, but with a large force of state militia in Berkshire County, no one thought they would return. The county's pro-government volunteers departed Stockbridge and returned

4. A New Life and America's Second Rebellion

to their homes. Theodore left for Boston to consult with the governor. As a result of this miscalculation, Elizabeth and the other citizens of Stockbridge would experience the most terrifying night of their lives.[40]

Freezing in his camp in the wooded highlands just over the New York border, Hamlin decided his position was untenable and that a bold stroke was required. He had a particular hatred for the Ruffled Shirts in Stockbridge, Theodore Sedgwick prominent among them, and also Jahleel Woodbridge, a judge of the Court of Common Pleas, who had refused to sign an oath demanded by the mob at Great Barrington the previous fall.[41]

Making their way through the snowy woods, Hamlin and his men entered the sleeping village of Stockbridge in the predawn hours of February 27, 1787. At first fairly well organized, they formed themselves into three groups at the Red Lion Inn and made their way to the homes of the town's most prominent citizens.[42]

Many years later, Judge Woodbridge's son, the Rev. Timothy Woodbridge, recalled being awakened that night by the shouts of armed men who were standing over the bed he shared with his father when he was a small child. He "shrieked in an agony of terror; and my father passed me between the guns to the arms of my sister. This is the first memory this poor world has left engraven on my heart." Before the home invaders hustled young Timothy's father into the street in his bed clothes, they plundered the house "most unsparingly."[43]

On the hill overlooking Plain Street, some of Hamlin's men entered the home of Pamela Sedgwick's elderly mother and Pamela's brother, Dr. Erastus Sergeant. Sergeant and his two medical students were taken prisoner. Here, too, the marauders seized plunder, including ripping the silver buckles off the shoes of a local seamstress, Mercy Scott, who was a house guest of the Sergeants.[44]

Next door, Hamlin's men invaded the home of the Jones family. They seized the father, who was an officer of the pro-government volunteers, his two sons, Josiah, age twenty, and William, age twelve, as well as an African American hired man named Backus and a young European indentured servant. The insurgents appropriated military stores that Captain Jones had on his property and helped themselves to a conch shell and a wampum belt that the Stockbridge Indians had given Jones as gifts.[45]

At the Sedgwick house, Elizabeth awoke in her room to hear a commotion below. Henry Hopkins, Pamela's nephew, and Ephraim Williams, her cousin, both law clerks of Theodore, were being abducted from their sleeping quarters on a lower floor of the house. Enraged at seeing the clothing they wore to court in their drawers, the intruders dumped the contents into the street.[46]

Rather than cower in her bed and hope the marauders would go away, Elizabeth, with her characteristic courage, quietly made her way to the kitchen and managed to arm herself with a fireplace shovel. When the insurgents found her there, they demanded to know where Theodore was hiding. Not believing that he was in Boston, they went through the house thrusting bayonets into likely hiding places in search of him.[47]

Then turning their attention to what could be stolen, they told Elizabeth to hand over the key to the cellar. Most women would have given them the key and fled while they rummaged the Sedgwicks' stores. But as Catharine Sedgwick explained many years later, "The supplies of to-morrow, now sent from New York on the order of to-day, were then laid in semi-annually, and Mr. S.'s cellar was furnished for six months' unstinted hospitality."[48]

Elizabeth was not about to allow Theodore and Pamela to suffer such a loss uncontested. Sizing up her opponents, she escorted them downstairs to the cellar, still clutching the fireplace shovel. The men made it clear they were interested in liquor. Using the darkness of the candlelit cellar to her advantage, Elizabeth directed them to a crate of bitter brown stout. One of the men broke off the neck of a bottle to drink. Sensing that large-scale vandalism was about to ensue, Elizabeth told the men she would fetch a corkscrew if they wanted to drink, but if one more bottle was broken, she would lay flat with her shovel the man who did it.[49]

As Elizabeth had hoped, upon tasting it, the men proclaimed the stout "bitter stuff" and asked, "Is there nothing better here?" She contemptuously replied, "*Gentlemen* want nothing better."[50]

The intruders decided to go upstairs to look for valuables. Not happy about Elizabeth's lack of enthusiasm for their cause, they began to insult her with vile names as they roamed the house. She in turn told one of them, whom she recognized, that he had sold her inferior brooms. At one point, the men threatened physical violence, and she asked them if they were the kind of men who would strike a woman. The intruders were disappointed in the few valuables they found in the house. Theodore had turned over his papers to the Reverend West for safekeeping. Pamela had given Elizabeth a few items of jewelry and the family silverware to be locked in Elizabeth's own oaken chest in her bedroom.[51]

When the men finally reached Elizabeth's bedroom and discovered the locked chest, they demanded Elizabeth give them the key. According to Catharine Sedgwick, who heard the tale many times from Elizabeth, she turned to the broom maker and said, "Ah! Sam Cooper, you and your fellows are no better than I thought you. You call me 'wench' and 'nigger,' and you are not above rummaging my chest. You will have to break it open to do it!" Apparently, she was still carrying the fireplace shovel, because none of them tried to force her to give the key to them. Elizabeth said of Sam Cooper, "He turned and slunk away like a whipped cur as he was!"[52]

Out on Plain Street, order was beginning to break down. The insurgents had broken into Timothy Edwards's general store and appropriated his entire stock of liquor.[53] For amusement, some of the insurgents tied to a rail Pamela's nephew, young Harry Hopkins, son of a man who ten years before had died in the Patriot cause, and carried him up and down Plain Street to the delight of their comrades.[54]

At one point, forty-one Stockbridge men were being held prisoner in the street or at the Red Lion.[55] In the confusion, a few slipped away, including Captain Jones, whom the Widow Bingham hid in the Red Lion's chimney closet. Out on the street, Jones's elder son Josiah convinced one of the insurgents to let his twelve-year-old brother, William, and Backus, the family's lame hired man, go home.[56]

As the sun rose, the insurgents and their prisoners marched south to Great Barrington, seemingly unaware that, in the chaos, messengers had been able to slip out of Stockbridge and inform militia commanders in Sheffield of the raid.

At Great Barrington, Hamlin's men broke into the jail and freed the debtors, then took another opportunity to refresh themselves at the Public House. It was late morning before Hamlin decided it was time to head west for the safety of the New York border.[57]

By about 1 p.m. in Sheffield, John Ashley's son had been able to assemble a force of about eighty militiamen. Perceiving that the insurgents would head for the border, Ashley Jr. was able to position his men in the woods on both sides of the road that ran west from Sheffield to Egremont, a town near the New York border. The militia arrived only shortly before the insurgents and their prisoners.[58]

It is not clear whether the insurgents were given an opportunity to surrender, but shots were fired. Fifty to sixty prisoners were taken by the government force. Thirty insurgents, including Hamlin, were wounded. Three insurgents were killed, together with one Stockbridge hostage, Solomon Glezen, the village's schoolmaster. On the government side, one militiaman was killed and a second was wounded.[59]

Late that afternoon, Elizabeth and the other residents of Stockbridge experienced the relief of standing at their front doors and watching a mile-long procession of sleighs transport the prisoners through Stockbridge on their way northward to the jail at Lenox.[60] Perhaps with the safe return of Henry Hopkins and Ephraim Williams to the Sedgwick household, Elizabeth slept well that night.

Thus ended Shays' Rebellion and, in many ways, the American Revolution in western Massachusetts. The government of Massachusetts decided to show leniency. Two hundred seventy men were pardoned. Initially, fourteen men were sentenced to death, but of those, nine were pardoned, and the remainder had their death sentences commuted to prison time, the longest serving seven years.[61]

Theodore agreed with the policy of leniency for all but the highest-ranking rebels. He was appointed to represent some of the Shaysites and secured them a fair trial. He also wrote letters to Governor James Bowdoin II for three of the insurgents, urging clemency.[62] This was broad-minded thinking for a man who had extended family members and friends kidnapped from his home and the homes of neighbors and who had to explain to his children why the village schoolmaster was dead. But he had lived through the polarizing period of the Revolution, and he understood that if Massachusetts was to move forward, it could not do so with 20 percent of the population in the western part of the state embittered.

5

Raising a Family and Building a Government

THOUGH HE WAS WILLING to extend an olive branch to the rebels in the aftermath of their defeat, Shays' Rebellion had a profound effect on Theodore Sedgwick's beliefs about the kind of federal government America needed, as it did for many others who would become Federalists. Prior to the rebellion, Theodore favored enhancing the federal government's ability to raise revenue. Now he realized that the federal government needed stronger powers for national defense, too.[1] He was profoundly alarmed that the federal government had been unable to send federal troops to aid the Massachusetts militia until February 9, two weeks after the insurgents' attack on the federal arsenal at Springfield and only three weeks before the end of the rebellion.[2]

Theodore concluded he must return to Congress as well as again stand for election to the Massachusetts House, so he could join the fight for a stronger federal government. This decision would change the lives of every member of the Sedgwick household, including Elizabeth's.

The previous summer, Theodore had told Pamela he was done with politics and intended to "return to the vale of private life for many years perhaps forever."[3] The decision was what Pamela had been praying for; he was both her lover and her best friend. She was achingly lonely when he was gone.

In thirteen years of marriage, Pamela had borne seven children, four of whom were living. Now weeks away from delivering an eighth baby, her husband was telling her he needed to return to politics for the good of the country.

Theodore was elected to the Massachusetts House of Representatives in the spring of 1787, and as was then permitted, he ran concurrently for the Confederation Congress, winning that office in June 1787.[4]

Theodore was away in Boston when Pamela gave birth on June 7 to a son they named Robert, with plans to soon depart for New York City where the Confederation Congress was sitting. Pamela was profoundly conflicted. She had feared for his life throughout the preceding months when he bravely helped lead the resistance to Shays' Rebellion. There were still Shays sympathizers who hated him in Berkshire County, so he was probably safer in Boston or New York than at home, but he was planning to be absent for many months, and the thought of the separation was close to unendurable.

Ten days after Robert's birth, she wrote Theodore of her longing for him. The needs of the country would not override it, but her fears for his safety did: "The time has been my love when I fondly hoped to see you.... Heaven forbid that I should ... wish you to return to be subject to the midnight robber or those shameless wretches who can boldly threaten assassination."[5]

Pamela was slow to recover from Robert's birth. This time she needed a wet nurse and had difficulty finding one. Elizabeth leapt into the breach with the older children, and Pamela's mother temporarily moved into her daughter's home to provide moral support and an extra pair of hands.[6]

Meanwhile, Theodore was deeply immersed in the struggle to scrap the Articles of Confederation and replace them with the Constitution. He was back in Stockbridge in November to convince his highly skeptical constituents that the Constitution should be ratified. In a marathon performance, he held the floor for upwards of eight hours at a town meeting, explaining the proposed Constitution point by point. His efforts paid off. The meeting voted sixty to thirty in favor of ratification and voted for Theodore as the town's representative to the state ratifying convention.[7]

In January at the state ratifying convention in Boston, he was a leader of the pro-ratification forces, who at the start of the convention were in the minority. He worked tirelessly on the committee that negotiated the compromise of ratifying the Constitution with recommended amendments, particularly an amendment that reserved to the states all powers not expressly granted to the federal government. In

5. Raising a Family and Building a Government

the end, the ratifying convention narrowly approved the Constitution by a vote of 187 to 168.[8] Theodore immediately traveled to New York and Philadelphia to help plan the next steps in the ratification fight.[9]

Elizabeth's contributions in the Sedgwick home were of immense importance at this time. With Pamela recovering slowly from Robert's birth and two-year-old Harry almost constantly ill, Pamela told Theodore, "Little Harry has been very ill is still in a poor way." Elizabeth's efforts kept Theodore from being summoned home.[10]

* * *

During the spring and summer of 1788, Elizabeth made it possible for Pamela to spend several weeks in Boston during the state legislative session in which Theodore served as Speaker. Pamela had concluded that if she wanted to spend significant time with her husband, she would have to set aside her reluctance to leave her children. Elizabeth's calm willingness to take on the challenge made it possible. The trip temporarily boosted Pamela's sagging spirits.

After a six-day coach journey back to Stockbridge, Pamela assured her friend Betsy Mayhew in Boston, "I know it will give my dear Betsy Pleasure to Hear her friend arrived at Stockbridge in safety … and was so happy as to find her little flock … all well accept her Babe who had been very Ill but was mending and is since restored to health."[11]

Theodore escorted Pamela home and then left immediately for New York, leaving Pamela to struggle with the reality of a solitary rural life without her absentee husband. She told Betsy Mayhew, who was younger than she was and still single, "You have no Idea of [how much] a Woman's happiness be affected with the absence of her husband."[12]

There is no record of what Elizabeth thought of Theodore's comings and goings. Her own experience with the father of her daughter was that men went away to do their duty, and women stayed behind caring for the children and keeping the home fires burning.

The realization that Theodore would now be absent from home most of the time probably took a while to permeate the Sedgwick household. Pressure was building on him to run again for Congress. Anti-Federalist sentiment was strong enough in Berkshire County that supporters of the new Constitution feared that Theodore was the only Federalist capable of holding the seat. Throughout the fall of 1788, Theodore promised his wife that he would remain in the new Congress for only one term.[13]

In late January 1789, Theodore again assured Pamela, "I hope your fears that I should continue in Public life will not create any considerable pain. Believe me my love your wishes on this subject perfectly coincide with my own."[14]

Meanwhile, Pamela kept Theodore informed of the constant activity in the frenetic household she and Elizabeth administered and of how difficult it was to find time to write him: "I snatch a moment from a crying Infant and the Noise of two or three ungoverned children."[15]

But Pamela's poor health placed much of the burden on Elizabeth, and Pamela knew it: "I have been so long of little use to them that their demands upon me seem to be greatly augmented. I often lament the Poorness of my Constitution as that ever deprives me of that Power that would render me Usefull."[16]

Theodore was back in Stockbridge during the spring to battle for his congressional seat. The county was so deeply divided that it took five ballots to determine the winner. Theodore eked out the victory with an eleven-vote margin.[17]

Pamela reported sadly to Betsy Mayhew, "Mr. Sedgwick left me 15 days since for NYork—I doe not expect to see him again until September and then but for a short time." She wryly advised Betsy, who was being courted by an admirer in Boston, "not [to] make Choice of one that is fond of Politics."[18]

In New York, Theodore's fellow Federalists in the new Congress quickly recognized his talents: "I have the vanity to believe my feeble aid in the important business in which I am engaged will not be altogether without effect," he proudly reported to Pamela.[19] Soon even George Washington was showing him attention. After the first presidential reception Theodore attended, he wrote to Pamela, "He did me the honor particularly to distinguish me, with great cordiality took me by the hand and expressed much satisfaction to see me here."[20] Before long, Theodore related that he was being invited to private conferences with the father of his country. "This morning I spent an hour with the president."[21]

5. Raising a Family and Building a Government

Theodore wanted Pamela to join him in New York for a few weeks, just as she had spent time with him in Boston the previous summer. Elizabeth would again manage things in Stockbridge while she was gone. He wrote, "I hope it may not be inconvenient to you to come down towards fall in which case I shall attend you home."[22]

But Theodore's visit home in the spring had once again resulted in pregnancy. Pamela concealed her disappointment and replied calmly, "I am affraid I shall not be able to comply with your kind invitation to attend you in NY—which if convenient would be pleasing to me."[23] A lady did not directly refer in writing to pregnancy, even to her husband. Theodore understood what she meant.

Instead, Pamela spent the summer of 1789 attending to her mother, Abigail, who was rapidly declining in health. Almost every day she left the children with Elizabeth to climb the hill to her brother's house, where Abigail was "in a very feeble state."[24]

As Pamela struggled with her loneliness, her mother's illness, and the prospect of another difficult pregnancy, Elizabeth grew ever more confident in the work she was doing and the life she was building. It had been eight years since she came to the Sedgwick household. To the rest of the staff, she was now "Madame Bet." As Henry Sedgwick later described it, "Without ever claiming superiority, she uniformly ... obtained an ascendency over all those with whom she was associated in service."[25] To the Sedgwick children, she was "Mumbet." Catharine Sedgwick later said, "The children under her government regarded it, as the Jews did theirs, as a theocracy; and if a divine right were founded upon such ability and fidelity, as hers, there would be no revolutions."[26]

Her own daughter, Betsey, was now about fourteen. As Elizabeth had hoped, Betsey barely remembered the Ashley household. There was, of course, an occasional reminder of the past. The Sedgwicks and the Ashleys remained friends. In late August, John Ashley, Jr., appeared at the door with a letter for Pamela. He had been in Boston, and Betsy Mayhew had asked him to carry it with him on the stage that passed through Stockbridge.[27] Elizabeth likely preferred to think of Ashley Jr. as Judge Ashley's son rather than Hannah's. She knew of his role in rescuing the Stockbridge hostages after Hamlin's raid, and she probably didn't mind his occasional visits.

A Revolutionary Woman

Despite her hard-won freedom and her professional success, Elizabeth must have struggled with the loneliness of a widow. Her position as governess to the Sedgwick children made an informal relationship with a man impossible. If she wanted a partner, a formal marriage would have been necessary. For a woman in eighteenth-century America who earned a salary and ordered her own life, that was a huge decision. The laws of the time decreed that a woman's wages belonged to her husband and that the decisions as to where she lived and whether she held a job at all were his. Elizabeth never found a man she was willing to trust with that power. She would remain a widow for the rest of her life.

Though Elizabeth lacked a partner, she did have the consolation of friends. About sixty African Americans were living in Stockbridge in the late 1780s, about twice as many as in Sheffield. Approximately half of these people lived in their own homes, and the other half, like Elizabeth, lived in the homes of their European American employers.[28]

Young Agrippa Hull, though an employee of the Sedgwicks, lived in his own home with his wife, Jane Darby. Not long after Elizabeth's freedom suit, Jane had fled her master, Mr. Ingersoll of Lenox. When Ingersoll tried to reclaim her, Theodore Sedgwick intervened at the request of Agrippa. Ingersoll backed off at the threat of a lawsuit, and Agrippa and Jane were wed. Agrippa sometimes accompanied Theodore on his travels. When he did, Jane was often in the Sedgwick kitchen assisting Elizabeth.[29]

Another of Elizabeth's friends was Rose Benny, who was once the slave of Jonathan Edwards. In 1756, Rose married Joab Benny, a former slave, who became a tanner, a blacksmith, and a farmer. Rose was freed upon her marriage or soon after. Joab subsequently became the wealthiest African American in Stockbridge. The younger of their two surviving daughters was a little older than Betsey Freeman.[30]

* * *

As the fall of 1789 transitioned into winter, Elizabeth must have noted with concern Pamela's exhaustion. Pamela went into premature labor, giving birth to Catharine Maria, her fourth daughter and ninth child, "in a bitter cold night" on December 28, 1789. Elizabeth and Pamela's brother, Dr. Erastus Sergeant, attended the birth, later telling Catharine she had been as "fair and handsome as a London Doll."[31]

5. Raising a Family and Building a Government

Despite the early birth, the baby thrived, but Pamela was again exhausted and bedridden. Theodore was present for the birth, but a month later he was back in New York, urging Pamela to find a wet nurse to preserve her health.[32]

An acceptable candidate could not be found, so Elizabeth and Pamela apparently decided to use cow or goat's milk to feed little Catharine.[33] Pamela understood that there were limits to even Elizabeth's strength and that after contending all day with the baby and five older children, she must have a good night's rest. Eliza, Pamela's firstborn, three months short of her fourteenth birthday, had recently returned from a year of school in Boston.[34] Elizabeth was, of course, available for emergencies, but as Catharine described in her autobiography, "My sister Eliza, through all that cold winter, slept in the room with my mother, and got up in the cold watches of the night to feed me."[35]

The strategy worked. By the first week in February, Pamela was up and about and able to receive visitors. Theodore, apparently unable to fathom how busy everyone was at home, complained, "You do not know how much I was disappointed on Wednesday in not having the pleasure to receive a single line from home. Mr. Jacob called on me this morning and said ... you informed him that the family was all well, and particularly observed that little Kitty appeared to grow finely." Theodore was, however, very impressed with how busy he was: "On Monday we shall enter on the all important subject of funding the national debt."[36]

By the end of February, Pamela was able to sit down and write Theodore a long letter. For the first and only time in their marriage, she was able to mock a bit the self-importance of Theodore and his colleagues: "nor will I make any great Pretensions to Public Spirit I am very willing to leve that Virtue to the Fathers of our Infant Nation and let them Bustle and wrangle about the Interest of their country at their Leisure." The work that she and Elizabeth were doing was just as important—no more important—than what the men were spending their time doing: "If I can still a squalling Infant and Settle a matter of Great Contention among a Company of unruly Boys—I feel myself as happy and as Great as an Empress."[37]

Pamela did not possess Abigail Adams's desire to share in her husband's diplomatic work or the social side of politics. But if, like Elizabeth Freeman, Pamela could have maintained the attitude that her work in caring for children was as important a calling as what men did, it might have preserved her mental health. Instead, her need for Theodore's companionship and her sense of guilt over her loneliness, as well as a growing sense that her beloved needed her less than she needed him, would soon launch her into a battle with depression that would last for the remainder of her life.

Meanwhile, she wrote of the daily onslaught of challenges she and Elizabeth worked together to confront: "The little Boys have been very unwell.... Little Catherine also who is still unwell." Eliza, who was such a help to them both, was in a sleighing accident, and she was "considerably hurt upon her head and her face very much.... Bruised."[38]

Theodore usually consoled himself with the knowledge that though he could not help Pamela personally, he had provided her with enough staff and enough money to deal with any problems that arose when he was away. Though he tended to discount the emotional stress of having to deal with these problems without him, if an issue arose that could not be solved through these avenues, he was willing to do more, as long as it didn't require him to come home.

Shortly after Catharine's birth, Robert, age two and a half, fell and injured his ankle. His uncle, Erastus Sergeant, and another local physician, Dr. Partridge, examined the boy. The ankle did not seem to be broken, but it did not heal. The problem went on for months. Either he dragged himself, or Pamela, Elizabeth, or Eliza carried him about. They were very worried, writing, "Almost we can perceive it grows less."[39] On two occasions, Theodore interrupted his congressional work to consult with doctors in New York. At one point, he suggested to Pamela, "It will be worth the attempt to bring him down here as soon as the river opens."[40] Pamela demurred. It was a big thing to ask of her brothers. She did not insist that, to avoid the risk of a lifetime of lameness, Theodore break off from his congressional work and come fetch him. Fortunately, by early May, when his father was home during a recess, Robert began to recover, and by the end of May, when Theodore was back in New York, Pamela could report that he was healed.

* * *

Theodore's talents as a negotiator, debater, and legal draftsman, together with his commitment to a strong federal government, were

5. Raising a Family and Building a Government

rapidly making him one of the administration's most valuable allies in Congress. Washington, Hamilton, and Knox all relied on his assistance, and Washington in particular was careful to cultivate him, as he did all his prized junior officers. Theodore shared with Pamela, "I spent two or three hours this afternoon with the Presidt. who treats me with a familiarity I have never before experienced, and with a confidence which was highly flattering to me."[41]

Hamilton's fiscal program was composed of three major elements: funding the domestic national debt, assumption of unpaid state war debts, and authorization of a twelve-million-dollar loan to pay America's foreign creditors.[42] This was a lot to swallow for those members of Congress, especially southerners, who were distrustful of a strong federal government. To win their support for his economic program, Hamilton struck a deal with the southerners. The capital would move to Philadelphia the following year, and in a decade, it would move to a new site on the Potomac River. The symbolism and convenience of a southern capital mattered deeply to southern legislators. Many of them agreed to support Hamilton's economic plan.[43]

Theodore understood the significance of the decisions: "A very few days will determine what will be the future complexion of the government," he excitedly informed Pamela.[44]

Theodore had been vaguely optimistic with Pamela about when he might return home. In late June, she received a visit from his friend, Cornelius Van Rennselaer, who injudiciously let the cat out of the bag. Hamilton's economic program was such a massive piece of legislation that Congress was very likely to be in session all summer. Elizabeth watched Pamela wilt before her eyes. Pamela wrote Theodore: "I sicken at the thought of your being Absent for so long a time.... I cannot Possibly reconcile my feelings or make myself Happy in this State of Widdowhood."[45]

Elizabeth, of course, had had to accept the permanent absence of her husband and true widowhood. Did she secretly scoff at Pamela's depression over long absences that eventually gave way to happy reunions? The evidence shows that Elizabeth genuinely sympathized with Pamela. Her own departed sister, Lizzie, was of a "timid" nature.[46] Elizabeth had loved and protected her all her life. Elizabeth was a caregiver and a healer by nature. She instinctively understood that some people were less equipped to deal with the challenges in their lives than others. The Sedgwick children, who were the primary witnesses to Elizabeth's care of Pamela over the next seventeen years as Pamela's physical and mental condition declined, were uniformly impressed with her sensitivity toward Pamela. Catharine Sedgwick later observed, "Mumbet was the only person who could tranquilize my mother when her mind was disordered—the only one of her friends whom she liked to have about her—and why? She treated her with the same respect she did when she was sane."[47]

Catharine wrote that Elizabeth, without medical training, intuitively understood how to calm her patient and reassure the confused young Sedgwick children who were forced to watch their mother's distress: "As far as was possible, she obeyed her commands and humored her caprices; in short her superior instincts hit upon the mode of treatment that science has since adopted." Hired to be the children's governess, Elizabeth compassionately guided both Pamela and her children through the dark days of Pamela's recurring affliction: "In addition to her other multiform services, she was my mother's nurse."[48]

When Pamela married Theodore, she did so knowing that she would never have been his wife if his beloved Eliza had not been struck down by smallpox. She had loved him enough to accept that fact, even naming their first child after her much-adored predecessor. Theodore knew he could not go through life without the love of a woman. He put aside his grief, and he and Pamela built a family together. Tearing down her body with what would be ten pregnancies, Pamela gave him the gift of the family. She never denied her body to him as a form of birth control as some eighteenth-century women did. He delighted in their intimate relationship and the children that came from it. At some point, Pamela dared to hope that she had become first in his heart as he was in hers. He certainly loved her dearly, but the opportunity to play a significant role in the making of the nation and the regard of great men that went along with it captured his imagination.

In the early years of the Revolution, Henry Knox, another Massachusetts man who rose to be Washington's second in command and later the first secretary of war, firmly told his wife Lucy that though she was the love of his life, she must accept their separation for a while

5. Raising a Family and Building a Government

as he helped found the nation. The separation lasted less than four years. As soon as it was safe, and indeed, a little before it was safe, she joined him in his military camp, and they were rarely separated thereafter. Once the war was over, Henry chose to live on the edge of bankruptcy in order to keep Lucy and their children with him in New York and Philadelphia as he continued his public service, first as the Articles of Confederation Secretary at War and later as George Washington's first Secretary of War. In 1795, when Knox came to see that continued public service was detrimental to his family's financial security, he retired from the administration. Though Henry Knox was far closer to George Washington than Theodore Sedgwick would ever be, there was nothing Washington could say to dissuade him. Lucy Knox knew that though she had lent her husband to the nation for a few years when they were young, his priority was her and their family.

For Pamela Sedgwick, it was very different. After sixteen years of marriage, it was almost as though America and fame were her husband's new mistresses, and she and her children could not compete with them. Pamela was profoundly shocked as she watched Theodore fall ever more deeply in love with his political career. Could he really feel so differently than she did?

If he wouldn't come back home for her sake, would he for their children? "My children want a father I everyday Sensibly feal what theay suffer from the Loss of the assid[u]ous care of a Wise and Tender Parent."[49] Would he not come home even for "sweet little Catherine who is finely grown and is now the Beautiful Likeness of her Pappa"?[50] Theodore was absent for more than eight months in the year 1790. For the period from 1789 to 1800, he would be absent from home more than half the year for eight out of those twelve years.[51]

6

"The main pillar of our household"

After the passage of Hamilton's economic program in September 1790, Theodore came home for most of the fall, but in December it was time for him to return to Congress, now located in Philadelphia, ninety miles more distant from Stockbridge than New York. To bolster Pamela's spirits, Theodore suggested that Pamela travel with him to Philadelphia for a short visit and then return via New York where she could visit friends, as he resumed his frenetic congressional schedule.[1]

Elizabeth was to manage the household and care for the couple's six children, ages fifteen, twelve, ten, five, three, and one, in their absence. Pamela's half sister, Electa Sergeant Hopkins, and Pamela's sister-in-law Abigail, Henry Dwight's wife, could be called upon in an emergency, and Eliza Sedgwick and Elizabeth's daughter, Betsey, both fifteen, were expected to be of some assistance with the younger children. Nevertheless, Pamela and Theodore were once again placing on Elizabeth's shoulders the daily running of their large household and the primary responsibility for the supervision, health, and safety of their family.

On Christmas Day, together with Abigail Adams and her son Charles, Henry and Lucy Knox, and other members of the political elite, Theodore and Pamela attended Martha Washington's first levee in the new capital.[2] Observers were impressed with Pamela: "Mrs. Theodore Sedgwick in whom were combined the finest graces of the New England matron, was conspicuous for a charming face, and an air and manner of singular refinement and elegance."[3]

At the end of the trip, Pamela was grateful to Elizabeth for the vacation, but she knew it was time to resume her duties as mother—a role she loved, although it was one she struggled to perform. It wasn't the glitter of social life in Philadelphia that she missed; it was Theodore. She shared with him, "I returned home & found my children theay were dear to me their company good their prattle diverting but still I found a Void in my heart."[4]

The duties that she found so rewarding when Theodore was at home were now exhausting for her. She wrote, "Theay look to me for gratification of every wish—I soon found myself week and Irresolute and wanted to repose my Anxious Heart in the Bosome of my Beloved friend & Protector but this alas was impossible."[5]

Pamela did her best to hide these feelings from her children. Her son Henry reflected after her death many years later, "Through a whole lifetime she never once expressed a feeling of impatience. Such was the strength of her submissive piety; but from the sensibility of her temper, she was often afflicted with the severest anguish, from an apprehension, that her life was useless."[6]

With little societal understanding of mental illness, Pamela looked to the tenets of her religion to explain her condition. As Catharine Sedgwick later noted, "She was overburdened with care and afflicted by the gloomy tenets of Calvinism, no abstractions to her sensitive nature."[7]

Her religion taught her that both her loneliness and her feelings of inadequacy were evidence of moral weakness. Good people suffered silently and carried on. Pamela confessed to her husband, "I grew dissatisfied with evry thing but most of all my Self—what dependent creatures we are ... not being able To govern our own Tempers and dispositions or of reducing our fealings under the control of Reason."[8]

In Philadelphia, Theodore was determined to explain away Pamela's letters as normal loneliness and too much humility. He was immersed in efforts to get the National Bank Act and an excise bill passed by Congress.[9] He was also enjoying Philadelphia's social whirl, attending a performance of Shakespeare's Taming of the Shrew, and he wrote, "Every day almost I have an invitation to dine and spend the evening."[10]

Back in Stockbridge, Elizabeth was severely overextended. Theodore had taken Agrippa Hull with him to Philadelphia, leaving an African American man named Ceaser as her assistant. Ceaser had concluded that, with Theodore gone, it was unnecessary to accept Pamela's instructions or to assist Elizabeth with household tasks. Elizabeth, a physically powerful woman who had stared down Hamlin's raiders, was not afraid of him, but he was completely useless to her. Though Pamela regularly dealt with the Sedgwicks' European American field hand when Theodore was absent, Ceaser intimidated her, and she could not work up the courage to fire him. She told Theodore, "I hope I shall have Patience to bear with [Ceaser's]—Pride and Negroisms until you return—and danger I know you will not wish me to."[11]

Not only was Elizabeth dealing with Ceaser's negligence and Pamela's distractedness, but Pamela's mother was in the final days of her life, and Pamela had to spend extended periods out of the house to be with her.[12] With so much to do, Elizabeth lost track of Catharine for a moment, and the thirteen-month-old baby sustained an injury. Pamela reported to Theodore, "Kitty is a fine little Girl—but since she has tottled about, has badly Burnt her Arm."[13] Pamela did not blame Elizabeth for the incident any more than she blamed Theodore for being absent (and taking Agrippa with him), but Elizabeth, who loved the Sedgwick children as her own and always required herself to be "up to the mark," a woman who as an adult Catharine would describe as embodying "ability, rectitude, and fidelity," probably felt it keenly.[14]

Theodore came home briefly in the spring before leaving for Boston to attend to a business matter.[15] The visit resulted in another pregnancy. It was to be Pamela's tenth and final pregnancy, and it would leave her once again in the throes of depression.

Back in Philadelphia that fall, Theodore made an off-hand comment to Aaron Burr, a grandson of Jonathan Edwards and a childhood friend of Pamela, that Pamela hated his absences and perhaps he should consider retiring from Congress. Burr passed the comment along to Pamela, and she leapt at the idea with renewed hope.[16]

Theodore quickly disabused her of the notion. Now chairman of the House Judiciary Committee, the legislative work he was doing was much more interesting to him than his legal career. He proposed to keep his Stockbridge legal office open by staffing it with a younger lawyer and a law clerk. He had also made some investments. He believed that the law office, investments, and his congressional salary should be sufficient to provide a comfortable life for his family.[17]

6. "The main pillar of our household"

Pamela tried once more to convince Theodore to give up his political career. She had given up the idea that he could be persuaded to relinquish his congressional seat to spend more time with her or their children, but what about his duty to provide financially for his family? Wasn't he taking a big risk by handing his legal practice over to others? "The Interests of your family deserve some attention ... should you find your circumstances straitened at a future day I know from the Tender affection you have for your children it would give you real pain—A return to Business would then be Painful and thought degrading."[18]

It was the final argument she could think of to convince him to come home. If he rejected it, Pamela stated, "I have not a distant wish that you should sacrifice your happiness to mine, or your inclination to my opinion.... Submission is my duty and however hard I will try to Practice what reason teaches me I am under obligation to doe."[19]

That kind of talk made Theodore uncomfortable. He didn't like to think of himself as some brute who was forcing his wife to submit to the gratification of his wishes over hers, and he wrote, "Nothing but a sence of my own honor which I know is dear to you and I may add a sence of public duty produced my ultimate determination." Buoyed by his role in pushing through federal assumption of the Massachusetts war debt, Theodore was reelected to Congress by a substantial margin.[20]

Pamela never again asked Theodore to withdraw from public life. Instead, now about six months pregnant, she began to sink more deeply into distraction and depression. Sixteen-year-old Eliza was visiting friends in New York. It was probably Elizabeth who encouraged thirteen-year-old Frances to write to her father and tell him how poorly Pamela was doing.

Theodore was shocked. He wrote Pamela on November 20: "Ever since I received Fanny's letter of the 9th I have been anxious about you, beyond any thing in my power to express." But was he to take a thirteen-year-old's word for it? "At some times I have been determined to set out imediately for home, and then again I hardly think my self justifyed in doing it."[21]

Pamela was humiliated. It was one thing to be physically dying from the complications of a pregnancy. A husband might be summoned home for that. But to be so filled with mental suffering as to be dysfunctional was a shameful weakness and dereliction of duty. On December 4, she confessed to her husband, "Friends would perswaide me I am not well but this I have no reason to Beleive but shall I tell you that I have lost my understanding what is my shame what is my pain what is my confusion to think of this what Evils will my poor Family without a guide without a head."[22]

Theodore wanted Pamela to make the decision about his return, but their correspondence shows that she was too distressed to make it: "For their Sakes I wish you at home—for your sake I wish you not to come you must not come it would only make us both more wretched."[23] Little Catharine, just short of two years old, would later record that among her first words were "Theodore" and "Philadelphia."[24]

Theodore wrote that he was in a quandary. "I do not know but that you and all my friends believe that I have been very deficient in performing my duty in not returning home at the first information of your illness. I am myself doubtful whether my conduct may not justly be charged with criminal neglect."[25]

Elizabeth and young Frances might recognize that Theodore should come home, but all the men in his life were saying otherwise. His close friend Van Shaack and Pamela's cousin, Elisha Williams, both wrote to say that Pamela was improving.[26] His colleagues in Congress were aghast. The chairman of the House Judiciary Committee couldn't abandon important legislative matters to run home and hold his pregnant wife's hand: "My friends here, however, have been so importunate as to induce me to put off the Journey at least for a few days."[27]

He was genuinely confused as to her due date. If she was actually *having* the baby, it would be a better excuse. "If I could know the time that would be most agreeable to you for me to be at home I would most certainly make a point of then being with you."[28]

But as Theodore wrote those words, Pamela was going into labor two months early. Elizabeth attended the birth, and on December 15, 1791, she delivered a baby so small she wasn't sure he could live.

To his credit, when he received word of the birth, Theodore immediately dropped his work and took an unpaid six-week leave of absence, departing Philadelphia on December 22, 1791.[29] Childbearing was so entirely deemed to be a woman's problem at the time that

6. "The main pillar of our household"

his political foes in Berkshire County mocked him for coming home in mid-session:

> Maria dear lady, how blessed is thy lot,
> O'er so noble a husband to bear such a sway.
> For sure very dear must that lady be thought,
> Who is valued at more than six dollars a day.[30]

The baby, who would later become in his parents' correspondence, "the good little man" and "our sweet little Charles," was struggling to survive in a world without incubators and other neonatal hospital equipment.[31] Catharine Sedgwick later wrote Elizabeth's account of Charles's early months. The account preserves both the drama of the situation and Elizabeth's dry humor as she retold the story many times to the Sedgwick children: "'The baby was nothing to look at,' said the dear old nurse, 'when he was born. The Judge (so she latterly styled my father) said he was not worth raising. Sir,' says I, 'I will try it.'"[32]

Charles was no project for elder sister Eliza. This time Elizabeth took the baby into her own bed. He was so small, she laid him on a pillow and put padding around his arms to protect his delicate skin from chafing.[33] During the day, assisted by three teens, her daughter, Betsey, and Pamela's daughters, Eliza and Frances, Elizabeth also cared for the bedridden mother and the four other Sedgwick children, ages two, four, six, and ten. Theoretically, she was entitled to Sundays off. Though she may have allowed herself an evening stroll once the younger children were in bed, she was on duty continuously during this period and many other times during her professional life with the Sedgwick family.

* * *

Meanwhile, Theodore returned to Congress, arriving in Philadelphia February 8, 1792. Ironically, as Elizabeth worked to keep his youngest child alive and the rest of his family fed and cared for, Theodore's Judiciary Committee was working on America's first Fugitive Slave Act.[34] Elizabeth probably didn't know it. She couldn't read newspapers.

Theodore didn't like the legislation, but he believed there was no choice. Article IV of the Constitution decreed that slaves fleeing from states where slavery was legal could not obtain legal refuge in states that had abolished slavery. The Fugitive Slave Act was intended to execute this constitutional provision. Whether slavery existed within its borders was a matter for each state to decide, and if slaves fled from a slave state to a free state, they had to be returned. That was the deal that had been struck with the South in order to obtain ratification of the Constitution.

Theodore was proud of his role in ending slavery in Massachusetts. He believed that there were other states, such as Pennsylvania, where public opinion was turning against slavery and where abolition was a real possibility. In October 1792, he joined the Abolition Society of Pennsylvania to encourage efforts in that state by Quakers and others to abolish slavery, but he had had enough conversations with southern legislators to be clear that there was no such sentiment in the South. In his view, if the Union was to stand, the North had to keep its word to execute Article IV.[35]

When Theodore returned home in the spring, what he regarded as a near miracle greeted him. As Elizabeth described it years later to the Sedgwick children, "when the Judge came home again I took him to the cradle where the baby was sleeping, and I threw off the blanket and showed him a plump, rosy boy—a perfect beauty, 'There, sir,' says I, 'is that boy worth raising?' Tears came in the Judge's eyes, and he took a silver crown out of his pocket and gave it to me, and I have it now in my trunk."[36]

Theodore wanted Elizabeth to have the money as additional compensation for her extraordinary efforts. To Elizabeth, what she had done was a gift of love. She kept the coin all her life as a kind of Olympic medal of nursing and bequeathed it to a great-grandchild when she died.[37]

Charles Sedgwick never forgot how Elizabeth saved his life as a baby or all her care of him and his siblings during their childhoods. After Pamela's death, he took to referring to Elizabeth as "mother" in his letters to his sister Catharine, and he regarded it as his sacred duty to be a staff of Elizabeth's old age.[38]

* * *

That summer, with Theodore mostly at home, Pamela's health improved. She was able to reopen her correspondence with her friend

6. "The main pillar of our household"

Betsy Mayhew, thanking her for "the kind concern you express at my loss of Health and the loss of my Reason a still heaveer calamety which it has Pleased God to bring oppon me for a Season." Always concerned to minimize others' anxiety about her, Pamela assured Betsy, "I am now the most of the Time free from any Pain or Destress and verry Comfortable."[39]

After consulting with Pamela and Elizabeth, Theodore devised a four-pronged plan to preserve Pamela's health while he attended the next session of Congress. Theodore had promptly discharged Ceaser upon his return home the previous spring. Now he realized that no one would be as helpful to Pamela and Elizabeth as Agrippa Hull. Theodore asked Agrippa to remain with the family for the winter rather than accompany him to Philadelphia. He hired another African American, John, to travel with him and serve as his valet.

Theodore eventually had to discharge John when he caught him stealing from him, but he did not report him to the law or try to ruin his chances of getting another job. He told Pamela, "Should John go home I wish at present it may not be mentioned—Perhaps he may repent & reform."[40]

Both Pamela and Elizabeth had told Theodore how much Pamela missed her deceased mother, Abigail. Prior to his departure, Theodore persuaded Pamela to invite her young, unmarried cousin, the children's beloved "Aunt Gray," for an extended visit during his absence. She would provide Pamela with the female companionship she had lost with her mother's death.[41]

Theodore and Elizabeth also persuaded Pamela that she should delegate many of her daily duties to seventeen-year-old Eliza. This was hard for Pamela because she already suffered from feelings of uselessness as a result of her extended illness, but it was probably presented to her as important training in household management for a young woman who could soon be expected to marry.

The final prong of the plan was the most important. Theodore wanted Pamela to come down to Philadelphia after the new year and remain with him until the spring recess. Elizabeth and Eliza would manage things at home. Pamela was worried about leaving the smaller children for so long. The four youngest were ages seven, five, three, and one. She and Theodore agreed that she would think about it and let him know in a few weeks if she would join him in Philadelphia.

Perhaps he was almost hoping that he would not be reelected to Congress. That certainly remained Pamela's wish. In early December, she glumly congratulated him upon the news that her hopes were once again dashed: "I Congratulate you my Dear tho I cannot my Self on your Re Election if it can give you pleasure."[42]

News of the reelection made Pamela realize again that her husband's long absences in Philadelphia were a permanent feature of their lives. Although some of the little ones protested, she decided she had to accept Theodore's invitation to make the trip to Philadelphia: "I think I must break away for I cannot think of not seeing you before next Spring."[43]

From Elizabeth's perspective, she now had able assistants in Agrippa, Eliza, and her own daughter, Betsey. Her biggest concern in contemplating Pamela's trip was the emotional toll it might take on the youngest Sedgwick children. Though Pamela had taken trips before, this one would be significantly longer. Three-year-old Catharine continued to talk about her father weeks after his departure: "Little Katherine is a fine child asks me evry morning for the Kiss Pappa sent her Says it is a sweet one Says I must tell pappa she is a good little daughter."[44] How would Catharine take her mother going away for such a long time too? And then there was one-year-old Charles. Catharine could at least be told her mother would return. To baby Charles, who, despite his prematurity, was beginning to walk right on schedule, it would be as though Pamela had simply disappeared. Of course, there were also seven-year-old Henry and five-year-old Robert. They were also missing their father, as well as their older brother Theodore II who was away at school, and they were enjoying their mother's recent return to functionality. How would they respond to her extended absence?

Having lived through the last three years of Pamela's illness, Elizabeth probably concluded there was no choice. Pamela's presence in the household caused all her children distress when she was in the throes of depression. If she needed this time in Philadelphia with her husband to stay sane, then it had to happen.

Mother Nature, however, had other plans. The winter of 1792–93 was among the warmest in living memory. There was no snow on the ground from Philadelphia to Stockbridge, making travel by sleigh

6. "The main pillar of our household"

impossible.⁴⁵ With the roads a foot or more deep in mud, Pamela's wrote that her journey was not to be: "Providence seems to deny me this Favour." She resolved to focus on Theodore's return in the spring: "I shall endeavour to quiet myself under this disappointment altho it is a severe one to me."⁴⁶

In Philadelphia, Theodore held his breath, wondering if this turn of events would cause Pamela to relapse. It was not pride, he assured his wife, that was keeping him away from her and their children. He was just too good natured to say no to his friends: "Shall I own to you my love the true cause that I have never as yet been able to decline being in public life? It is a kind of proshitute good nature which has always prevented my resisting the importunity of my friends."⁴⁷

Pamela must have wondered why his "proshitute good nature" allowed him to turn down her requests that he come home to his family, but she had resolved to view his ambition kindly, and she wrote, "You have been so long in the habit of Public Cares ... the mind gets innured to active scenes grows fond of them and grasps the country as its world, whare all that is dear is centered." She empathized: "A man who has faithfully served it as I know you my Love have feals that its Interests require his constant attention from which he cannot be separated without fearing a Distressing and painful Void—as a fond Mother does when she is by some misfortune Detached from the care of her family."⁴⁸ This is the closest Pamela ever came to expressing to Theodore what he was doing to her. She loved being a mother, but he was telling her that it was she who would have to face the void rather than him. She would have to choose between being a mother in Stockbridge or a wife in Philadelphia.

Elizabeth, too, was holding her breath as the winter proceeded, hoping that Pamela could get through it without another major period of depression. She did her best to keep the household as tranquil as possible. Henry and Robert were now attending Stockbridge's public elementary school. That was some help to Elizabeth, except they kept bringing illnesses home. In late December and early January, she nursed Henry through a serious case of the flu. Pamela shared the news with Theodore: "Dear little Harry is quite unwell ... his disorder is of the Rumatick kind he cannot walk is very uneasy and Restless."⁴⁹ Three-year-old Catharine was a delight, "a sweet little chatterer and amuses us all with her Spriteliness Vivacity and good nature." Catharine was already showing herself to have a mind of her own to a far greater degree than her two older sisters. Pamela was a bit taken aback: "She is seldom out of humour but a little two [sic] much indulgence makes her pritty noisey." Elizabeth, whose own daughter was still "rather impish" as a teen, encouraged this self-assertion. Catharine would later recall the joy of being allowed to run about the fields and woods of Stockbridge with her brothers and school friends when her mother was ill or not at home.[50]

In addition to taking satisfaction in her work, Elizabeth was beginning to enjoy the financial security that came with long-term employment. She dressed in tasteful black silk gowns and was able to make an occasional small loan to a needy friend.[51] She was also beginning to set aside money for her retirement. This was a very wise measure, because in 1793, the Town of Stockbridge included her on a list of people "warned out."[52]

The towns of Massachusetts had a system by which one was only eligible for town charity in the event of sickness or old age if one was a citizen of the town. Usually that meant either a person had to have been born in the town or be a member of the town's Congregational Church. Thirty-two African Americans, half of Stockbridge's African American population, were on the 1793 warned-out list, but it also included more than a hundred European Americans, many of them widows or unmarried spinsters. One of the unmarried European American women on the list was Theodore Sedgwick's niece, Betsey Sedgwick, who was staying with the family.[53]

Agrippa Hull was not among the African Americans on the list. Though he had been born in Northampton, he had been raised from age six as a foster child of Rose Benny, a member of the Congregational Church. Agrippa himself did not join the church until later in life, but Rose's membership, together with Agrippa being a small landowner, seems to have been sufficient to keep Agrippa from being warned out.[54]

Elizabeth probably huffed in disgust when either her daughter Betsey or a literate friend informed her that her name was on the warned-out list posted in several locations about the town. She had no intention of becoming a town charge. She was saving to buy property—a small farm. She didn't have enough money yet, but soon she would.

6. "The main pillar of our household"

She was so confident she could achieve this goal that she didn't go through the motions of joining the Congregational Church.

We do not know what caused Elizabeth's decision not to seek membership in the Stockbridge Congregational Church. Perhaps it was long hours as a girl on the back bench of the Sheffield Congregational Church on her only day off each week, listening to the fire and brimstone sermons of the Ashley family's minister. Perhaps it was knowing that the man who had helped her gain her freedom, Theodore Sedgwick, refused to join his wife's church and having an occasional opportunity to hear his thoughts on the subject. Elizabeth believed in God. She told Catharine Sedgwick so in one of the greatest moments of grief in Elizabeth's life. But she didn't like the Congregationalists' way of thinking about God, and she wasn't about to sign on to church membership to add to her financial security.

* * *

At some point before Theodore returned home in the early summer of 1793, Pamela experienced another serious bout of depression. This time it could not be attributed to childbirth. Theodore now had to acknowledge that Pamela required serious medical intervention. Pamela agreed to accept the rudimentary treatment that was available in Boston at the time. Her brother escorted her there. When Congress recessed, Theodore came back to Stockbridge and spent the summer and early fall helping Elizabeth and Eliza care for the younger children. He did this wholeheartedly. As his daughter Catharine fondly observed later, when Theodore was at home, "My father had the habit of having his children always about him." He allowed even the smallest ones to stay up late with him listening to him read aloud and tell stories. Deprived of his company for most of the year, the children soaked in his presence when he was at home.[55]

But as summer turned to fall, Theodore would soon need to return to Congress. He seized on word that Pamela seemed to be improving. The children were already protesting his departure. It would be so much easier if they had Pamela's return home to anticipate, and he wrote, "By your letters and what the Doctor says I perceive you do not expect, nor intend to return home before winter—I hope you will be both able and desirous of returning before that time." For the first time, he had a taste of the guilt Pamela faced each time she left the children to join him in Philadelphia: "You seem to suppose I shall go to Philadelphia before your return, but that will be impossible."[56]

Perhaps Pamela subconsciously knew it would do her good to be the one who, this once, decided when they next would see each other. But she could never bring herself to resist when he insisted. She came home, and Theodore soon left for Philadelphia.

At some point during the winter, Pamela suffered some sort of physical malady that required an operation. Eliza and Frances wrote to their father to inform him. Laden with guilt and not wanting his teenaged daughters to think ill of him, Theodore responded, "Had I believed that your dear Mamma was so soon to undergo so dreadful an operation, it would have been impossible to have left her and you." He was unwilling, however, to commit to requesting another leave of absence from Congress. Stalling for time, he told them, "If on the whole my return is thought advisable nothing shall detain me."[57] But upon talking to congressional and administration colleagues who insisted he was needed in Philadelphia, Theodore decided not to leave the matter to his daughters' discretion. Writing directly to Pamela, he laid the decision on her.[58] As he probably knew she would, the self-effacing Pamela opted to go through the operation without him.

Thanks to the doctor's skill and Elizabeth's fine nursing care, Pamela recovered sufficiently to travel to Philadelphia in mid-spring. Accompanied by Eliza, she was away from home for two months.[59] It would be the last time she would be well enough to make the long journey. Buoyed by her joy at seeing Theodore and the pleasure of showing her eldest daughter the capital city, Pamela had a very good time. Theodore was delighted to have his wife and daughter with him. Together they attended plays, tea parties, and "routs," and on at least two occasions stayed out "untill past one o'Clock."[60]

As usual, Elizabeth took care of the younger children and administered the Stockbridge family home. If she needed to communicate with Theodore and Pamela, which didn't happen often, she told one of the Sedgwick children to include the matter in their letters to their parents. In late April, Theodore assured nine-year-old Harry, "Mrs Freeman shall have what you wrote for."[61] The children had plenty of time to write because the Stockbridge elementary school closed for an extended

6. "The main pillar of our household"

recess in late May.⁶² Fortunately, Elizabeth had the assistance of her daughter, Betsey, sixteen-year-old Frances Sedgwick, and Theodore's niece, Betsey Sedgwick, in dealing with the four youngest Sedgwick children, but even so, her days were very full and the house was very noisy.

Agrippa Hull was also an important ally of Elizabeth in the task of raising the Sedgwick children. Especially when Theodore was absent, Theodore's children found "Grippy" a comforting presence and were riveted by tales of his Revolutionary War service under Kosciusko. Catharine Sedgwick recalled, "He had a fund of humor and mother-wit and was a sort of Sancho Panza in the village, always trimming other men's follies with a keen perception, and the biting wit of wisdom."⁶³

Portrait of Elizabeth's friend and colleague Agrippa Hull in the latter years of his life (*Agrippa Hull*, artist unknown, the Stockbridge Library, Museum and Archives: SLAHC Art Collection #47.002).

The trip to Philadelphia had a restorative effect on Pamela. For the next year and a half, she was in relatively good health and was able to resume some of her household duties.⁶⁴

7

A Brilliant Career, a Blind Eye

ELIZABETH WAS A VALUED employee, and when Pamela was well, she tried to make sure that Elizabeth was not overburdened. Aware of her critical role in raising the children, Pamela was anxious to ensure Elizabeth wasn't required to do more than supervise heavy housekeeping tasks. During February 1795, Pamela wrote to Theodore to inform him they needed more domestic help and suggested he inquire at the New York City poor house. Later that month, Theodore responded, "I have already written to Mr. Penfield to request him to procure for you a girl & boy from their poor house. I will again write him on the subject by this post."[1]

The marriage of Elizabeth's daughter, Betsey, to Jonah Humphrey may have occasioned the need for additional household staff. We do not know the precise date, and no record of a religious ceremony survives, but sometime in the mid–1790s, Betsey, then about twenty, married Jonah, about three years her junior. Jonah was the third of five children of Enoch Humphrey, Sr., sometimes referred to as Humphry Negro in town records, and Penelope "Nell" Fortune Humphrey.[2] Enoch Sr. was a free man prior to the Revolution. He owned land in Stockbridge as early as 1771, probably purchased from the Housatonic Indians. Like Agrippa Hull, he served as a soldier in the Revolutionary War.[3]

Elizabeth and Betsey Freeman may have first met the Humphrey family when they moved to Stockbridge with the Sedgwicks in 1785, but it is possible that Enoch Sr. served with Betsey's father during the war and that this was a bond between the two families. Certainly Enoch's war service was something with which Elizabeth would have identified.

7. A Brilliant Career, a Blind Eye

Upon her marriage, Betsey apparently went to live with her husband's family. There was no room for the young couple at the Sedgwicks. The Humphrey homestead was less than two miles from the Sedgwick house, so Elizabeth still saw her daughter frequently.[4]

Betsey was soon pregnant and gave birth to Elizabeth's first grandchild, a girl. The only official records of her life that survive refer to this eldest grandchild as Mrs. Harry Van Schaack.[5] Though some students of Elizabeth Freeman have suggested that her given name might have been Elizabeth like her mother and grandmother, according to Catharine Sedgwick, who knew her well, her name was Lydia Maria.[6]

As the joys of young love and childbirth played out in Elizabeth's family in Stockbridge, the fortunes of the Federalist faction in the U.S. House of Representatives were declining. Faced with the probability of a Democratic-Republican majority in the House in the Fourth Congress and the loss of his chairmanship, together with the recent resignation from the Washington administration of Alexander Hamilton and rumors that Henry Knox would soon follow suit, Theodore wrote Pamela, "Shall I now tell you a Secret? it must remain as secret with you. I have determined the next election to decline."[7]

Alas, President Washington and Federalist stalwarts in Congress had other ideas. The Senate was currently battling out the Jay Treaty. The treaty was ratified in June by the bare margin required, but Democratic-Republicans were already threatening to use the appropriations power of the House to strangle execution of the treaty. This was no time for the House's leading Federalist debater and strategist to retire. As usual, Theodore's "proshitute good nature" prevailed, and at the same time as Henry Knox was leaving the Washington administration to better secure his wife Lucy and their children's future, Theodore accepted reelection to his House seat.

It may have been the raising and dashing of her hopes or perhaps simply the certainty of another prolonged separation, but soon after Theodore headed back to Philadelphia in November 1795, Pamela was once again in the throes of a major episode of depression. This time, Theodore hardened his heart to the painful situation at home. There was no dithering about conflicting obligations or talk of deferring to others' wishes. When twenty-year-old Eliza and seventeen-year-old

Frances each wrote to tell him in early December that he must return home, he responded unequivocally: "I beleive a superior duty fixes me here at present, and here I must remain untill the great question of executing the treaty shall have been determined."[8]

Despite evidence that Pamela usually improved when he was at home, he had decided that her mental illness was God's will and that his presence or absence would not change it. Theodore didn't understand why this was happening to Pamela: "Of all our race none has appeared less to deserve chastisement.... Kind, generous, benevolent, compassionate, amiable ... in all her dispositions. Correct and pure in all her conduct." But he had had to accept the death of his young first wife so many years before, and painful though it was, he now decided he had to accept his second wife's mental illness. Rather than become an unbeliever, he told his daughters he would "more fully ... confide in that source of consolation to a wounded spirit, in a future distribution where every inequality will be corrected."[9]

While these reflections may have helped his eldest children to cope more philosophically with the tragedy they were facing, they did little to calm the terror of his younger children, who desperately needed the security of his comforting arms as their mother's sanity deteriorated before their eyes. Instead, it was Elizabeth Freeman who stepped into the breach. As Catharine Sedgwick, who was just about to turn six, later wrote, "Then came thronging recollections of my childhood, its joys and sorrows—'Papa's going away,' and 'Papa's coming home;' the dreadful clouds that came over our sunny home when mamma was sick; my love of Mumbet, that noble woman, the main pillar of our household."[10]

Elizabeth maintained a respectful affection for both Theodore and Pamela throughout these crises. Like Theodore, she made it clear to the Sedgwick children that their mother was sick and couldn't help being unable to take care of them. Though Elizabeth believed that Theodore's children should keep him informed of Pamela's condition, and she probably disagreed with some of his decisions not to come home when his daughters asked him to, her loyalty to him for helping her achieve her freedom, combined with her experience of Shays' Rebellion, also gave her real respect for Theodore's public service.

Elizabeth's attitude, combined with the love that Pamela showed

7. A Brilliant Career, a Blind Eye

the children when she was well and the good job of fatherhood Theodore did when he was at home, resulted in the children being able to love not only Elizabeth but both of their parents, too. As an adult, Catharine was able to say of her parents: "Her sufferings are past, and I doubt not, prepared her to enjoy more keenly the rest and felicities of heaven. The good done by my father in contributing to establish the government, and to swell the amount of that political virtue which makes the history of the Federal party the record of the purest patriotism the world has known—that remains."[11]

What Elizabeth also did for the Sedgwick children, especially Catharine, was to provide the model of a strong, independent woman who was a survivor. Though Catharine Sedgwick grew up loving both her parents despite their frailties, she did not love their marriage. She understood perfectly the power dynamic that existed between them. In writing of her parents' union, she quoted Pamela's surrender line on the question of Theodore's political career: "Submission is my duty."[12] As Catharine grew up to become America's leading female novelist of the 1820s and 1830s, Elizabeth's life provided not only themes for her writing but also a concrete example of a productive, loving life lived much differently from that of Catharine's mother.

Pamela hated the distress she saw in her children's eyes as they watched her suffer. She would once again leave home to seek medical attention. Theodore thought Boston was too far away, so it was decided that Pamela would take up residence in the home of Doctor Waldo in nearby Richmond.[13] For six-year-old Catharine and four-year-old Charles, it was all a blur: "She had two or three turns of insanity, which lasted each, I believe, some months; I know not how long, for I was too young to remember anything but being told that my 'mamma was sick and sent away to a good doctor.'"[14]

In Philadelphia, Theodore oscillated between justifying his refusal to come home and reporting to his daughters all the expressions of regard he was receiving from the great. He had once again been given the honor of sitting at the head of George Washington's table. "It is some, and indeed considerable compensation for the sacrifices which I have made in public life to have been treated with the distinction I have always experienced from that good man."[15]

In Stockbridge, Elizabeth and Eliza, with the help of Henry Dwight's wife, Abigail Wells Dwight, had the situation under control. An African American woman named Katy, hired to assist Elizabeth, proved unsatisfactory. With Elizabeth's approval, Eliza dismissed her. Theodore, surprised that his assessment of Katy had proved incorrect, was uneasy, but having told Eliza she and Elizabeth could manage things, Theodore had to accept their decision. Katy would probably not have been happy if she had remained in the Sedgwick household. Elizabeth had found her wanting. She did not abide incompetence or dishonesty. As Catharine Sedgwick noted, "Mumbet had a clear and nice perception of justice and a stern love of it, an uncompromising honesty in word and deed."[16]

In Richmond, Pamela had good days and bad days. At the end of January, she had improved sufficiently that her brother, Henry Dwight, and Doctor Waldo discussed the possibility of a home visit, but shortly thereafter, Dwight informed Theodore, "It was proposed & intended to have her visit her Family last week, but it had a very disadvantageous effect upon her, and was therefore given up—any of her friends calling there operates in a degree, the same way."[17] Henry Dwight, proud of his brother-in-law's status and accomplishments, shared Theodore's view that Theodore's presence at home would not change Pamela's condition and that he should therefore remain in Philadelphia.

Theodore was preparing for one of the greatest moments of his political career. On March 2, 1796, Edward Livingston, a Democratic-Republican from New York, made a motion on the House floor that President Washington be required to hand over all papers related to the Jay Treaty negotiation for study by the House so that body could better decide whether the treaty should be executed.[18] Debate went on for days. On March 11, Theodore delivered what was regarded as the best of a number of speeches for the Federalist position. In a ninety-minute tour de force, he gave a point-by-point refutation of the theory that the House had any role in treaty making.[19]

When he concluded, a grateful Vice President Adams took him by the hand and said, "From my heart I thank you.... I never flatter ... but your speech for matter, style and delivery exceeds anything I have ever heard, and I have heard much good speaking."[20]

The Federalist ladies of Philadelphia were also quick to signal their approval, and Theodore couldn't keep from telling his daughters about it. During his lengthy speech, "Miss Paterson" sent him

7. A Brilliant Career, a Blind Eye

an orange to soothe his parched throat along with an admiring note. At Martha Washington's drawing room that evening, he was "covered with confusion by the compliments I had & particularly from the ladies who had attended the house."[21]

In Stockbridge, Elizabeth nursed eight-year-old Robert, who had been ill for several weeks, with what was probably influenza. Informed of Robert's illness and that Pamela had suffered a relapse, Theodore told Eliza and Frances, "Let me hear particularly of Robert," and "Would to God I had humble resignation your angelic Mamma would practice were our fates transposed." But the treaty battle held precedence over these personal concerns: "I dare not desert the path assigned to me, when a single vote may save my country from that ruin with which the passions & ambition of wicked men threaten it."[22]

This engraving of Theodore Sedgwick portrays him near the end of his distinguished political and judicial career (*Hon. Theodore Sedgwick* by John Rubens Smith, copy after Henry Williams and Gilbert Stuart, 1813, National Portrait Gallery, Smithsonian Institution NPG.84.14).

Theodore was not exaggerating the closeness or ferocity of the appropriations battle in the House. Livingston's motion to demand more information from the administration passed sixty-two to thirty-seven on March 24. Using the arguments marshaled by Theodore in his March 11 speech, Washington rejected the demand as unconstitutional. The House grudgingly backed down, and on April 30, it passed the appropriation resolution to execute the Jay Treaty fifty-one to forty-eight.[23]

Massachusetts Federalists were as pleased with Theodore's role in the victory as were Washington and Adams. When Caleb Strong resigned his U.S. Senate seat a few weeks later, the Massachusetts House and Senate each voted to have Theodore Sedgwick complete Strong's term. Theodore resigned his House seat in June 1796, and when he returned to Congress that fall, it was as a United States Senator.[24]

Pamela returned home during the summer of 1796; she had apparently again recovered from her depression. Henceforth, Pamela's ailments tended to be physical rather than mental. In January of 1797, Theodore wrote, "I was very much distressed by Mr. Williams's last letter to learn that you was again too unwell to write me. I had hoped those paroxysms of illness were becoming less frequent, and less painful."[25]

Pamela was showing the early signs of a condition that, within a few years' time, would result in a debilitating stroke, which was beyond the medical knowledge of the time to properly diagnose or treat. Theodore therefore relied on traditional remedies in advising his wife about treatment for her symptoms, urging her to use her fine carriage to get plenty of fresh air: "As soon as the weather will permit ride and that frequently—Say not that the horses are wanted—Interpose no other consideration or excuse."[26]

* * *

Despite her poor physical health, Pamela was absorbed in planning for her elder daughters' futures. Eliza had recently become engaged to Thaddeus Pomeroy, an Albany doctor. In January, Pamela wrote Theodore a newsy mother-of-the-bride letter updating Theodore on her efforts to obtain kitchen equipment for Eliza's dowry.[27] She also engaged in a long-distance discussion with Theodore about the romantic life of their second daughter, eighteen-year-old Frances.

The previous summer, Theodore had been appalled to notice a growing fondness between Frances and Loring Andrews, Stockbridge's postmaster and the publisher of Berkshire County's only newspaper, *The Western Star*. In his mid-twenties and without family in the small village, Andrews spent more time than Theodore thought acceptable in the taproom of the Red Lion Inn.[28] There may also have been a class bias operating in Theodore's estimation of Andrews. He was not a professional man like Theodore and Eliza's fiancé, Thaddeus Pomeroy, and he was of modest means. In short, Theodore thought Frances could do

7. A Brilliant Career, a Blind Eye

better. When Theodore left for Philadelphia, he insisted that Frances accompany him for a year of school, where she could be introduced to better prospects.[29]

Frances went unwillingly, and Pamela was concerned. Her mother, Abigail Dwight, had initially disapproved of Theodore but had given way in the face of her daughter's unhappiness. Andrews continued to call at the Sedgwick home, hoping to enlist Pamela's aid. The drama heightened when Andrews told Pamela he had written Theodore asking for Frances's hand and had been rejected. Pamela certainly discussed the situation with Elizabeth, who cared deeply about all the Sedgwick children and was witness to Frances and Andrews's despair.

Initially, Pamela, perhaps buoyed by Elizabeth's concurrence, attempted to advocate for the young lovers: "We had Letters from Frances last week She appears to be very far from being Happy." Pamela testified to Andrews's improved behavior: "I believe he has been very Circumspect in his Conduct this Winter … he is certainly in many respects an amiable Character and is greatly attached to Frances."[30]

But Theodore remained firmly opposed to the match. In a time when a woman lost virtually all of her civil rights upon marriage, including control of inherited property, Theodore believed it was a dereliction of his duty as her father to permit Frances to marry a man with almost no assets and a taste for alcohol. Pamela continued to sympathize with Frances, but she had learned through hard experience that opposing Theodore's will was a losing proposition.[31]

Whatever Elizabeth thought of the twists and turns of Frances and Andrews's romance, she had to focus on tending to Pamela's health, the needs of the younger Sedgwick children, and preparing for Eliza's nuptials. Eliza was planning to move to Albany, forty miles from Stockbridge. Not only would Elizabeth miss Eliza, whom she had helped raise and who had been so much assistance to Elizabeth during Eliza's teen years, but Elizabeth surely feared the effect Eliza's departure would have on Pamela and the younger Sedgwick children.

Eliza's company was a prop to Pamela's fragile mental health when Theodore was away. Though gamely proceeding with the wedding preparations, Pamela admitted her despair to Theodore and probably to Elizabeth as well: "I do not know how we can do without our dear Eliza my heart Sinks when I think of parting with her."[32]

The effect of Eliza's departure on seven-year-old Catharine was also a cause for concern. Catharine had slept in the same bed as Eliza since infancy. The adults of the household were beginning to talk to little Catharine about the upcoming wedding, but not wanting to upset the child, everyone was emphasizing the fun of the wedding celebration and post-wedding visits to Albany. How would Catharine react when she finally understood that she would be apart from Eliza most of the time?

Elizabeth did not have to wait long to find out. On the day of the wedding, the guests assembled in the Sedgwick family's west parlor to watch Pamela's uncle, Dr. Stephen West, join Eliza and Thaddeus in matrimony. Catharine stood beside Elizabeth. As Catharine recalled in her autobiography, "When the long consecrating prayer was half through, I distinctly remember the consciousness that my sister was going away from me struck me with the force of a blow, and I burst into loud sobs and crying."[33] Both Elizabeth and Theodore attempted to quiet the bawling child, but to no avail. To prevent Eliza's wedding ceremony from being ruined, Elizabeth swept Catharine into her arms and brought her to the east parlor. Decades later, Catharine remembered, "Mumbet whispered her 'hush' but for the first time it was impotent."[34]

Catharine's emotional display was the opening Theodore needed. He was home only for a short time and would be returning to Philadelphia soon. He already feared Pamela would break down when he and Eliza left, and now this. Shamelessly, as soon as the ceremony ended, he asked Thaddeus if Eliza could remain with her family for a while. Thaddeus's reply endeared him to his father-in-law but did little to mollify Catharine: "Then came my new brother-in-law—how well I remember recoiling from him, and hating him when he said to me, 'I'll let your sister stay with you this summer.' He let her!"[35]

Elizabeth probably admired little Catharine's keen perception of the unfair power dynamics between men and women of the time, but like Theodore and Pamela, she must also have been relieved that Eliza could remain for a few weeks. But even with Eliza staying for a while, it was still a challenge for Elizabeth to get Catharine through the transition: "I was undressed and put into bed, and I cried myself to sleep and waked crying the next morning."[36]

7. A Brilliant Career, a Blind Eye

As usual, Theodore told himself he was leaving his children in good hands and departed for Philadelphia, where being a U.S. senator in the opening days of the Adams administration suited him very well indeed. Prior to John Adams's election, Theodore had flirted with Alexander Hamilton's idea that Thomas Pinckney, former minister to Great Britain, might be a better choice for president, but other than a few letters to friends that hinted at this thought, as soon as it became clear that Adams would prevail, Theodore quickly fell into line.[37]

The major issue facing the federal government was relations with America's erstwhile ally, revolutionary France. For the time being, Theodore, Hamilton, and Adams all agreed that war with France was to be avoided.[38]

Friendly as fellow Massachusetts Federalists during the Washington administration, Theodore and Adams now became even closer. A talented member of the Federalist majority in the Senate who was known to have Alexander Hamilton's ear, Theodore was someone John Adams was anxious to cultivate.[39] Senator Sedgwick dined frequently with the new president and first lady, gushing to Pamela, "Mrs Adams appears to me one of the most exalted characters I have seen."[40]

He was not above using his position as pater familias to get other people to cover for him in Stockbridge, even if their own responsibilities were elsewhere. Informing Pamela in mid–June that Congress would be in session for another two weeks, he proclaimed rather than requested, "I wish Eliza may find it convenient to stay with you till that time."[41]

As for Elizabeth, her constant presence was a given. If she ever yearned for some time off, she never said so to the Sedgwicks. She felt needed, loved, and respected, and her savings for the farm continued to grow. It would be another decade before she informed Theodore Sedgwick of her limits.

At last Eliza was permitted to join her husband in Albany, and a pregnancy soon resulted. It was traditional for the expectant mother's mother to be present for the birth. At first the prospect excited Pamela, but fearing that the sight of her daughter in labor might trigger an episode of depression, she soon confessed to Theodore, "I cannot feal otherwise than unhappy while I think I am of no use to my Children no blessing to you or my family indeed it Poisons all my comforts and makes me miserable."[42]

Finally Pamela found the solution. She would ask Elizabeth to accompany her. She could be with her daughter at this critical moment, but it would be Elizabeth who would take primary responsibility for helping Eliza through the labor and delivery, just as she had helped Pamela so many times.

Before returning to Congress the previous December, Theodore had told Pamela he intended to retire when his Senate term expired in 1799.[43] Now once again, he was having so much fun he began to equivocate: "To the President I have not yet communicated the decision I have taken no[r] do I believe I shall do it until it becomes irrevocable." This time Pamela did not even protest. She knew all too well that her concerns would be sympathized with and ignored.[44]

The snow was sparse again that winter in Stockbridge. Pamela wanted to set out for Albany in early February as soon as possible after a light snow, but she delayed doing so because Elizabeth was busy caring for the wife of an African American member of the Sedgwicks' domestic staff. "I should go sooner But Bet Intends going with me She can not leve home sooner as Moses wife has been put to bed but a week and she does not Like to leve her—She has got a fine Boy and is very well."[45]

One can scarcely imagine Hannah Ashley abiding such an excuse, even from a free employee. It wasn't just her loyalty to Theodore Sedgwick or her love for the Sedgwick children that kept Elizabeth with the Sedgwick family for decades. These were important factors, but her working relationship with and affection for Pamela Sedgwick mattered, too. Pamela was an intelligent and decent human being who respected Elizabeth's judgment and who acknowledged the debt she owed Elizabeth for the life-saving care Elizabeth had given to Pamela and her children over the years. The scope of judgment and authority Elizabeth wielded in the Sedgwick household as a result was a source of satisfaction to Elizabeth that she would be unwilling to relinquish after Pamela's death.

The plan was that Frances would oversee the Sedgwick household while Pamela and Elizabeth were gone. At the last minute, Frances begged to accompany them, proclaiming dramatically that it might be the last time she would see her sister Eliza alive. Pamela was not fooled. Loring Andrews was now living in Albany. Making the decision without consulting Theodore, she told Frances she could come

7. A Brilliant Career, a Blind Eye

for a few days but then must return home to care for the younger children. Pamela informed her husband, "I did not think it best positively to refuse her I am perswaded that opposition to her seeing Andrews has no good affect."[46]

The three women managed well on the bumpy, day-long sleigh ride to Albany. They were probably driven there by Elizabeth's son-in-law, Jonah Humphrey, who would be asked to perform this job a number of times during Eliza's years in Albany: "We found the road very Indifferent but got there comfortably. Found Eliza in fine Health and good spirits."[47]

It was no small thing to ask free African Americans to make the journey into slaveholding New York, and it is further evidence of Elizabeth's natural courage and devotion to the Sedgwick family that she was willing to do it. Abductions sometimes occurred with victims being sold to the West Indies or southern plantations. As a woman in her mid-fifties, Elizabeth was at less risk than young Jonah, but no one was entirely safe. During her visit there, Elizabeth probably did not stroll around Albany unaccompanied by some member of the Sedgwick or Pomeroy clan. Jonah stayed at Eliza's home the night they arrived and probably returned to free Massachusetts the next day.

The delicacy of writing one's due date in a letter extended not only to husband and wife but also to mother and daughter. It was only when Pamela and Elizabeth were able to speak to Eliza personally that they concluded she probably had about another month to go before the baby would arrive. Knowing that Theodore continued to worry about proximity to their pregnant daughter triggering an episode of depression, Pamela reassured him: "I brought Mamma Bet with me—so you see we are in forse here."[48]

As agreed, Frances returned to Stockbridge to supervise the household after spending several days visiting Eliza and seeing Loring Andrews. In her gentle way, Pamela was defying Theodore and giving Frances a chance to take her future into her own hands. A few days after Frances's departure, Pamela confessed to her husband, "Andrews is gone to Stockbridge," and "after all that has been said to her I thought she had better Act for herself."[49]

Andrews did indeed go to Stockbridge and ask Frances to elope with him. Unfortunately, Frances could not work up the courage to oppose her father's will. Within a year, she and Andrews broke off their relationship, and Frances soon accepted a man her father wanted her to marry, who would prove to be a very bad husband.

What Frances Sedgwick did was a common phenomenon in late eighteenth-century America. Told throughout their lives that men's judgment was superior to their own, few teenaged girls of the time were prepared to substitute their judgment for that of their fathers, even in this most personal decision, and to accept the financial and social consequences of doing so.

With Elizabeth's assistance, Eliza delivered her baby in early March 1798. "Eliza is now very comfortable and in a fine way the little Boy is a fine one and Perfectly Well," Pamela joyously informed her husband.[50] In an indication of his affection for Theodore but also of what an eminent man Theodore had become, Eliza's husband agreed that his firstborn son would be named not for his own father, as was traditional, but for Eliza's father.

Far from bringing on an episode of depression, the trip to Albany was a tonic for Pamela; she told Theodore, "I have enjoyed more health than usal since I came here."[51] Together, she and Elizabeth provided the young mother much-needed assistance in the weeks after the baby's birth: "My little grandson is endeeard to me every day and feals to me much as my own Little Boys did at his helpless Age."[52]

Delighted though he was to become a grandfather, Theodore did not let his absence from the happy event diminish his enjoyment of social life in Philadelphia. Beset by failing eyesight and an attack of gout, he seemed to find it necessary to prove to himself that he was still a young man.[53] Perhaps to confirm to himself that he wasn't doing anything wrong, he also felt the need to tell poor Frances about it. He informed his daughter that, at the president's most recent drawing room at the end of March, the ladies "flattered me by graciously receiving my attentions, and in some instances they seemed condescendingly to court them."[54] It is unlikely that Theodore was ever physically unfaithful to Pamela, and his adult children did tend to laugh off such statements as minor vanities, but as Pamela's physical infirmities increased, Theodore unquestionably developed a social life separate and apart from her that allowed him to make abrupt changes when she eventually predeceased him.

7. A Brilliant Career, a Blind Eye

* * *

Pamela and Elizabeth returned to Stockbridge by stagecoach in mid–April. They "had a fatigueing ride home ocasioned by the badness of the roads." Neither of them was too surprised to find that in their two-month absence, "the children seem to have run pretty wild."[55]

After the brazen seizure of an American ship by a French privateer in the coastal waters off Philadelphia,[56] Theodore took a major role in drafting the Alien Acts of 1798: "I shall be every moment engaged this day in framing a bill to authorize the President to send out of the country the French rascals who disturb our repose," he told Pamela.[57]

By mid–June, the remission in her health problems that Pamela had enjoyed for several months was over. Elizabeth's burden increased during a brutal heat wave as Pamela again became an invalid.[58]

Elizabeth continued to enjoy vibrant good health. As peers with easier lives passed away, including Mary Ashley Fellows, who died in 1797, and John Ashley the younger, who would die in 1799,[59] Elizabeth, about fifty-four, an age considered old at the time, managed a heavy workload with vigor and resolve, providing an example of character and strength to everyone around her. As Henry Sedgwick later observed, "She claimed no distinction but it was yielded to her from her superior experience, energy, skill and sagacity."[60]

By the time Theodore came home for the summer recess, he was squarely in the camp of those Federalists, led by Alexander Hamilton, now a private lawyer in New York, who believed America should declare war on France. The previous summer, President Adams had sent a three-man delegation to France in an attempt to peacefully resolve issues between the two nations. In June 1798, two members of the delegation, John Marshall and Charles Cotesworth Pinckney, returned to America and reported that the French foreign minister had refused to enter into negotiations without the payment of a substantial bribe.[61]

This treatment of the American envoys, which became known as the XYZ Affair, together with fears that French spies might be trying to stir up insurrection among subsistence farmers and the urban working class in America, was viewed as the last straw by many members of the Federalist-controlled Senate. The House, which contained a higher proportion of members who were pro–French

Democratic-Republicans, remained unconvinced that war was necessary. So did President Adams, who had held several diplomatic posts in Europe and understood that bribe-taking did not necessarily signify hostile intentions.[62]

While Adams was performing diplomatic duties for America in Europe during the 1780s, Theodore had been on the front lines of Shays' Rebellion. It had been a life-changing experience. Personally threatened with assassination by Shaysites, his home violated by them, and friends and neighbors kidnapped, his view of the bloody French Revolution was that it could happen in America and that it would be directed at families like his. Before Congress adjourned for the summer, Theodore cast a vote to declare null and void the 1778 treaty of alliance between America and France.[63]

Nevertheless, Theodore was not yet prepared to break with Adams over this significant policy disagreement. On a personal level, now less than a year away from the expiration of his Senate term, he faced up to the fact that he did not want to retire from public life. Supreme Court Justice James Wilson had recently died. In late September, Theodore wrote to Adams requesting that Adams consider him for the lifetime appointment. It is likely that Theodore did not tell Pamela he was doing this, probably preferring to give her the bad news that he would be permanently spending nine months a year in the new federal capital of Washington, D.C., only if he was successful.

Adams deeply respected Theodore's legal abilities, but southern Federalists were a crucial part of his majority in the Senate. Wilson was a southerner, and the southern Federalists expected a southerner to replace him. Adams gave the nomination to Bushrod Washington, nephew of George Washington and James Wilson's former law clerk.[64] Theodore probably understood the political necessity of Adams's decision, but it meant he continued in the Senate, where his sincerely held views about the inevitability of war with France would now play out.

Pamela by now apparently understood that Theodore was considering running for a House seat when his Senate term expired in the spring. Her reaction was to reflect on how unimportant she was to his life and on how her problems were simply a blight on his happiness. She sometimes refrained from writing even when she was physically able, confessing: "I consider you as always engaged in something of Consequence to Yourself or the Public or that you are engaged with some agreeable company—and that my Letters will for a moment interrupt your happiness."[65]

Theodore viewed these sentiments as a possible harbinger of another episode of depression. Unwilling to take any responsibility for her unhappiness but also remarkably advanced in his understanding that depression was an affliction for which she was not responsible, he told her, "You are suffering under a depression of Spirits—This we both know to be a disease—would to God we could discover a remedy." Having over the years discussed her condition with doctors in Boston and Philadelphia, he advised, "Some thing may be done by your own exertion not, indeed, by attempting directly to encounter those feelings & to subdue them, but by diversion to other & more cheerful subjects."[66]

Their son Theodore was about to travel to Albany to begin a law clerkship. Theodore suggested that Pamela go with him so she could visit Eliza and their grandson. In a stunning display of selfishness and male privilege, he added, "If you should go I hope it may be convenient to you to return by the time of my arrival—It shall be very solitary without you."[67]

As Elizabeth did her best in Stockbridge to ease Pamela's physical symptoms and help her manage her mood disorder, in Philadelphia Theodore moved toward an open breach with President Adams. Many Federalists in Congress were insisting on preparations for war with France. An army reorganization bill was being considered, and a commanding general and deputy had to be appointed to lead the greatly enlarged force. George Washington, now sixty-six, was the obvious choice for commander, but the choice of deputy was less clear. Should it be Henry Knox or Alexander Hamilton? Though Adams did not object to Washington's appointment, he believed Hamilton was both personally hostile to him and determined to create an incident that would make war with France inevitable. Adams favored the appointment of Henry Knox as deputy, the same position he had held at the end of the Revolution.[68]

Washington knew, however, that Henry Knox, now almost fifty, was fully committed to the development of his lands in Maine. It had been Alexander Hamilton who had acted as Washington's deputy during the Whiskey Rebellion, when Secretary of War Knox, late in his tenure and on leave to attend to his Maine estate, had been unable to return in time to assist Washington in the field. Washington wrote Adams of Henry Knox, "I can say with truth there is no man in the United States with whom I have been in habits of greater intimacy, no one whom I have loved more sincerely nor any for whom I have had greater friendship," but nevertheless, continued Washington, it was Hamilton who was currently the best man to be his deputy.[69]

Theodore agreed that Hamilton would be a more focused and vigorous deputy; he backed his appointment despite Adams's preference for Knox.[70] Perhaps even more critically, Theodore and other high Federalists opposed Adams's proposal to send William Vans Murray as envoy to France in a last-ditch effort to avoid war.[71]

In an explosive meeting between Adams and Theodore on February 18, 1799, the president accused Theodore and the other high Federalists of trying to dilute his power as commander-in-chief in favor of Washington and mocked their fears of possible domestic insurrection incited by French provocateurs.[72]

With Theodore helping to lead the charge, the Senate rejected Vans Murray's appointment. Eventually, a compromise between the president's adherents and the high Federalists was worked out, and a three-man commission was authorized to resume negotiations, but the breach between Theodore and Adams was permanent. The refusal of Theodore and other members of the pro–Hamilton wing of the party to get behind Adams in the election of 1800 would result in the end of Adams's presidency and of Theodore's congressional career, as well as the demise of the Federalist party.[73]

But all of this would take a year to play out. Meanwhile, Theodore decided that he did indeed want his old House seat back and that the speakership might be within his grasp.[74] The House currently had a narrow Federalist majority thanks to anti–French war anxiety. When Theodore returned to Philadelphia in December 1799, he was elected America's fourth Speaker of the House, defeating Democratic-Republican Nathaniel Macon of Georgia by a vote of forty-four to forty-two.[75]

From Albany, Theodore II sent his father ecstatic congratulations: "It is the triumph of honesty over villainy, of virtue over vice & is equal

7. A Brilliant Career, a Blind Eye

to anything but a victory against the regicides in France."[76] Despite young Theodore's enthusiastic assessment, his father's victory was a hollow one. Now devoid of any influence with the president, faced with a narrow House Federalist majority badly split between high Federalists and supporters of the president, and with fear of war with France declining after the success of Adams's peace mission, Theodore spent his fifteen-month speakership competently executing its parliamentary functions but accomplishing little else.[77] He admitted to Pamela, "Had I known how it was so, no consideration would have induced me to accept the office of speaker. It is the most unpleasant political situation I have been in."[78] Disgusted, he decided not to run for reelection.[79]

8

A Place of Her Own and a Long Goodbye

IN STOCKBRIDGE, AS THE Sedgwick children grew older and Pamela grew more feeble, Elizabeth's role gradually shifted from primarily being the children's governess to primarily being Pamela's nurse and household administrator. Shortly after Theodore's election to the speakership, eight-year-old Charles informed his father, "Mumbet helps Mama very often twice in the evening I sleep in Mama's room with her."[1]

During the summer of 1800, Pamela, age forty-six, suffered a stroke that caused her to have difficulty walking and resulted in the permanent loss of the use of her right hand. Theodore was home for the summer recess when the stroke occurred but departed for Washington, D.C., the new federal capital, in November.[2]

Over the next seven years, Pamela became the victim of a series of frightening seizures. Elizabeth's job was to both ameliorate Pamela's physical discomfort and calm the fears of the younger Sedgwick children while maintaining a happy and optimistic atmosphere in their home. She and the children frequently talked about how much fun it would be when their father came home. Eleven-year-old Catharine, who particularly pined for her father, wrote excitedly in January, "The spring is fast advancing when my Dear Papa will return from Congress never to go again."[3] Perhaps because the night duty with Pamela was exhausting and because Elizabeth wondered if Theodore's retirement would really happen, on February 1, 1801, Catharine informed Theodore, "Mumbet wishes to be remembered to you she longs to have you come home she says."[4]

Later that month, the drama of the president and the Speaker's

8. A Place of Her Own and a Long Goodbye

bitter dispute entered its final act. Not only had the Federalists lost their majority in the next Congress during the fall elections, but Thomas Jefferson, the "wretch," as Theodore referred to him, was elected president over Burr and Adams in the House of Representatives.[5] Theodore left Washington, D.C., before dawn on the morning of Jefferson's inauguration. By chance, he got into the same stagecoach as now-former President John Adams. They spoke not a word to each other on the long ride north.[6]

Though Elizabeth now thought it was necessary for Theodore to come home due to the severity of Pamela's condition and the joy his presence brought to young Catharine and Charles, she may have been less happy that his homecoming all but guaranteed Frances's final acquiescence in a marriage to Ebenezer Watson. In the year since Frances's final break with Loring Andrews, Theodore had been the enthusiastic advocate of Watson, a New York City merchant and bookseller from a Connecticut family, whose father was a friend of Theodore.

Frances, still heartbroken over Andrews, was distinctly unimpressed by Watson, writing her father in February 1799 that she would be perfectly happy if he would stop corresponding with her: "I can lament it—only as rather disappointing the wishes & pleasure of Yourself & Theodore—my two beloved Friends."[7] Though such a letter would have placed doubt in the minds of many fathers, Theodore remained blissfully certain that Watson was the right choice for her. With Theodore's persistent cheerleading, the courtship had progressed by January 1800 to a desultory marriage proposal, but as Theodore II reported to his father on the 26th, the engagement was soon hanging by a thread after Ebenezer, "requesting in his cool moderate manner to name the time when the marriage should take place. She was offended by the indifference with which he treated such a subject." According to Frances's brother, who was acting as his father's lieutenant in the matter, "Even so trifling an incident created an almost unconquerable aversion."[8]

Two months later, Theodore II remarked uneasily, "From what little I know of him I suspect he will make a better husband than lover. He seems not to possess those attractions which engage a young & fervent mind. But he has solid virtue discretion prudence industry & talents."[9] In a time when a young woman was supposed to enter marriage without prior relationships, Theodore feared that the rumors swirling around Frances and Loring Andrews in both Albany and Stockbridge were endangering Frances's reputation and marriageability. He was determined to close the deal with Watson. The pair was married shortly after Theodore's return to Stockbridge.[10]

As Elizabeth hoped, Theodore's presence at home meant that she temporarily had some assistance with Pamela's care. Though she required an arm to lean on and probably walked with a cane, Pamela still enjoyed carriage rides and visits to friends and family. In July, Theodore drove her a half-day's journey to northwestern Connecticut, where they spent a few days with his brother John's family. Theodore reported triumphantly to his son Henry at school in Williamstown with Robert, "Your Mamma bore the journey very well."[11]

But this was only a short respite for Elizabeth. Theodore resumed the practice of law, and Elizabeth soon resumed the full-time care of Pamela. Theodore frequently spent the day in Lenox, seven miles from Stockbridge, where the Berkshire County courthouse was now located.[12] He was under some pressure to make money. Though he had made successful investments, he no longer had his congressional salary. His oldest son, Theodore II, was completing his legal training and would soon need money to set up a law practice. His three younger sons all needed to be sent to college and to be launched in their careers. His youngest daughter, Catharine, would require a dowry at some point, and Frances's husband had asked him to loan him money for a business venture. How could he refuse Ebenezer after virtually insisting that Frances marry him based on Ebenezer's trustworthiness and business acumen?

Theodore confessed anxiously to his eldest son, "For several years … my expenses have tho' not greatly exceeded my income. Perhaps I ought not to have expected to educate my children without some diminution of my capital, but at my time of life, and circumstances as your Mamma is, a lessening of my income cannot but produce, when reflected on, unpleasant feelings."[13]

* * *

Frances's move to New York City would soon present an interesting travel opportunity for Elizabeth. Like her sister Eliza, Frances became pregnant shortly after her marriage. Pamela was now

8. A Place of Her Own and a Long Goodbye

physically past the point where the long journey from Stockbridge to New York was possible or where she could be of any use to Frances once she arrived. Neither parent was willing to trust a stranger to assist their daughter. It had to be Elizabeth.

It was out of the question for Elizabeth to make the trip alone. Women did not commonly travel unescorted at this time, and an African American woman's chance of insult or worse was far greater than a European American woman's—not to mention that the risk of kidnapping in New York City was greater than in Albany.

It was an important professional moment for Theodore. Thomas Dawes had recently decided to retire as an associate justice of the Massachusetts Supreme Judicial Court, the state's highest court. Though defeated at a national level, the Federalists were still in control of the Massachusetts state government, and Theodore was being considered for the lifetime appointment. Nevertheless, believing that Elizabeth's care could make a critical difference in his daughter and grandchild's chances of survival, he agreed to personally escort her on the 150-mile out-of-state journey. At a time when Theodore's political enemy, President Jefferson, was being mocked in Federalist newspapers for his relations with Sally Hemings, Theodore decided to bring along his thirteen-year-old son Robert, too, so the trip would set no tongues wagging.

It fell to twelve-year-old Catharine, who was visiting Frances and Ebenezer, to inform her father that the moment for departure had arrived, the topic of a woman's labor being completely out of bounds between a father and son-in-law: "Mr. Watson sends his respects to you. He is very much obliged to you for attending to Mumbet's coming here he wishes to have her come as soon as possible."[14]

In mid-winter the stagecoach was probably not feasible. Theodore, Elizabeth, and Robert likely took a sleigh to Hudson, New York, formerly Claverack, and from there a packet boat to New York City. What emotions did Elizabeth feel as she made the reverse journey to Claverack, a place she had probably not seen in forty years? Her parents were almost certainly dead. There was no one to visit on the way to the boat landing. Did she reflect that as painful as that long-ago parting had been, had she remained in New York, she and her daughter and even her granddaughter would still be slaves?[15]

A Revolutionary Woman

Such bittersweet thoughts soon gave way to the sights and sounds of New York City. Elizabeth had lived her entire life on farms and in rural villages. The only city she had ever seen was Albany. She must have been impressed with the sheer scale of New York and its urgent pace. There would be time to explore, but first there was important business at hand.

On George Washington's birthday, Elizabeth helped Frances deliver a healthy son. The maternal grandfather was again honored with a namesake, Theodore Sedgwick Watson.[16]

Theodore had needed to return to Stockbridge almost immediately. Theodore II kept him informed of events in New York: "Frances is better and will be down today Mr Watson's ship has this moment left the wharf."[17] Now Elizabeth had time to play the tourist. Escorted by Theodore II and accompanied by young Catharine, she visited shops, made some purchases, and had her first glimpse of the Atlantic Ocean.

At the end of April, Elizabeth returned to Stockbridge accompanied by Theodore II. It was not a moment too soon. Theodore's nomination to the Supreme Judicial Court had been approved. He would be riding circuit in eastern Massachusetts for the next several months, and Pamela could not be left alone.[18]

The Supreme Judicial Court held two terms a year. Some sessions were held in Boston, but the justices also rode circuit from town to town. The job did not require as much time as a seat in Congress. Instead of being absent eight to nine months a year, Theodore would now be gone a total of five to six months annually. For Pamela this was still bad news, having had her husband at home full-time for the past year.

Now fifty-six, though still vigorous, Theodore was beginning to suffer from recurrent attacks of gout and asthma, as well as diminishing eyesight.[19] Riding circuit certainly required considerable energy, but as he aged, the judicial post would provide a steady income that did not require him to be in constant quest of clients as a law practice would. Moreover, with Berkshire County becoming steadily more Democratic-Republican, Theodore must have worried whether five years hence an old Federalist would be able to bring in much legal business there at all. He had already had to tell Theodore II that he

8. A Place of Her Own and a Long Goodbye

could only help him set up a legal practice in Albany, not the more expensive New York, as they had previously planned.[20] He probably told Pamela that this new judicial post was a sacrifice they must make to ensure their children's futures. It was indeed a wise financial decision, but he would soon find that he didn't mind spending half the year away from sleepy Stockbridge.

* * *

As Elizabeth enjoyed a reunion with her daughter and granddaughter and slipped back into the routine of caring for Pamela, ten-year-old Charles, and an ever-shifting cast of elder Sedgwick children who spent various portions of the summer at the family home, Theodore was adjusting nicely to life as a justice. At first he was homesick, but courteous and outgoing by nature and determined to establish a higher level of civility in his courtroom than was the norm, he soon developed friendly relations with many members of the eastern Massachusetts bar. Moreover, it turned out there was an active social life in his new role, not only in Boston but also riding the circuit. He wrote that in one town, "every evening in the week I was in large parties of Ladies and Gentlemen." Maine, still a part of Massachusetts, was in the circuit. Determined to maintain relationships from his days as an influential member of Congress, he planned to "spend a day or two at General Knox's if he has returned home from the General Court."[21] Though Henry Knox, now a Massachusetts legislator, probably knew Theodore had supported Hamilton over him for the post of Washington's deputy during late 1798 and early 1799, the socially adept former Secretary of War was not one to hold a grudge.

Theodore was back in Stockbridge by late summer. There, he and Elizabeth received news of John Ashley's passing in Sheffield on September 1, 1802. Age ninety-three at the time of his death, Colonel Ashley may have felt he had lived too long, surviving not only his wife Hannah, who died in 1790, but also three of his four children and several grandchildren.[22]

Though Elizabeth retained a residual affection for Ashley, who had sometimes acted as a buffer between her and Hannah Ashley's vindictiveness, Elizabeth must have shuddered to think how many more years of her life and Betsey's could have been spent in servitude to the Ashleys had she not taken their fates into her own hands and sought out Theodore Sedgwick's legal assistance that long-ago summer day in 1781.

Yes, that had been a critical decision, as had been the decision to accept employment with the Sedgwicks. Economic exigency had forced her fellow slave, Zach Mullen, to return to work for the Ashleys in 1789. Never paid enough to save anything; every year his debt at the Ashley general store exceeded his wages. Ashley's heirs eventually would even evade the provision of John Ashley's will that provided a small pension to Mullen, setting it off against his debt to the store.[23]

Though there wasn't enough money in the world to pay Elizabeth for all that she had done for the Sedgwick family, she had been paid decently by local standards over the years, and now she was in a position to secure her own and her family's future. She would not end up like Zach Mullen. Betsey and Jonah Humphrey were currently tenant farmers on land owned by Thomas Peters, an African American. He had indicated a willingness to sell them some of the land. On September 29, 1803, for $75, Elizabeth and Jonah took a deed to the house the Humphreys were occupying, together with a parcel of land consisting of five acres and twenty-three rods. Elizabeth probably paid most or all of the purchase price, with Jonah contributing his labor for his share of the farm.[24]

The farm, on present-day Cherry Hill Road, was two miles south of the Sedgwick home and just north of Monument Mountain and Negro Pond, now Agawam Pond. The family's closest neighbor was Archibald Hopkins, son of Pamela's half sister, Electa Sergeant Hopkins. As indicated by the name Negro Pond, at the time of Elizabeth's purchase, several African American landowners were also in the vicinity, including Jonah Humphrey's father, Enoch Sr., and Agrippa Hull.[25]

Though Elizabeth continued to spend most nights at the Sedgwick house in order to care for Pamela, she now knew that when the time came to retire, she had a place of her own.[26] It probably gave Elizabeth particular pleasure to provide this added security to her daughter's family at this time as well, because shortly after the purchase, probably in 1804, Betsey Humphrey gave birth to Elizabeth's second surviving grandchild, a girl Betsey named Mary Ann.[27]

8. A Place of Her Own and a Long Goodbye

At the Sedgwick household, Pamela's health continued to decline. To supplement Elizabeth's efforts, Theodore did not hesitate to fire off letters from Boston and various cities and towns on the circuit, shaming or pressuring his adult children to take turns altering their schedules to be with Pamela when he wasn't. He probably felt justified doing this because of the financial help he was giving to all of them except Eliza. In Eliza's case, he had the good fortune to have a dutiful eldest daughter, despite Eliza's having a family of her own that would grow to twelve children and an extremely affectionate relationship with her husband, Thaddeus Pomeroy.

With her husband frequently away and only twelve-year-old Charles still at home most of the year, Pamela relied heavily on her grandchildren's company, often insisting that one or another of them be left with her when it was time for one of her elder daughters to conclude a visit. When this happened, Elizabeth cared for both the invalid grandmother and the active grandchild. In March 1804, it was four-year-old George Pomeroy who was Elizabeth's charge. Theodore II told his father, "Eliza was very unwilling to leave him, but the solicitations of Mama and Catharine prevailed."[28] Theodore was conscious of the added burden and was willing to reciprocate by doing an occasional personal errand for Elizabeth in Boston: "Mumbet thinks she shall want two pieces of linen," Catharine informed her father during little George's stay.[29]

Though Pamela was physically weak, her mind remained sharp. Her teenaged children spent increasing amounts of time away from home, but she did her best to supervise them from a distance. When fourteen-year-old Catharine set off for Boston to spend the 1804–05 social season at the home of Theodore and Pamela's friends, John and Sarah Tucker, unable to write, Pamela dictated a detailed letter for transmittal to Sarah Tucker.[30]

Pamela was also well enough that fall to pass along Theodore's instructions for the farm to their European American hired man, Crocker, but the neurological condition that would eventually take her life flared up again in late autumn.[31] Around the time she and Theodore received word of the death from whooping cough of Pamela's namesake, Eliza's toddler daughter, Pamela suffered a "dreadful fit" that affected her speech for several weeks.[32] In addition to caring for Pamela during this crisis, Elizabeth also had the care of Eliza's three-year-old son, Egbert, who was staying with his grandparents at the time.[33]

We do not know whether Elizabeth connected Pamela's latest fit to her palsy, but when Pamela was able to speak "nearly as well" as she had prior to the episode, Theodore convinced himself that it wasn't another attack of the palsy that had crippled the right side of her body for the last several years but rather the effect of the "extremely cold weather" that Stockbridge was experiencing. His solution was to install in her bedroom a stove that he had shipped from Albany. Whether Elizabeth agreed with Theodore's diagnosis or not, she was undoubtedly happy to have the stove in a room in which she and Pamela spent so much time.[34]

By late 1805, Theodore had apparently accepted that Pamela's condition was permanent, and he chafed under the restrictions it placed on him. During his public service in Philadelphia and Washington, D.C., he had always told himself and his children that he was providing Pamela with the best care and every possible comfort while he performed important duties for the nation. Now, he seemed to feel that Pamela shouldn't mind his spending his leisure time apart from her, too. Home from his judicial duties for a three-week vacation in October, with most of the children elsewhere, he was soon bored. Though he knew it would wound her, he asked Pamela if she would mind if he visited Eliza and Theodore II in Albany for a few days. She knew saying no would not change the result.[35]

Apparently relieved to be back in Boston in early December, Theodore described two dinner invitations to Catharine, who was staying with Frances in New York, and noted happily, "The dissipation of the season is hardly yet commenced."[36] Members of Theodore's vibrant social circle in Boston included Catharine and Penelope Russell, the spinster daughters of a Tory doctor, Charles Russell, and his wife, Elizabeth Vassall. The Russell sisters had spent a portion of their childhoods in exile in Antigua during the Revolution.[37] Several of Theodore and Pamela's children were introduced to the Russell sisters by their father during the teens' various visits to Boston. It would not be long before the Sedgwick children would have a closer and undesired relationship with them.

8. A Place of Her Own and a Long Goodbye

* * *

As 1806 dawned, two things happened that both the Sedgwicks and Elizabeth Freeman could celebrate. Eliza and Thaddeus Pomeroy decided to move their family back to Stockbridge, and Frances gave birth to a healthy daughter she named Catharine for her younger sister.[38]

Both Theodore and Pamela were overjoyed to have their eldest daughter and her children in a home just down the street from them. For Elizabeth, it meant that she could spend more nights at her own home. That was a very good thing because her son-in-law, Jonah Humphrey, was contemplating an extended journey to upstate New York, and Betsey would certainly be more comfortable with another adult in the house at night with her and her two young children.[39]

When Frances gave birth to her daughter in mid–January, Theodore paid her a visit but this time did not bring Elizabeth with him to act as midwife and nurse.[40] The decision that Elizabeth would remain in Stockbridge probably reflected both the reality that Pamela was now too feeble to do without her primary caregiver for several weeks or more and Elizabeth's reluctance to leave her own family for an extended period when big changes were about to occur for them.

Elizabeth's son-in-law spent a significant portion of 1806 in Clinton, New York. Clinton was one of ten townships that a group of investors from Stockbridge, including Theodore Sedgwick, purchased from the Oneida Indians in 1786 or 1787 in a transaction known as the Chenango Purchase.[41] Samuel Kirkland, missionary to the Oneidas, had for many years spent half the year with the Oneidas and half the year in Stockbridge, where his family resided, before permanently moving to Clinton in the early 1790s. He undoubtedly helped to mediate the Chenango Purchase.[42]

For Theodore, the land was an investment, but as settlement moved farther west after the Revolution, some residents of Stockbridge left western Massachusetts to settle there. Among them was Sewall Hopkins, son of Pamela's half sister, Electa Sergeant Hopkins, and brother of Archibald Hopkins, the Humphrey-Freeman family's next-door neighbor.[43]

Perhaps as the result of conversations with the Hopkins family, Jonah decided to make the journey to Clinton to test his prospects there. By 1806, the farmland of Berkshire County had been under continuous cultivation for seventy years, and the land's fertility was declining.[44] Jonah may have been having trouble eking out a living on the small farm Elizabeth had purchased for the family. He was probably also running up against the reality that other employment opportunities for African Americans in western Massachusetts were limited. Mill jobs were beginning to come into existence in the towns, but those jobs usually went to European immigrants.[45]

Jonah probably accepted an offer to work as a laborer for the 1806 cultivation season on Joel Bristol's lands, with the idea that he might be able to purchase his own land in central New York with his earnings. Bristol was a former Stockbridge resident who had moved to Clinton. He was a close friend of Samuel Kirkland, serving as a trustee for Kirkland's Hamilton Oneida Academy, which later became Hamilton College.[46]

We do not know whether Elizabeth or even Betsey approved of Jonah's plan. It is unlikely Elizabeth could have been very happy about the idea of her only child and only grandchildren potentially moving nearly a hundred and fifty miles from Stockbridge. Nevertheless, an arrangement was apparently made with Jonah's brother, Enoch Jr., for Enoch to perform the labor on Elizabeth and Jonah's farm in Jonah's absence.[47]

Whatever Jonah's hopes were, things did not go well in Clinton. He returned home indebted to Joel Bristol for $26.10.[48] Elizabeth did not pay the debt for him, but probably to address his concern that their farm was too small to produce an adequate living, on December 1, 1807, she purchased an additional parcel of twelve and a half acres for $49.00. This parcel consisted of woodlands and was likely intended to serve as the source of the family's fuel supply and to permit Jonah to sell excess lumber for additional income for the family.[49]

Theodore continued to occupy his judicial post. In mid–1806, after being passed over for the chief justiceship in favor of Theophilus Parsons, he briefly considered retirement, but urged on by friends and some family members other than Pamela, he decided for financial, intellectual, and social reasons to remain on the court as an associate justice.[50] He did this with full knowledge of the strain his absence from Stockbridge placed on his family as Pamela continued to decline.

8. A Place of Her Own and a Long Goodbye

On a night in February 1806, before Eliza and Thaddeus had completed their move back to Stockbridge, and on a night that Elizabeth was apparently at her farm, a "trembling and pale" fourteen-year-old Charles Sedgwick ran across the street to the home of Mary Gray Bidwell, Pamela's cousin, seeking help for his mother. Before Mary Bidwell was able to put on her cloak, twenty-one-year-old Henry appeared "exhausted with agitation" to say their mother's situation was critical. Mary spent the night caring for Pamela, believing several times she was about to die. When Elizabeth arrived in the morning, Pamela continued to suffer "repeated fits" for an additional day and night, intermittently reviving to ask why so many friends and relatives were in her room.[51]

Despite needing to spend some nights at the family farm during 1806, Elizabeth's relationship with the Sedgwicks remained strong. Back home in Stockbridge, sixteen-year-old Catharine informed her brother Robert, who was studying law with his elder brother in Albany, "Mumbet has made me break open my letter to tell you you must get her a pair of English morocco shoes, with sharp toes and let Theodore try them on." Theodore Sedgwick II, twenty-six-year-old attorney at law, apparently tried on a pair of women's shoes in an Albany store for his former governess and sent them along to her.[52]

Ever conscious of the financial obligation of her husband to her father but also susceptible to Pamela's piteous pleas for company, Frances reluctantly left her "sweet little Eben" in Stockbridge when she returned to New York after a visit to her parents that fall. With her youngest child, Charles, now at boarding school in Connecticut and her husband heading back to his judicial duties, Pamela's loneliness overwhelmed her, and she pried the three-year-old away from his mother. Frances was in agony over it but, as usual, gave way to a parent's wishes. Pamela's need must have been great that she could bear to read from Frances, "I thought my little boys lamentations were the sources of any grief in the seperation—but all the Mother fills my heart–& I find my own loss almost inexpressibly painful." It was perhaps justice for Pamela to be informed by her daughter that it was Elizabeth, not she, who Frances relied on to sustain her little boy during the forced separation: "Mumbet has my sincerest gratitude for her goodness to him–& I have the utmost confidence that she will at all times exercise the affection and kindness of the tenderest Mother towards him."[53]

The last winter of Pamela's life passed much like the previous one. When she displayed reasonably good health in January, although Pamela was far from being well enough to travel, Theodore, home between court sessions, seized on the opportunity to leave her for a six-day trip to Albany. This time he had the excuse of escorting seventeen-year-old Catharine who wanted to visit Theodore II and Robert in Albany. He knew Pamela would have to accede to that.[54]

When she was at home, young Catharine both assisted Elizabeth with Pamela's care and kept the rest of the family apprised of the family matriarch's condition: "She sits in the East room entirely, sleeps very well, and has quite as much appetite as usual," she reported in mid–March to Henry, who was in Boston making contacts with a view to setting up a legal practice there.[55] Catharine was doing her best to be helpful to Elizabeth and her mother, but even with Eliza and her family now living down the street, she longed for her turn away from Stockbridge. "You know I have no great penchant for solitude, and I never was so weary of it as at present," she confessed to Henry.[56]

For Pamela, with her restricted movement and long days spent sitting in her parlor waiting for letters that came too infrequently, it must have been even more tedious, but perhaps she had a growing sense that her long travail was almost over. Catharine wrote in a letter to Henry, "Mama begs you will give her love to Papa and desire him to write her. She is quite as well as she was before her last illness and is very cheerful."[57]

Elizabeth was too busy to be bored, and unlike Catharine, she did not have the alternative of flight to a vibrant social and cultural life in New York or Boston. For the present, she still had a deep sense of being needed by the Sedgwicks, though even with her prodigious energy, she must have sometimes wished for a rest. Perhaps now, though, she sometimes looked at frail Pamela and the often-empty Sedgwick house and realized that a long, fulfilling chapter in her life might be coming to an end. Did she regret it, or now that Jonah had given up on the idea of moving Betsey and the children west, did she welcome it? As with most significant life transitions, probably a little of each.

But as spring gave way to summer, there was little time to think

8. A Place of Her Own and a Long Goodbye

about it. Frances arrived with her three children for her annual summer sojourn, and Henry returned from Boston. Robert and Theodore II were also expected for the family's usual late-summer reunion.

The family was excited. Over the opposition of her stepfather, John Livingston, Susan Ridley, Theodore II's longtime sweetheart, had agreed to marry him. Theodore, who believed it was high time his twenty-seven-year-old son was married, thought highly of Susan and was deeply pleased that Livingston, who had not thought Theodore's son good enough for her, was being defied. It was one thing for Theodore to reject an impecunious suitor for his daughter—how dare Livingston reject his marvelous son?[58]

Almost before everyone knew it, the long summer days waned. In mid–September, Theodore departed for Boston. It would be the last time Pamela would have to bid him farewell. Some of the family stayed on for a little more time together. There was no sense of an impending loss. On September 17, Henry wrote Theodore II in Albany, "We are all well…. The shooting is fine & Mr. Watson [Frances's husband] enjoys it highly … Mama particularly desires her love to You & wishes You to come down."[59]

On the morning of Saturday, September 19, Elizabeth, as usual, began to get Pamela ready for the day. As Mary Gray Bidwell later described to her husband, Elizabeth "was alarmed while dressing her that morning by the appearance of a livid spot over her right eye." When Elizabeth pointed it out to Pamela's children, they decided it was merely "some slight contusion." Pamela seemed fine, and because of her partial paralysis, bruises were not unusual.[60] Perhaps it was just as well that this is what they believed, because even if they had thought otherwise and summoned a doctor, there was nothing that the medical science of the time could have done to save their mother. As it was, "she supported her customary pleasantness throughout the day."[61] Late in the afternoon, a neighbor, Sally Fairman, came to visit Pamela. The young Sedgwicks and some of their friends were in the front parlor "in a high scene of mirth." When Pamela's visitor asked if the noise bothered her, she said, "No, I am pleased to find they are cheerful and happy." When Elizabeth helped her into bed that evening, she was "without special complaint."[62]

At about 2 a.m. on Sunday, the 20th, Pamela jolted from sleep and suffered a series of seizures. Mary Bidwell describes them as about twenty in number and similar "to those which have so long afflicted her." At some point Pamela slipped into a coma. At daybreak someone fetched Elizabeth, and messages were sent to Theodore in Boston and Theodore II and Robert in Albany. Elizabeth was by her side when Pamela died shortly before 8 a.m. She was fifty-four years old.[63]

Catharine was inconsolable, crying for hours, "sobbing over my dead mother." At last Elizabeth said to her, "We must be quiet. Don't you think I am grieved? Our hair has grown white together." Catharine recalled decades later, "Even at this distance of time I remember the effect on me of her still, solemn sadness."[64]

Theodore arrived by stagecoach from Boston on Tuesday afternoon. The funeral was held the following morning. Henry wrote his mother's obituary, describing her "submissive piety" and her "apprehension that her life was useless." Henry could not put a name on a condition that clearly had some biological components but, to modern eyes, also involved depression stemming from a life framed by submission to a husband less devoted to her than she to him—a life in which her ambition to raise a large family side by side with him was subordinated to his political ambition and the needs of the new nation. When Pamela married Theodore in 1774, he was a country lawyer with a home office who rode several miles to court each day when court was in session. Many modern marriages have foundered because of the determination of one of the spouses to pursue career opportunities far from home. In the late eighteenth century, it was always the man who could make such a choice and the woman who had no choice but to submit to it.

Pamela's youngest daughter, while continuing to idolize her father, would take from her mother's life that marriage was a fate to be avoided. Pamela's son Henry concluded simply, "Her sufferings in degree and duration, have been perhaps without parallel, but they reached not the measure of her faith and her patience."[65]

9

Big Decisions

THEODORE, EVER THE PATRIARCH, was insistent that his children tailor their lives to his new circumstances. A plan to send Charles to New York for training in business was abandoned. Henry's proposal to move to Boston was deferred, and Catharine's usual winter sojourn with Frances's family was severely truncated. The two youngest children, Catharine and Charles, just turning eighteen and sixteen, tried to be sympathetic to their father's wishes in the face of his bereavement. Henry, at twenty-two, was beginning to chafe at his father's manipulations, complaining to Theodore II, "You know how extremely unpleasant it is to argue with him on these subjects, and how difficult to make him think at all upon them."[1]

Elizabeth, anxious to help the sorrowing Sedgwick children adjust to life without their mother, continued as a steadying influence in the household, drafting Catharine to help her make mince pies and focusing her on the present.[2] The week before Christmas, with Catharine assisting, Elizabeth helped Eliza deliver her seventh child.[3]

In the spring, when Theodore returned to Boston, he allowed Catharine to accompany him, installing her at the Tuckers while he took up quarters at a nearby boarding house. This arrangement allowed him to see Catharine when he wished but to pursue a separate social life. Catharine loved staying with the Tuckers, who had a daughter her age, but she was also a little puzzled by her father's new life, writing Henry, "I meet him now and then in parties except that I hardly ever see him."[4]

In Stockbridge, Elizabeth continued to run the Sedgwick household for Henry and Charles, who remained to oversee the farm at their father's insistence. Probably at Elizabeth's request, but certainly with her consent, Henry dismissed a male house servant named Jo for poor performance in late April.⁵ At about the same time, Henry assured Catharine, "Mum Bet desires me to inform you what I know to be the fact that she has preserved more than a bushel of cranberries for You."⁶

When Theodore left Boston to ride circuit, he told Theodore II that he had allowed Catharine to remain at the Tuckers, "tho I have given her a strict injunction not to delay her return much beyond the period of my arrival at home."⁷ In addition to his usual imperiousness, Theodore had good reason to want as many of his children at home as possible when he returned in the spring, because he was about to announce astonishing news: He had proposed marriage to Penelope Russell, and she had accepted.

All of Theodore's children were shocked. Pamela had been dead for only a little more than eight months when he broke the news in early June 1808. The news hit the unmarried children the hardest, but even twenty-eight-year-old Theodore II, who planned to marry Susan Ridley in the fall, wrote Henry, "To tell you that I was as astonished and afflicted is unnecessary—I was totally unprepared to hear of such an event, as I had not the slightest expectation of it." It came, not only so soon after their mother's death, but also "I see in it the certainty of the breaking up of the family.... That Miss R will not live in S is I think certain."⁸

Catharine, unwilling to ascribe precipitousness or disloyalty to her beloved father, even decades later blamed his Boston social circle: "My father was flattered into this marriage by some good-natured friends who believed he would be the happier for it, and knew she would. Like most second marriages where there are children it was disastrous."⁹

If Elizabeth's more mature perception saw in the speedy engagement the certainty that Theodore had emotionally distanced himself from the physically and psychologically wounded wife who adored him long before her death, she said nothing to the reeling Sedgwick children. As to what she herself would do, a big decision was looming. Theodore and Pamela Sedgwick had employed her since 1781, the year Theodore helped her gain freedom for herself and her daughter. She would never forget that and would always be grateful to him. But in the intervening twenty-seven years, she had spent most of her waking hours with Pamela, delivering her babies, worrying together over sick children, and nursing Pamela as best she could through the throes of mental and physical illness. Pamela was almost a sister to her. Could she accept a new mistress of the household, especially one installed with such disrespectful dispatch? And if she did, what would she have to tolerate from this woman? Would she have to pretend that it was Penelope who was supervising the household and attempt to get her to make the correct decisions?

She realized from Catharine's description that Penelope knew nothing about running a household: "a Boston woman, of a highly respectable family, an agreeable exterior, and attractive vivacity.... The Poor lady was put into a life for which she was totally unfitted. She knew nothing of the business of country domestic life."[10] Unwilling to immediately cause the Sedgwick children further pain in the wake of the betrothal announcement and perhaps wanting to give herself additional time to reflect, Elizabeth decided to bide her time.

* * *

Elizabeth soon received additional information. Despite Theodore II's fears, Theodore told Penelope he wished to spend the periods between court sessions at Stockbridge in order to maintain ties with his children. This caused enough anxiety in his city-loving fiancée that she required more information about his rural retreat before entering the bonds of matrimony. It was agreed that Penelope's elder sister, Catharine Russell, would make a visit to confirm that the home was as gracious and comfortable as Theodore insisted it was. Penelope did not think it proper for her to visit her betrothed prior to the marriage, and she also may have wished to avoid the long stagecoach ride from Boston to Stockbridge. Catharine Russell was curious about Theodore's fiefdom, so she agreed to perform the inspection on her sister's behalf.[11]

Theodore and Catharine Russell were great friends. Though in-laws of the opposite sex sometimes corresponded with each other in the early nineteenth century, Catharine and Theodore's letters display a warmth, humor, and easy familiarity that was independent of the marriage connection.[12] It is possible that Theodore first cast his eye on Catharine when thinking about a third wife but, receiving no encouragement, transferred his attention to Penelope.

A Revolutionary Woman

Penelope, at thirty-nine, was still potentially capable of having one or more children. This was probably not a plus in Theodore's eyes. He was under grave economic pressure providing for the seven children he already had. The prospect of needing to divide his estate further could only have caused him anxiety. He must have known, too, that the matter was of deep concern to Pamela's children, who were relying on him to fulfill his financial commitments to them. But Catharine Russell apparently enjoyed her independence, while Penelope looked forward to the prestige of being Justice Sedgwick's wife. She may have also hoped for the late blessing of motherhood.

By the conclusion of Catharine Russell's visit, Miss Russell had decided that her sister's future country seat was quite acceptable, and Elizabeth Freeman had decided that Penelope Russell would never be her employer. As Catharine Sedgwick described it many years later, "She felt she could no longer maintain the authority into which she had gradually grown—and saying she 'could not learn new ways' she went to live at the little place which she had earned with the sweat of her brow."[13]

It is doubtful that the reason she gave the Sedgwick children was the only reason why Elizabeth left the Sedgwick household. She was well aware of the bargaining advantage she held over Penelope, had she wished to stay on. As would soon become obvious, no one in Berkshire County could play the role that Elizabeth filled in the household. She also had on her side all the Sedgwick children, who would make it clear to Penelope that Mumbet was more a member of the family than an employee. Elizabeth's position would not have been diminished in a household that continued to exist mainly because Theodore wanted to maintain close ties with his children.

The idea that Elizabeth wanted to retire because of advancing age does not seem likely either, because after she left the Sedgwicks, Elizabeth maintained an active private nursing and midwife practice for more than a decade. The familiarity between Theodore and Catharine Russell on display during her visit may have played an important role in Elizabeth's decision. It forced Elizabeth to see for the first time that all those years when Pamela was suffering in his absence, Theodore wasn't just selflessly serving the nation; he was also having a good time. As she told Catharine the day Pamela died, their hair had

9. Big Decisions

"grown white together." Theodore's children might have to accept this new reality that had been thrust upon them, but she didn't, and she wasn't going to, especially since the Sedgwick children were mostly grown up, with many of them planning their own departures. That didn't mean she would abandon the Sedgwick children, whom she loved so much. She made it clear they could call on her if they needed her, and she kept that promise throughout Theodore's third marriage and beyond.

Elizabeth apparently waited until Miss Russell departed before speaking to Theodore. She wanted no bad feelings between them. Though she would later be a little more frank with the Sedgwick children, she simply told Theodore that the time had come for her to retire. She was now about sixty-four, so Theodore could hardly dispute that she was entitled to retire if she wished, but he asked her to think it over. He was himself about to leave for Boston, and he probably thought that Henry, Catharine, and Charles would talk her out of it.

He was already in a glum mood, and the conversation with Elizabeth could only have depressed him further. He was by now painfully aware that none of his children welcomed his remarriage. Having their beloved Mumbet's retirement connected to it would make matters worse. He was also fully aware that Penelope had some trepidation about living part of the year in Stockbridge and that she knew nothing of household management. Without Elizabeth to run the place, what would happen?

On October 20, he wrote Theodore II, telling him he would leave for Boston the following week: "I shall probably while there be married." And yet, the prospective bridegroom was having some doubts: "There is much, in my circumstances in this solemn event, to make me thoughtful and gloomy; and it does make me gloomy. I have, indeed, a high opinion of Miss R. but I hardly know what to say or think—she is sensible, and I believe amiable, yet I can foresee events which would render the connexion a source of uneasiness and misery." Nevertheless, he didn't exactly want to back out: "I know not a woman in the world with whom I could expect more satisfaction."[14]

Theodore respected his children's feelings sufficiently not to force a celebration on them. He timed his nuptials in Boston for the same week that the rest of the family was gathering in New York City for Theodore II's wedding to Susan Ridley.

For their part, his adult children decided to pose no further obstacle. In mid–October, Theodore II wrote to his father asking him to "present my most affectionate remembrance to Miss Russell."[15] Two weeks later, he requested a loan from his father. The economic downturn caused by the Embargo Act, America's response to British violations of American neutrality leading up to the War of 1812, was putting the viability of his law firm in doubt.[16] Henry, perhaps perceiving that his father's marriage would at last free him to begin his life in Boston, wrote him the day before the nuptials: "None of us affect not to have feelings on this occasion which we believe to be natural and unavoidable, yet none of us pretend to question that You are the sole judge with respect to the propriety of the choice."[17]

As for Elizabeth, she had come to a final decision, and not even her beloved Henry, Catharine, and Charles could talk her out of it. On October 30, Henry informed Theodore II, "Our family establishment is about to undergo a very unpleasant alteration in the loss of Mum-Bet."[18] He delayed an additional week before finally telling his father, "I believe that Mum-Bet is resolutely determined to leave the family."[19]

* * *

Theodore replied to Henry on November 12, by this time, a married man. As he had always done during Pamela's lifetime when making a decision against her wishes, he proclaimed how difficult doing what he wanted to do was for him: "Had I imagined it possible that the harmony of the family could have been disturbed by this event, or the happiness of my dear children impaired I would have preferred death to it." Still, having now participated in marital congress with Penelope, he had decided to live: "I believe my companion to be kind, gentle, affectionate and good. She is infinitely anxious as to the impression which her character may make upon the family. I hope and pray that it may be just and favorable."[20] With respect to Elizabeth's departure, he wrote tersely, "I hope you will be able to procure a successor to Bet so as to prevent the necessity of taking a woman from Boston."[21]

Henry probably sighed in frustration when he read that line. Was

9. Big Decisions

he a miracle worker? He turned the business over to his busy elder sister, Eliza. A few days later, Eliza appended a postscript to a letter to her father from young Charles. With Aunt Dwight's help, she found in Pittsfield an African American woman named Lilly. Lilly had a twelve-year-old daughter who would accompany her, but she was only willing to work for the Sedgwicks for the winter. It was a stop-gap measure, but the woman had worked previously for Aunt Dwight, who was happy with her, and as Eliza optimistically concluded, "It is possible that Bett will be willing to return next spring."[22]

Theodore was relieved. He had dreaded having to tell Penelope that the family housekeeper had left her position. The whole premise of their splitting time between her beloved Boston and his Stockbridge home was that life would be restful and enjoyable for her there while giving him time with his children. The last thing he wanted to do a few days after their wedding was to make her responsible for interviewing domestic help or to embarrass her by having to do this traditional upper-class woman's task for her.

Regardless, he was by now very glad he had cast his doubts aside and entered the marriage. This is what he had wanted for years—a woman unfettered by the obligations of motherhood who could be his constant companion. And given his proclivity to believe that other people would eventually agree to do what suited him, when he set out on the circuit with Penelope, he may have told himself that Eliza was absolutely right: Bet would probably come back in the spring.

Back in Stockbridge, in addition to making herself available for private nursing and midwife assignments, Elizabeth had more time to address a festering problem.[23] Betsey's husband, Jonah, continued to struggle with the labor demands of their farm. To address the issue, on April 1, 1809, Elizabeth and Jonah deeded a one-eighth-acre house lot to Jonah's brother, Enoch Jr., for $250 but took back a purchase money mortgage. The arrangement was apparently that, in exchange for the house lot, Enoch Jr. would help Jonah work the farm.[24]

Meanwhile, Theodore and Penelope arrived in Stockbridge. Henry reported the scene to Catharine, who was wintering with Frances in New York. On the whole, it went reasonably well. "Partly by forcing our feelings and partly by yielding to the impression naturally made by the social … qualities which Mrs Sedgwick eminently possesses we have for a considerable part of the time since her arrival passed our time in that hilarity which usually characterizes the meetings of our family." Still, there was no denying that it was a strain for everyone involved. The sight of his sixty-three-year-old father playing the lover with a woman seven years older than his eldest daughter was jarring. It was hard "to see our revered father caressing a woman with any other sentiment than that of paternal affection."[25]

For the sake of her continuing relationship with the Sedgwick children and in recognition of Theodore's role in gaining her freedom, Elizabeth agreed to come by the house and greet the newlyweds. Later, in Boston, Penelope hyperbolically reported to her friends how much all the Sedgwick children loved her and that their beloved governess, Mumbet, highly approved of her. When these reports eventually circled back to the Sedgwick children, they were the occasion of a good deal of mirth among the siblings.[26]

With views on the question of paternal prerogatives similar to those of many other upper-class men of his time, Theodore continued to use a combination of financial leverage and his children's natural affection to get them to abandon their own plans and be available to keep him company when he was in Stockbridge. Heavily imbued with the patriarchal notion that ultimately his happiness was more important than his children's, or rather, that they must be happy because he was happy, he complained to Catharine, "The utmost extension of my wishes ... is to have all my children about me, but the boys continually complain of the dullness of the scene—so much so as to give me a great deal of pain."[27]

He still had it in his power to pressure seventeen-year-old Charles to abandon his plans to move to New York to undertake a business apprenticeship, and he did so without regret. Ignoring the fact that Eliza and her growing brood lived just down the street, he told Catharine, "Under the circumstances I cannot consent to have Charles go to N York. I cannot willingly be bereaved of all my children; and Charles excellent young man consents cheerfully to stay with me."[28]

Catharine did not debate the point then, but many years later she wrote of her brother Charles, "From that time he devoted his life to his father. For him he threw away every personal consideration. He steadily refused a collegiate education, because it would take him from home."[29]

9. Big Decisions

In May, Theodore and Penelope's temporary housekeeper, Lilly, left, and despite Eliza's optimism the previous fall, Elizabeth remained firm in her decision not to return to her old position. Theodore was forced to write to Theodore II in Albany asking if his wife, Susan, could find someone for them there: "The woman who is coming is engaged only for a month. We have a girl engaged at Boston, she is not acquainted with cooking. This is a case of difficulty … and we are obliged to tax our friends to aid our own resources."[30]

But Elizabeth meant what she had promised the Sedgwick children when she left the household. She would always be there for them when they needed her. Theodore II's wife, Susan, was to give birth to their first child in early December 1809. A few weeks before, accompanied by Jonah, Elizabeth made the trip to Albany to care for Susan. It turned out that her services were gravely needed. In what was probably a case of preeclampsia, Susan delivered a stillborn baby and was delirious for days. Elizabeth was at her side throughout the ordeal. As Catharine wrote many years later, Elizabeth's nursing decisions were often critical at such times: "More than once, by a courageous assumption of responsibility, by resisting the absurd medical useages of the time, in denying cold water and fresh air to burning fevers, she saved precious lives."[31] On December 17, Catharine was able to assure Frances, "I found her recovered astonishingly & Mumbet said she was stronger … than you were in the same time."[32] Elizabeth remained with the bereaved young mother for two months. Her father-in-law, Theodore, was grateful for Elizabeth's tender care of Susan and helped arrange transportation for Elizabeth when she was ready to return to Stockbridge.[33]

Back at home, Elizabeth found that financial problems continued to plague Jonah. Joel Bristol was again pursuing him for the debt Bristol claimed he owed him. In April 1810, Bristol renewed the claim in a Berkshire County court.[34] For whatever reason, Elizabeth did not help Jonah resolve the matter. Perhaps it was because he and Betsey were having marital difficulties. On January 14, 1811, Elizabeth bought back Jonah's share of the farm from him. Jonah left Stockbridge, failing to appear for the hearing in the matter with Bristol. A default judgment was entered against him. Jonah would not return to Stockbridge for more than two decades, and then only briefly. Betsey and her two daughters continued to live on the farm with Elizabeth.[35]

Jonah's brother, Enoch Jr., also remained on the farm with his wife, La Minta Elkey, and their five children. From this time on, it was Enoch Jr., with the help of his sons, who worked the farm for Elizabeth.[36] Electa Jones described Enoch Jr. as "a man of much sound sense and general intelligence."[37]

Probably feeling she had done all she could to help Betsey resolve her marital crisis, Elizabeth traveled again to Albany in the latter part of January 1811 to assist Susan Sedgwick with her second delivery. On January 27, Theodore II wrote triumphantly to his brother Henry: "Susan presented me with a fine son, this morning at half past seven— She is now in the best possible way—Never did any body get through such a peril this far, more fortunately. The boy is one of Mum-Bet's best."[38] Susan expressed her own appreciation for Elizabeth's care a few months later when she painted a watercolor miniature portrait of Elizabeth, the only likeness posterity has of her.[39]

Though young Theodore's father also greeted the news of another grandchild with joy, this was not a happy time for him.[40] Theodore was beginning to question his continued tenure on the Supreme Judicial Court. The rising tide of Democratic-Republicanism had finally reached Massachusetts, particularly the district of Maine, which remained a part of the state until 1820. Theodore began to complain not only of the "exhaustion of riding the circuit" but also of the "degradation to which I have been subjected" as subsistence farmers crowded into rural court rooms to jeer judicial enforcement of debtors' obligations.[41] He decided to soldier on for financial reasons: "My expenses are enormous, and I know not how to retrench. I know no human state more miserable than that of an old man who has been accustomed to affluence at the close of life reduced to straightened circumstances."[42]

If he had asked his wife, she probably would have suggested selling the house and farm in Stockbridge and buying a smaller house in Boston. But Theodore's sense of himself as a country squire and his desire to preserve the family home as a place for family reunions made such an idea unthinkable. Nevertheless, had Theodore let Charles go to New York and live with Robert while he undertook business training as originally planned and sold the Stockbridge estate, he would probably have improved his financial position considerably. Instead, he continued to require his wife, who by now was suffering from a serious stomach

9. Big Decisions

condition, to undertake the long journey there between court sessions while telling himself and anyone who would listen that she loved being in Stockbridge.⁴³

* * *

Theodore could take pride in one professional achievement in that difficult year of 1810. His blistering dissent in the case of *Greenwood v. Curtis* argued forcefully for the proposition that contracts to buy and sell slaves in Africa could not be enforced in a Massachusetts court. Theodore insisted the slave trade was completely illegal in Massachusetts, and any contract with respect to it involving a Massachusetts merchant, though executed elsewhere, was void. Going beyond statutory interpretation, Theodore also argued more broadly that the slave trade opposed all the "just principles" on which the Revolution had been based. The only question was whether the settled law of the Commonwealth could be twisted "for the gratification of our unlicensed avarice" for the purpose of enslaving "beings, who, in their material form, and essential character (whatever our supercilious arrogance may suggest to the contrary) bear equally with ourselves the impress of Divinity, and are equally entitled to all the rights of humanity."⁴⁴ It was certainly Elizabeth Freeman and Agrippa Hull who came to Theodore's mind as he wrote those words.

Though Elizabeth was unable to read the newspaper reports of the case, the Sedgwick children followed their father's judicial career

Elizabeth Freeman was approximately sixty-seven when Susan Sedgwick, Theodore II's wife, painted her portrait (*Elizabeth Freeman*, watercolor on ivory by Susan Anne Livingston Ridley Sedgwick, 1811, Massachusetts Historical Society).

assiduously, and it is very likely that one or more of them told her about it. As the daughter of two people probably stolen from Africa in their youth, Elizabeth probably found it particularly meaningful that Theodore continued to fight to eradicate any abetting of the slave trade by the Commonwealth of Massachusetts.

His dissent in *Greenwood v. Curtis* was the most significant accomplishment of Theodore's last years on the court. His financial problems and his own and Penelope's health issues were now his main preoccupations. Penelope's now-chronic stomach condition was affecting both her appearance and her behavior.[45] Unable to keep food down, she had lost a great deal of weight and was drinking significant amounts of brandy for the pain, as recommended by her doctor.[46] She had always drunk more alcohol than the Sedgwick children were used to seeing their Congregationalist mother imbibe. Early in the marriage, Theodore had joked casually with Catharine Russell about her drinking habits, which were probably similar to Penelope's: "I had the pleasure to receive your letter, and it was a good one, though you insinuate that you had drank a glass of wine too much."[47]

But now in constant pain, bored by country life in Stockbridge, and perhaps coming to recognize that her illness precluded any chance of motherhood, Penelope was sometimes obviously tipsy. When under the influence of alcohol, the veneer of sociability she had struggled to maintain with the Sedgwicks dropped away, and she could be petulant and whiny. Catharine, Henry, and Charles regularly shared their feelings about her, with Theodore II sometimes chiming in. In June 1811, Catharine, writing to Henry in Boston, assured him she had burned his letter lest their father ever see it and noted stoically, "Wisdom and religion impose upon us the obligation of silence and submission. This is the alloy that must be thrown into our cup of happiness my dear brother."[48] When Theodore and Penelope journeyed to central New York to inspect Theodore's land holdings there, Theodore II noted sarcastically to Henry, "I presume that Mrs Sedgwick has from her excessive love of home taken him to Niagara."[49] Mild-mannered Charles expressed his relief "to get rid of the society of one for a little while whose selfish and uneasy temper is death to domestic comfort."[50]

9. Big Decisions

* * *

Theodore's health was beginning to give way under the personal and professional stresses he was experiencing.[51] In July 1811, Theodore confessed to Henry that he was up to his neck in guarantees of Eben Watson's failing business enterprises: "Mr. Watson when he entered into partnership with Mr. Whiting engaged to advance 20,000$ as his part of the stock.... On his application to me I agreed to guaranty $10,000. At the same time I am bound for him to nearly 9000 on a former guaranty to Mr. Wolcott." Theodore had all but forced Frances into the marriage, and he couldn't bring himself to abandon her now that his judgment was proving wrong: "This is going as far, and perhaps further than prudence would dictate. But it seemed a last chance to him and that the future welfare of the family depended on rendering this scheme effectual."[52]

As Elizabeth listened to Catharine and Charles complain about Penelope on their frequent visits to her farmhouse, she doubtless congratulated herself on having decided not to work for her. She was also certainly sorry to hear of Theodore's health problems. She would always care deeply about the man who had so significantly affected her life for the better.

In her own family, there was something to celebrate. At about this time, her elder granddaughter, Lydia Maria, married Harry Van Schaack. In short order, the pair made Elizabeth a great-grandmother, not once but twice, with a girl named Lydia Maria Ann and a boy named Amos Josiah Van Schaack.[53]

Perhaps it was because the young couple moved into the Freeman farmhouse and things were getting a bit crowded that Elizabeth's daughter, Betsey, decided to make another try at domestic happiness, apparently becoming the partner of Jackson "Jack" Burghardt, a maternal great-grandfather of W.E.B. DuBois, and moving to Burghardt's farm in neighboring Great Barrington.[54] By the 1820s, Betsey was again living at her mother's farmhouse, and legal documents continued to refer to Elizabeth's daughter as Elizabeth Humphrey, so it is likely that the domestic partnership with Burghardt was not a legal marriage and that it occurred for a period of several years beginning no earlier than 1811, when she separated from Jonah Humphrey.[55]

The Sedgwick children's opinion of their stepmother continued to deteriorate throughout the fall of 1811. Theodore was neutral in the matter, content that his children were formally polite to her and unwilling to press them for anything more.

When Penelope asked Theodore's old friend, Judge Egbert Benson, to lecture twenty-six-year-old Henry about their coldness, twenty-one-year-old Catharine responded sympathetically, "We could be amply revenged by disclosing a <u>few facts</u> but this would be a miserable triumph." Catharine, probably the closest of all the children to Theodore, urged patience for his sake: "We owe to our Father a <u>perfect self conquest</u> in this affair, for we cannot more than fill up the sum of our duties to him, by the most painful and constant exertions."[56]

And yet, even Catharine found these exertions too painful to be constant. Her solution was to escape Stockbridge whenever possible by wintering in New York with Frances or in Albany with Theodore II's family.[57]

Theodore, himself, was chafing at the boredom of wintertime in Stockbridge and a nearly empty house: "I am very desirous of going to Albany, but I do not chuse to leave her, and she, certainly is not able to accompany me."[58] By mid-January his husbandly resolve had crumpled. "Last week I spent in Albany," he informed Henry.[59]

As for Elizabeth, she avoided Penelope but, on February 4, helped Eliza deliver her ninth child, a girl Eliza named Julia.[60] Just as Elizabeth was helping Eliza bring a new Sedgwick into the world, Theodore was beginning a slow but inexorable final decline. The same month little Julia was born, Theodore suffered a gout attack so severe that Charles had to carry him from room to room.[61]

In early April, Theodore recovered sufficiently to return to Boston with Penelope, but when Theodore headed for Worcester later that month, Penelope, still suffering from her stomach condition, elected to remain in Boston. Charles told Theodore it was a good thing, believing Theodore "too feeble" to handle any responsibilities but his judicial duties.[62]

Plagued by asthma, Theodore was able to perform his spring circuit schedule, but when he returned to Stockbridge that summer, he was exhausted. "I find that all serious mental application is fatiguing and injurious to me," he told Henry.[63]

Though debilitated, Theodore was still well enough to follow the

9. Big Decisions

news. Like most Federalists, he opposed war with Britain and was confident that New England's opposition would prevent it.[64]

But not even his interest in war and peace could push aside his presentiments of mortality, writing to Henry, "Whether I shall ever be better God knows, but I hope I shall not only be resigned to whatever may take place but grateful for the many and great mercies which I have received."[65]

All of the children made a point of coming home for the annual end-of-summer reunion. Many of the young Sedgwicks took the opportunity to make the two-mile walk down to Elizabeth's farmhouse. It wasn't just duty. As Henry said many years later, "She could neither read nor write; yet her conversation was instructive, and her society much sought. She received many visits at her own house, and very frequently received and accepted invitations to pass considerable intervals of time in the families of her friends."[66]

These young people she loved so much would have told her of their fears for their father. She undoubtedly accepted their invitation to come by the Sedgwick house to partake in the hospitality that characterized these family get-togethers. It was probably on one of these sociable occasions that she saw for the last time "the Judge" as both she and his children referred to him—the man with whom she had made history and with whom for three decades she had shared so many interlocking obligations and so many triumphs and sorrows.

10

A Mother to Them All

THEODORE RALLIED SUFFICIENTLY in September to perform circuit duties in nearby Lenox.[1] In November, he was determined to return to Boston for the court term there. He asked Catharine to accompany him and Penelope rather than go to New York. She confessed to Robert that it was "the frustration of all my plans of happiness for the winter," but she was resigned to doing it: "I am more and more convinced that my going to Boston is almost necessary to Papa You know Mrs Sedgwick."[2] Catharine requested that Henry inquire if she could stay at the Tuckers while looking after their father: "Papa says I could stay at his lodging but that is out of the question."[3]

It was a difficult journey. Theodore was so weak that the three nearly turned back at Springfield, but Theodore insisted on pressing forward.[4] While he still clung to the idea that he could take the bench when he arrived, perhaps what impelled him now was a desire to die in a place where there would be public recognition of his distinguished career upon his death. They made it to Boston, but after attending court for only a few days, Theodore was confined to his bed at his lodgings in Bowdoin Square with what may have been bronchial pneumonia.[5]

By the end of November, all his children recognized that Theodore might be nearing the end of his life. Charles arrived from Stockbridge. Theodore II, whose wife gave birth to a daughter in December, sent anxious requests for news.[6] Eliza, at this time still a confirmed Congregationalist, wrote her father a distraught letter expressing concern for his soul, and Frances, who shared Eliza's conservative religious views, exhorted her siblings in Boston to bring a minster to their father's bedside.[7]

Theodore desired spiritual consolation, but not of the sort Eliza

10. A Mother to Them All

and Frances had in mind. Even while a student at Yale, he had possessed progressive religious ideas that had not endeared him to Yale's president. A few years later, his vision of his first wife shortly after her death confirmed for him that the fire and brimstone teachings of the Congregational Church could not be correct. In 1805, he told Henry, "I do in my heart and understanding believe ... the Christian system ... because it is a system of love, of benevolence, of grace and mercy which no mind but one infinitely kind would have determined, and no power less than infinite can effect."[8]

Theodore knew both Henry and Catharine had grown close to Boston's preeminent Unitarian minister, William Ellery Channing, and that both of them often attended his church. One day in early January, Penelope went out for a walk, leaving Catharine and Theodore alone. Theodore suddenly told Catharine why he had never joined a church: "He had feared giving pain to Dr. West and many good people in Stockbridge by joining any other than their church, and he could not bring his feelings to joining that."[9] Now, he was interested in joining Channing's church: "Mr. Channing's belief ... agreed with his better than any other Clergyman's in Boston."[10]

Soon the Reverend Channing visited Theodore's bedside and explained to Theodore "his understanding of this holy sacrament which agreed entirely with Papa's—He then proceeded to administer it in the most solemn and affecting manner."[11]

In Albany, Susan Sedgwick was making such a slow recovery from childbirth that Theodore II was afraid to leave her. Henry assured his brother that he was doing the right thing to remain with his wife and wrote, "I am glad that Mum Bet is at last with her."[12]

It may be that Elizabeth's granddaughter gave birth to her first child at about the same time as Susan's delivery. Whatever the reason for Elizabeth's inability to attend the birth of Susan's baby, she was with her by early January. Theodore II would have immediately shared with Elizabeth all the news from Boston. She would have learned of a second visit by the Reverend Channing and that Theodore was being given laudanum. She would have been told that Henry believed, "His strength is nearly exhausted his constitution is gone—each moment may be his last, & the closing moment cannot be long deferred."[13]

Robert had arrived from New York the last week in December.

Eliza left her eight surviving children with her husband and, escorted by her uncle, Henry Dwight, arrived at her father's bedside on January 22. To everyone's joy, "He affectionately recognized Eliza."[14]

On the evening of January 28, Theodore II received a letter from Henry that he read to Elizabeth. On January 24, Theodore II's father and Elizabeth's emancipator and friend "expired almost without a struggle a little before 7 o'clock in the evg."[15]

Communications were so slow that by the time Theodore II and Elizabeth received word of Theodore's passing, his funeral had already taken place. Probably as he had hoped, a committee of the Boston Bar asked permission to help make the arrangements. Resolutions by both houses of the legislature were issued proclaiming him "an able judge and a distinguished patriot." The funeral was held at 4 p.m. on Wednesday, January 27, at the Reverend Channing's church on Federal Street. It was attended by the entire Massachusetts House and Senate as well as all the members of the Boston Bar, with each of the attendees wearing a black crepe band on his left arm.[16] The following day, most of the family, including Penelope, left for Stockbridge, where Theodore's will was to be read.[17]

In Albany, Susan was still so weak that Theodore II and Elizabeth delayed telling her about Theodore's death. Theodore didn't think he could come to Stockbridge for the reading of the will, telling Henry, "Susan has been very ill, and although considerably better, is still so.... She is very feeble, has some pain, and has lost her spirits in a great measure."[18]

In retrospect, Theodore II may not have been sorry to miss the reading of his father's will and the days that followed. While the Sedgwick children were satisfied with the terms of the will, Penelope was not. She was to receive an annual income of $550, but her property in England, estimated at a value of $4,800, was to constitute part of the capital fund that was to produce income for the estate. She was also given use of her bedroom at the Stockbridge house, with appurtenant privileges in the cellar, kitchen, and gardens during her life, and one-third of Theodore's books, as well as a portrait of Theodore. Charles was to inherit the house, most of the land, and his father's law books. Eliza was bequeathed $5,000, Frances $6,000, and Catharine $8,500. Theodore II, Henry, and Robert were to receive the remainder of the estate.[19]

10. A Mother to Them All

Though this was a fairly standard method in the early nineteenth century of dividing an estate when there were both children from a first marriage and a second wife, Theodore had apparently failed to discuss the plan with Penelope. Understandably, it came as a very unpleasant surprise to her that the law of the time provided that the property she brought to the marriage was included in her husband's estate.

As Catharine reported to Frances in New York, "Mrs S... expressed her dissatisfaction with the provision made for her." There were displays of anger: "By giving her reason up to her ruling passion she removed the tight veil that hid the deformity of her heart." Perhaps misunderstanding where the loyalty of the domestic staff lay, or perhaps hoping her words would find their way back to the Sedgwick children, "She has even said in so many words, that she had made no money marrying, that she has had a life of slavery, and got nothing for it at last—Such expressions betraying her object and her disappointment have poured into the ears of servants that despised her."[20]

A week after the will was read, Henry arrived in Albany to consult with Theodore II. It was at this time that Elizabeth got a full report of Penelope's histrionics and again congratulated herself for having refused to work for her. As for the Sedgwicks, they were prepared to sweeten Penelope's financial deal if they could be done with her once and for all.

Together, Theodore II and Henry came up with a proposal. Leaving Susan and the children in Elizabeth's capable hands, on February 15, the two brothers returned to Stockbridge and presented to Penelope the outlines of a deal. She could have her property in England free and clear and also receive the annual payment of $550 from Theodore's estate, but she must give up any claim to occupy a room in the family home, her share of Theodore's books, and the portrait of Theodore he had bequeathed her.

Though she "unhesitatingly avowed her intention of breaking the will provided her friends should advise it," she now had something substantive to discuss with her Boston counsel.[21] It was Henry's unpleasant task to escort her back to Boston, but as he told Catharine, "she was at least decently civil which was more than I expected, and as much as I wished."[22]

A Revolutionary Woman

* * *

After the stress of her father's death and its aftermath, Catharine needed the comfort of the woman she regarded as her second mother. As soon as Henry and Penelope departed, she was off to Albany to help Elizabeth care for Susan and her children. Soon her good humor returned, joking with her lawyer brother: "My time is chiefly spent in the Nursery (the details of which/Mumbet to the contrary notwithstanding) would not much interest you."[23]

As this quote indicates, Elizabeth found early childhood development fascinating and the care of young children very rewarding. Susan Sedgwick's confidence in her was such that when Elizabeth needed to return to Stockbridge, Susan agreed that Elizabeth would bring Susan's six-month-old daughter, Maria, with her and that Susan would follow several weeks later for her annual summer visit accompanied by two-year-old Theodore III.[24]

With Penelope no longer mistress of the household, Elizabeth was willing to resume some of her old duties on a flexible basis, helping twenty-one-year-old Charles, the new owner, and twenty-three-year-old Catharine manage things while supplying the connection to their childhood that these grieving young people longed for. As Catharine shared with Henry, "I confess Mumbet's powers, and I am often charmed into forgetfulness of past sorrows and absent friends by her tales of other times—She sends her best love to her pet-child Mr. Harry, and desires him to come home and see his little niece!!!"[25]

Soon Susan arrived with little Theodore, and Frances arrived from New York with her two youngest children. With several of Eliza's children constantly there playing with their cousins, the house was once again as it had been twenty years before. Elizabeth was in her element, laughing as the "dumb little plagues," many of whom she had brought into the world, swirled around her. Catharine, who was about forty-five years younger and a fond aunt, was exhausted. She assured Henry in Boston so many children were in the house that childless couples could come and select from any age and sex, and there would be plenty left over.[26]

Though Elizabeth was a second mother to the Sedgwicks, the constraints of class and race nevertheless tinged aspects of their

10. A Mother to Them All

relationship. As the Sedgwick children reached adulthood, Elizabeth felt compelled to add "Mr." and "Miss" to their given names, and none of them felt comfortable telling her to stop. As mature adults, Catharine, Henry, and Charles all became committed abolitionists. Henry pointed to Elizabeth's life and character as proof that claims of racial inferiority as a justification for slavery were false. In 1831, he wrote, "Having known this woman as familiarly as I knew either of my parents, I cannot believe in the moral or physical inferiority of the race to which she belonged."[27] In 1854, having described Elizabeth's moral triumphs over Hannah Ashley, Catharine asked, "Which was the slave and which was the real mistress?"[28] And yet, some of them could be oblivious to the damage inflicted on African Americans by racism, and Elizabeth could demonstrate confusion about its effects on her fellow freedmen. Thus, in 1818, Catharine was capable of relating an insensitive story to her brother Robert about one of their Aunt Dwight's servants, prefacing the story by assuring him that Elizabeth also held him in contempt.[29] As she aged, Catharine in particular, though always ascribing the cause to "injustice and oppression," continued to show impatience with the "petty reprisals" of Black servants, describing the actions of these victims of abduction, slavery, and racism as "vices of a degraded and subjected people."[30]

As Elizabeth and the female members of the Sedgwick clan attended to Theodore and Pamela's numerous grandchildren, Henry Sedgwick successfully concluded his negotiations with Theodore's widow. In the end, Penelope's lawyer advised her to accept Henry and Theodore II's proposal as financially favorable to her. When the evidence of her unpopularity with the Sedgwick children caused gossip in Boston, Penelope salved her embarrassment with a three-year sojourn in Naples. After she departed, the Sedgwick children quietly had their father's body exhumed from the Granary Burial Ground in Boston and reburied beside their mother in Stockbridge. While in Naples, Penelope recovered from her stomach condition. She returned to Boston in 1818, never having more than a nodding relationship with any of the Sedgwicks again. She died in 1827.[31]

The younger Sedgwick children entered adulthood as the War of 1812 raged. The battles of that conflict were fought far from Stockbridge. Its effect on the village's inhabitants was mainly economic.

The war took on a more personal cast in 1814, however, when twenty-seven-year-old Robert Sedgwick volunteered for military service. Elizabeth was all too aware from her own past experience that young men who went off to war sometimes did not return. Late that summer, Catharine informed Robert, "Mumbet has just come in and says 'if you are writing to Mr Robert Do tell him he had better have minded me, and staid at home, poor Boy. I think on him all the time.'"[32]

Elizabeth's fears for Robert Sedgwick proved short lived. He survived the war and went on to marry, have children, and resume his successful legal practice. It was not long, however, before Elizabeth suffered one of the great tragedies of her life. In January 1815, Elizabeth's elder granddaughter, Lydia Maria, only about twenty years old, died unexpectedly. According to Catharine Sedgwick, Lydia had given birth about three weeks before her death. This child was probably Amos Josiah.[33]

Lydia's recovery was going so well that Elizabeth felt comfortable two weeks later turning her attention to Eliza Pomeroy, who was approaching the due date of her final pregnancy. Suddenly Lydia "got an ague in her breast." As Catharine related it to her sister Frances, "Mother returned to her—and in a few days she was again doing well." But a few days later, "after sitting with the family, and eating very well, she was preparing to go to bed, when she complained of faintness, and swooned for a few moments—she came to again said she was quite recovering & fell into a gentle sleep, which continued 5 minutes, when she opened her eyes, and breathed her last without a struggle or a pang."[34] The cause of death may have been an undetected heart condition.

Catharine rushed to Elizabeth's farmhouse to comfort her: "I remember Mumbet walking up and down the room with her hands knit together and great tears rolling down her cheeks, repeating, as if to send back into her soul its swelling sorrow, 'Don't say a word; it's God's will!'"[35]

Catharine told Frances, "I never saw a family more tenderly affected–& poor Mumbet tho' the most calm among them, was the most deeply wounded." Elizabeth had a special bond with Lydia, who was very much like her grandmother in character and personality.[36]

10. A Mother to Them All

As the burial rituals were performed, Elizabeth could not contain her grief. Catharine brought her the shroud: "Mother took it to put it on, and when she raised the cold body to put it on, her feelings which she had til then restrained and moderated burst out into an overwhelming torrent of expressions 'Oh' said she 'my child'/and her head fell onto Lydia's bosom/'I dressed you first, and I dress you last, you should have done this for me, I thought you would.'" Catharine told Elizabeth she would place Lydia in the shroud for her. "'Oh no, she is my child I will do everything for her. I can do it.'" Catharine told Frances, "I think Mother has shown Christian submission to an event that wrested from her, her all."[37] Elizabeth and Betsey now became the primary caretakers of Lydia Maria's two small children.[38]

* * *

The economic effects of the War of 1812 continued to have a devastating effect on Ebenezer Watson's publishing business. In settling their father's estate, the Sedgwicks did their best to keep Frances's husband afloat. Eliza generously agreed to give up her bequest of $5,000 so that the money could be credited to her father's guarantees of Watson's firm. Catharine, who, as an unmarried woman, was completely dependent on her bequest of $8,500, agreed to loan Watson $3,500, with Theodore II, Henry, and Robert guaranteeing repayment of Watson's bond to Catharine should he fail to redeem it. The three brothers would have to make good on that promise when Watson's firm dissolved in 1816.[39]

Watson, who had used Frances's inheritance to pay some of his obligations, could not accept that these significant gestures by her siblings were all they could do to help save his foundering business. During the spring and summer of 1815, he began to argue with his brothers-in-law and to physically abuse Frances when she defended them.[40]

The abuse came as a shock to all the Sedgwicks, but especially to Catharine, who had spent winters with the Watsons since she was eleven and who had always considered Eben a very good man. With Watson no longer able to support his family and the marriage deteriorating, in May 1816, Frances and her five children moved back to the Stockbridge family home to live with Charles.[41] Elizabeth was certainly glad Frances was no longer subject to Watson's abuse. She probably also reflected sadly that Pamela's inclination to let Frances follow her heart and marry Loring Andrews had been correct.

Despite the failure of the Watson marriage, Elizabeth hoped that the four younger Sedgwick children would soon enter into happy marriages, and she did not hesitate to tell them so. She got her wish with respect to Henry when he became engaged to Jane Minot in the summer of 1816. Jane was a friend of Catharine's, and Catharine enthusiastically supported the match.[42]

The courtship had taken place in Boston, and the couple planned to move to New York after the nuptials, but first they came to Stockbridge to introduce the bride to Elizabeth and the rest of Henry's siblings. Soon after the marriage took place, the new bridegroom rhapsodized to Catharine, "She is everything that I anticipated & I do not know that she could be more." Paraphrasing Elizabeth's wishes for him, he added, "Tell Mumbet that I got a nice wife."[43]

Charles became engaged in March 1819 and was married on September 30, 1819, to Elizabeth Buckminster Dwight, a maternal cousin. At about the same time as Charles's engagement, his sister Catharine was also coming to a decision about her future. Courted by both Edward Channing, a younger brother of the Reverend Channing, and William Cullen Bryant, a noted Berkshire poet and author, Catharine reluctantly became engaged to Bryant during the summer of 1818.[44] In some ways, it was a good match. They were friends, and they were both literary people who liked to winter in New York and summer in the Berkshires.

There was family pressure to get on with it. Catharine's sister-in-law, Susan Sedgwick, was worried about Catharine's biological clock, and Elizabeth, who loved motherhood and the care of young children, probably told her it was an experience not to be missed. Nevertheless, the terms of early nineteenth-century marriage appalled Catharine. An acute observer from childhood, she had loved her parents but not their marriage. The shock of seeing her respected brother-in-law, Eben Watson, turn into a domestic tyrant a few years past was also a stark reminder of how few rights a married woman possessed. Even Eliza's marriage, though happy, was based on patriarchal principles that Catharine found disturbing.[45] In the end, she concluded she liked Bryant but did not love him. In March, she broke off the engagement, telling Robert, "He has been so generous as to relinquish the promise I then gave him and all is now ended forever— He is very unhappy.... Susan mourns over my obduracy."[46]

Catharine had already published a number of poems and reviews. Soon, encouraged by Henry, she converted an essay about Calvinism into a novel.[47] In the summer of 1822, the same summer her last unmarried brother, Robert, wed Elizabeth Dana Ellery, the first of Catharine Sedgwick's six novels, *A New-England Tale*, was published.[48]

Literary historians describe Catharine Sedgwick as the most important American female novelist of the early nineteenth century and rate her work as the equal of James Fenimore Cooper, Washington Irving, and her beau, William Cullen Bryant.[49] Catharine's female protagonists were often poor orphans who succeeded through integrity and intelligence. It is believed that Elizabeth Freeman served as a model for these characters. A theme running throughout Catharine's novels was the right of women to make their own choices. Though Catharine's observation of the lives of many contemporaries informed this theme, Elizabeth's bold assertion of her right to be free from slavery was certainly an important influence.[50]

Though Elizabeth probably mourned Catharine's decision not to become a mother, she was doubtless very proud that the child she raised from infancy had become a famous author. Catharine certainly read the books to her when she returned

Catharine Maria Sedgwick was America's most famous female novelist in the early decades of the nineteenth century (*Catharine M. Sedgwick*, engraving by Asher Brown Durand after a portrait by Charles Cromwell Ingham, 1832, Metropolitan Museum of Art, Gift of Mrs. Frederic F. Durand, 1930, Accession Number 30.15.25).

to Stockbridge each summer, and Elizabeth's chest must have swelled with pride when Catharine read the passage from her third novel, *Hope Leslie*, in which the Native American protagonist, Magawisca, protects a friend by raising her own arm to receive the blow intended for him.[51]

And there was certainly no dearth of babies and small children for Elizabeth to love in the last decade of her life. Elizabeth's younger granddaughter, Mary Ann Humphrey, married Andrew Drean in about 1820. In addition to Lydia Maria's children, Lydia Maria Ann and Amos Josiah, in the early 1820s, Mary Ann gave birth to three more great-granddaughters, Sarah, Mary Elizabeth, and Wealthy Ann Drean. Elizabeth certainly helped deliver them all. In 1826, a fifth generation was added to Elizabeth's family when her great-granddaughter, Lydia Maria Ann Van Schaack, and her husband, George Cato Van Allen, presented Elizabeth with a great-great-grandson, Gilbert Van Allen.[52]

Nor was she done helping to bring Sedgwicks into the world. In 1820, at about seventy-six, she guided Charles's wife, Elizabeth, through a thirty-hour labor that resulted in a healthy baby girl. Catharine reported to Henry's wife, Jane, "Mumbet says 'She is the most resolute Gal she ever saw, she behaved charmingly & never thought of such a thing as giving out.'"[53] The same could be said of Elizabeth Freeman.

11

Sunset

With long life came the loss of more people that Elizabeth never expected to outlive. In March of 1820, Frances's son, Theodore Watson, the child she traveled to New York City to deliver, died at age seventeen. In 1824, Elizabeth's great-granddaughter, Sarah Drean, died at age nineteen months, probably the victim of a childhood disease that today would be prevented by immunization.[1]

By 1825, now about eighty-one, Elizabeth had retired from her nursing and midwifery practice and was beginning to feel some effects of old age. Catharine, recently returned from a gala celebration of the fiftieth anniversary of the Battle of Bunker Hill at the home of Daniel Webster in Boston, and Charles, who had sold the family home in Stockbridge to Theodore II and who was now living in nearby Lenox, were determined to repay some of the loving care Elizabeth had lavished on them.[2] In October of that year, Charles reported to his wife, who was away visiting relatives, that he, Catharine, and their little daughter Kitty had a house guest: "Mumbet is with us, and it is really delightful to be able to contribute so much to anyone's pleasure, especially those to whom we owe so much." The visit had improved her health and spirits: "She is happy as a child, and the Congress Water [Saratoga Springs mineral water] and good tea make her head as 'clear as a bell.' She will stay the week out, and we must have another visit from her if possible this fall."[3]

These visits were opportunities to reminisce about old times. They may also have been opportunities to talk about spiritual matters with some of the people Elizabeth cared about the most. Calvinism still held a firm grip on Berkshire County in the first half of the nineteenth century. In 1827, Elizabeth's friend and colleague, Agrippa Hull, would join the Stockbridge Congregational Church, accepting that congregation's conservative views on salvation.[4]

On the other side of the theological divide, Catharine and Charles Sedgwick were Unitarians. They believed in a loving God and rejected the idea that only the elect would enter heaven. The summer following Elizabeth's visit, Charles reported to his brother Robert an unpleasant visit to Charles's in-laws in Northampton, which summed up the disagreements between the two denominations. Describing his stay as "a perpetual camp meeting," Charles expressed his revulsion for the idea that God expected the elect to accept a nonelected loved one's consignment to eternal flames: "How is it possible that one ... who has a particle of benevolent feeling ... who might be persuaded ... to go with him through the journey of life, and part with him at the last just as he was embarking for the gulph of fire, shouting hosannas to the glory of the Being who, by plucking them as brands from the burning, had severed the chords of nature, and even put to scorn all the ties of blood and kindred!"[5]

Elizabeth would declare her own spiritual views on her deathbed. Catharine and Charles Sedgwick already knew what they were. Not only did she share Catharine and Charles's view of a loving God, but the racism of some members of the Stockbridge Congregational Church offended Elizabeth and made it unpleasant to contemplate worshipping with them. Though many members welcomed him, Agrippa Hull had to suffer the prejudice of others in order to join the congregation. The nineteenth-century Stockbridge historian, Electa Jones, reported that once after attending a service presided over by a visiting biracial preacher, a European American congregation member accosted Agrippa Hull and asked, "Well, how do you like nigger preaching?" Agrippa responded, "Sir, he was half black and half white; I liked my half, how did you like yours?"[6]

* * *

In 1827, Elizabeth faced the final two tragedies of her life, both visited on the children of Theodore and Pamela Sedgwick. Over the previous several years, Henry Sedgwick, Elizabeth's "pet-child," had suffered vision problems so severe that he had consented to have an operation on each of his eyes. Neither operation was successful, and by early 1827, he was close to blind. A lawyer and an editor, he was unable to pursue his professions or to support his family. To compound his financial difficulty, an investment that he had made in a coal operation failed.[7]

The effect of all these misfortunes was to drive him into deep depression.[8] When he and Jane were forced to give up their home in New York and move to Stockbridge that summer, Catharine reported to Robert, "He is not as weak and imbecile as he was before he left NY and sometime when he is with strangers he makes an effort to calm."[9] But Elizabeth knew his illness, and she saw with a sinking heart the same symptoms that had made Henry's mother an invalid at about the same age.

To compound the gloom, Eliza Sedgwick Pomeroy, the eldest Sedgwick child, died of a stroke that October at age fifty-two. She left behind her grieving husband, Thaddeus, and nine surviving children, the youngest of whom was twelve years old.[10]

Soon after Eliza's death, Henry seemed to improve, but it quickly became clear that his condition differed from that of his mother. Pamela's illness had manifested solely as depression. Henry's condition swung between depression and mania: "His mind is perpetually suggesting new & illimitable projects," Catharine told Frances.[11]

Even in the 1790s, the Sedgwicks had viewed Pamela's condition as a disease and had sought out the most humane treatment then available. Now, a generation later, they once again sought out cutting-edge treatment. In December 1828, Jane and his siblings persuaded Henry to become the patient of Dr. Rufus Wyman at McLean Hospital in Boston. Formerly known as the "Asylum for the Insane," it had been renamed in 1823. Unlike many of his contemporaries, Wyman did not believe in restraints, and when patients were well enough, they sometimes dined with his family.[12]

When Jane and Charles brought Henry to Boston that bitter December, they had real hope Wyman could help Henry. Unfortunately, that hope would fade away during the year as Henry failed to improve. We now know that bipolar disorder has a biological basis and responds well to lithium and other drugs. Without these medications, kind, intelligent Henry Sedgwick continued to suffer severe mood swings. Soon he was begging to come home.

As winter turned to spring and then summer, Elizabeth began to feel unwell herself. At first, she told no one. Now about eighty-five years old, she had enjoyed robust health throughout her life, and it was not her habit to complain about aches and pains. At the end of August, Catharine, at home in Stockbridge for the summer, was unaware that there was anything other than old age ailing Elizabeth. She wrote Robert saying she planned to return to New York sometime between October 20 and October 31.[13]

But a week later, Catharine had bad news for Robert: "Mumbet is very unwell—She has a singular local disease—We fear of a cancerous nature—She has made up her mind to the result with her characteristic magnamity."[14]

Catharine insisted she see a doctor and decided to delay her return to New York until mid–November. Mary Curtis Hopkins, Elizabeth's next-door neighbor, was also concerned. Mary, the wife of Mark and Electa Hopkins' son Archibald, was the mother of three sons, two of them with scientific backgrounds. Mark Jr. was a doctor then practicing in New York City who would later become president of Williams College. Albert had just been promoted from tutor to Professor of Mathematics and Natural Philosophy at Williams College.[15]

Mark Hopkins examined Elizabeth when he was visiting Stockbridge at the end of the summer but could offer no solution to what was then an incurable condition. A few weeks later, two doctors were visiting Albert at his mother's farmhouse for the purpose of performing some pharmacological experiments, which Albert described to Mark: "We brought in our crucibles and salts of iron, roots and plants—and having first initiated the painter, proceeded to action." Mary asked the two doctors, Clarke and Sergeant, if they could spare some time to visit Elizabeth. They agreed to do so.[16]

The doctors discovered that in addition to her internal condition, which was probably stomach or intestinal cancer, Elizabeth had a painful external sore on her abdomen.[17] The doctors could do nothing about the cancer, but Clarke applied an herbal remedy to the sore, which proved effective. Mark wrote to the third Hopkins brother, Harry, at the beginning of October, "If Clark[e] has brought that swelling of Mum Bet's to a head he has done well.... I have never seen a similar one."[18]

A few weeks later, Harry informed Mark, "Mumbet is alive but failing, the ulcer is entirely healed. What Clarke used was the Baptista tinctoriam applied to the Ulcer as I understand and taken internally."[19]

11. Sunset

At some point, not long after Clarke and Sergeant's visit, Elizabeth decided that nothing more could be done and that it was time to wrap up her affairs. Harry Hopkins told Mark, "I believe however that Clarke never visited her but twice. Granny [Betsey Humphrey] then dismissed him."[20]

Elizabeth now requested the Sedgwicks' assistance. It was time to make a will. One day in mid–October, Charles and Catharine rode down from Lenox accompanied by Charles's nine-year-old daughter, Kitty. Frances Sedgwick Watson, who was staying in Stockbridge with Henry's wife, Jane, after another failed attempt to reconcile with Eben Watson, also joined them at Elizabeth's farmhouse.[21]

Charles, a lawyer and clerk of the Berkshire County Court, wrote down Elizabeth's bequests. Charles was to act as trustee of her real property (her house and land) for the benefit of her daughter Betsey and Lydia Maria's minor children, Amos Josiah and Lydia Maria Ann Van Schaack. These were the family members who lived on Elizabeth's farm. Elizabeth divided her personal property among Betsey; Amos Josiah; Lydia Maria Ann; Elizabeth's granddaughter, Mary Ann Drean; and Mary Ann's surviving daughters, Mary Elizabeth and Wealthy Ann Drean. When the will was probated in January 1830, Elizabeth's estate was valued at about $400. It was the fruit of more than forty years of hard work and prudence.[22]

Among the personal items Elizabeth bequeathed to her daughter were a gown "recd. of my father" and a "short gown that was my mothers," items lovingly preserved over the decades as her only material link with the parents she had been separated from so many years before. The gold piece that Theodore Sedgwick had given her for saving the infant Charles's life in 1792 was bequeathed to Amos Josiah. Charles was named executor of the will. Catharine, Frances, and Kitty acted as witnesses when Elizabeth solemnly made her mark at the bottom of the document.[23]

It was probably at this time that the question of Elizabeth's burial was broached. The Sedgwicks requested the honor of laying her to rest in the Sedgwick family plot, where Pamela, Theodore, Eliza, and several Sedgwick grandchildren were already interred. Catharine, a confirmed spinster at age thirty-nine, may have told Elizabeth then that she wished to lie beside her when her own time came. Elizabeth gave

Catharine "a necklace of gold beads" as a keepsake. After Elizabeth's death, Catharine had it made into a bracelet, which she wore frequently. The bracelet was passed down to Kitty and Kitty's daughter and was eventually donated to the Massachusetts Historical Society.[24]

The settling of Elizabeth's affairs put her mind at rest. Her serenity as she faced eternity struck Catharine, who visited her daily: "I felt awed as if I had entered the presence of Washington. Even protracted suffering and mortal sickness, with old age, could not break down her spirit."[25]

Mary Hopkins, a God-fearing Congregationalist and sincerely fond of Elizabeth, was convinced that no one could enter paradise without being a member of her church. She insisted that her pastor, David Dudley Field, who had replaced Dr. West, pay Elizabeth a visit. Years later, Catharine recalled the meeting: "When Dr. F. said to her, with proud assurance of his spiritual office, 'Are you not afraid to meet God?' 'No sir,' she replied, 'I am not afeard. I have tried to do my duty, and I am not afeard!'"[26]

In mid–November, Catharine decided to leave for New York City. She never explained in either her autobiography or her journal why she did not remain in Stockbridge for Elizabeth's final days. Catharine did mention in a letter to Charles from New York shortly before Elizabeth died that Elizabeth was well taken care of by Betsey and Lydia Maria Ann.[27]

It may be that Catharine began to feel that her daily visits were impinging on Betsey's prerogative to oversee her mother's care or that she sensed uneasiness in Betsey about her level of involvement. Throughout her life, Catharine had felt something akin to sibling rivalry with Betsey.[28] Catharine loved Elizabeth like a daughter, but it was Betsey who actually was her daughter. Catharine mentioned several times in her writings that among Elizabeth's biological progeny, it was only her deceased granddaughter, Lydia Maria Van Schaack, who was a hard worker.[29] Catharine disliked the idea that even in Elizabeth's old age, the financial security of her family rested on Elizabeth's shoulders. Catharine failed to accept two important truths: Elizabeth loved being a nurse midwife. She didn't want to stop doing it. Also, Elizabeth derived great pleasure from providing for Betsey. Thanks to Elizabeth, Betsey was a farm housewife throughout her adulthood,

11. Sunset

just as middle-class white women were. Born a slave in the Ashley household and a domestic assistant to her mother in the Sedgwick household during her teen years, as an adult, Betsey never had to perform domestic service for others. That was a source of pride for Elizabeth and probably something Catharine didn't like to think about.

But now, knowing that it was she who would be buried beside Elizabeth and perhaps not wanting to inject any drama into Elizabeth's last days, Catharine decided to delay her departure no longer and let Betsey have these final days with her mother. Before they parted, Elizabeth comforted Catharine, saying of her imminent passing, "It is the last stroke and it is the best stroke."[30]

Despite having made the decision, it was still difficult for Catharine to execute it. While waiting for the stagecoach that would take them to New York, Charles, who was escorting Catharine, stopped by Elizabeth's home to check on her. Elizabeth was apparently having a bad day and told him they should stay because she was about to pass. When Charles told Catharine, they let the stagecoach leave without them. A day or two later, when Elizabeth was feeling better, Charles promised to visit her upon his return, and he and Catharine departed.[31]

Charles kept his promise to Elizabeth. He reported the visit to Catharine in New York: "When I saw Mumbet she was calm & perfectly self-possessed though she has at times been somewhat delirious—She enquired 'how they all did in New York' & twice particularly after you."[32] It was a slow decline that Elizabeth was handling bravely, but with the anticipation of release: "She is confined to her bed suffers a good deal of pain & is very desirous to get at the end of her trial & when I said to her that it was a comfort to think that the time which once seemed so long seems very short to look back upon she said 'O yes it was a great comfort.'" As Catharine already knew, Betsey and Lydia Maria Ann were taking good care of her: "Betty told me that Mother still takes great pleasure in Lydia & assured me most solemnly that Lydia did not neglect her."[33]

Catharine responded, "I shall grieve for it, but I shall be thankful to hear of her dismissal—Would not her pain be alleviated by giving her more of the black drop?" (laudanum).[34]

As Charles and Catharine grappled with Elizabeth's imminent

death, they were also struggling with decisions about Henry's care. After a year at McLean Hospital, he was still no better, and he was now demanding to come home. Jane traveled to Boston to see him. Dr. Wyman told her frankly that Henry was unlikely to recover and that she should abandon any idea of bringing him home. Jane was not willing to go home and simply forget about Henry. She told Catharine, "I have no hope of his recovery & I do not think Wyman has any—but surely we must make some effort to lessen his misery."[35]

Unfortunately, a wife in the early nineteenth century did not have legal authority to make the decision. She needed the approval of Henry's brothers. Jane also needed the financial help of Catharine and the Sedgwick brothers to execute her plan to bring Henry home.[36]

Catharine completely agreed that her brother should be removed from Wyman's care, but "it does not seem to me possible that Harry could be managed out of a public institution with as little suffering as in it—unless we had unlimited means." She was willing to help pay for a sea voyage, and if that was ineffective, for care by Dr. Eli Todd in Hartford.[37]

The stress created by Elizabeth's impending death and the need to make a decision about Henry was intense. Catharine told Charles, "I find it absolutely necessary to make exertion to avoid continual gloom."[38] Charles told Catharine he was having chest pains. He was in anguish over the correct course to take with respect to Henry and with respect to Elizabeth: "I sometimes feel that thro ignorance of her condition & her wants we are prevented from offering all the alleviation that her case admits of—offering some service that she in similar circumstances wd have deprived herself of rest & sleep every comfort to bestow on us."[39]

Jane did not dare tell Henry that Elizabeth was near death, but even in the midst of his own suffering, his thoughts were on making her happy. Jane reported to Catharine: "He was more wild than in the first interview but I was able to part from him very comfortably after promising to buy for him innumerable presents for the children & a velvet gown for Mumbet."[40]

As the year 1829 ebbed toward its close, so did Elizabeth's life. Charles saw her for the last time on the afternoon of Sunday, December 26. He told Catharine, "She spoke with difficulty then & I doubt

11. Sunset

whether she knew me tho she replied that she did when I asked her the question."[41]

Elizabeth died at 8 a.m. on Tuesday. Betsey immediately sent word to Charles. There may have been some disagreement between Charles and Theodore II in the preceding days over whether to consent to Jane's plan to remove Henry from Dr. Wyman's care, because Charles chose to send a letter to Thaddeus Pomeroy, "the Doctor," rather than his brother, informing him of Elizabeth's death. Charles requested that Thaddeus and Theodore II begin making the funeral arrangements. Apparently unwilling to ask his older brother for any favor at that moment, he noted in his letter to Thaddeus that if he had still owned the family home, he would have held the funeral there, but since he did not, the funeral could be held at the church or the schoolhouse.

When Susan Sedgwick got wind of this idea, she promptly dismissed it. The woman who had helped Susan through dangerous childbirths and who had lovingly tended to her infants and so many other Sedgwick babies would, of course, have her funeral rites at her longtime home. Susan probably also told her husband that it was time for his tiff with Charles to end. Charles reported gratefully to Catharine: "He [Thaddeus] sent my letter to Sister Susan & she instantly & with her accustomed kindness threw open her house that one which of all others should be the scene of the last poor honors that we could pay to our good benefactor."[42]

The funeral was held at 3 p.m. on the last day of the year. Charles told Catharine, "I wish dear Sister that you could have stood by me, & enjoyed with me, in looking upon her great & noble face, tranquil & beautiful ... the memory of those great qualities and beneficent deeds which place her in our hearts by the side of our parents."[43]

There was no Unitarian minister in Berkshire County, and there was no question in 1829 of holding a memorial service without the assistance of a clergyman. The only option was David Dudley Field. It was probably Theodore II or Susan who asked him to perform the service.

Charles was uneasy. He wanted this done right, and he wasn't sure Field could balance Elizabeth's refusal to join his church with her goodness and her many services to the community: "I never longed more to have an occasion rightly used & it was so much better done than I expected that I felt absolutely grateful."⁴⁴ After an introductory prayer, "he spoke of her temperance—industry—prudence—faithfulness—her strong judgment & common sense & her almost unrivalled excellence & renown as a nurse with something like enthusiasm."⁴⁵ Field did not stint his praise during this part of his oration. Elizabeth's obituary, which appeared in the *Berkshire Journal* on January 21, 1830, quoted him as saying, "Hundreds of persons at this moment attribute the preservation of their faculties—the health of their bodies and the perfection of their limbs, under God, to the faithful care and judicious treatment of this excellent woman."⁴⁶ Field's own wife, Submit Dickinson Field, may have been one of these persons. She gave birth to three of her nine children in Stockbridge.⁴⁷

There was no possibility in the second quarter of the nineteenth century of a Congregational minister limiting his remarks to such thoughts: Charles knew what was coming next: "When he came to speak professionally as he must do, of the state of her soul, he expressed doubts upon the subject it affected me for a moment as we are sometimes affected by a frightful dream."⁴⁸

But Field's words could not long shake Charles's confidence in God's love or in the extraordinary goodness of his beloved Mumbet: "Her brow & forehead were as smooth as an infants it seemed to me a fit emblem of the repose which should come at the close of such a life & a beautiful presage of the joyful tranquility with which such a spirit should return to God who gave it, having fulfilled to the utmost measure allowed to mortals the beneficent commission with which it was sent upon the earth."⁴⁹

And indeed, the group assembled in Theodore II and Susan's parlor that winter afternoon was an extraordinary testament to the fulfillment of Elizabeth's beneficent commission: Her daughter Betsey, who grew up a free woman because of her mother's determination; Elizabeth's great-grandchildren, two of whom she raised after their mother's tragic death; Charles Sedgwick, so premature as a baby, his own father had no hope for his survival; Jane Sedgwick and her children, whose husband and father, Henry, was so sickly as a toddler that the family believed he would not have survived childhood without Elizabeth's care; and Susan Sedgwick, who twice needed Elizabeth's

11. Sunset

nursing to survive the rigors of difficult childbirth. Crowded into the room, too, were people whose names we do not know who were grateful to Elizabeth for their lives or the lives of loved ones.

And of course, there were those who could not be there. Catharine Sedgwick, for whom Elizabeth was the person to whom during her childhood she "clung ... with instinctive love and faith," and who, during Catharine's adulthood, was the inspiration for several of Catharine's literary heroines as well as a model for Catharine's own independent single life.[50] Pamela Sedgwick, who relied on Elizabeth for almost two decades as the only caregiver who knew how to soothe her during the worst of her mental and physical agonies, and Theodore Sedgwick, who could not have performed his considerable services to the nation throughout the 1790s without "that noble woman the main pillar of our household," who gave his needy children stability and love and his suffering wife emotional succor and physical care during his long absences from home.[51]

There were also the thousands of former slaves across the Commonwealth of Massachusetts who gained their freedom years earlier than they might have, because a few determined people, such as Elizabeth Freeman and Quok Walker, dared to believe that the right to liberty and equality proclaimed in the Massachusetts Constitution applied to them too.

When the funeral service was over, her loved ones carried Elizabeth down Plain Street to the cemetery. The emotion of the day and Susan's insistence had broken the ice between Charles and Theodore II: "I spoke to Theo abt the kind of monument & he agrees with me that a plain simple stone, similar to that of Sister Eliza & Egbert wd be best, but of this you shall decide," Charles told Catharine.[52]

Charles did not think he was a good writer, though his letters are often eloquent. He asked Susan to write the obituary that appeared in the *Berkshire Journal*, and he wanted Catharine to write the epitaph that would appear on Elizabeth's gravestone.[53] But Catharine was in Philadelphia, and the engraver needed the words. Catharine later said that Charles wrote the epitaph, but the draft of the epitaph in the archives of the Massachusetts Historical Society bears the initials "JS."[54] Apparently it was Jane Sedgwick, having heard countless tales of Elizabeth's deeds from Jane's husband, Henry, and the other

Sedgwicks, who composed the words on Elizabeth's gravestone, the first erected for an African American in the Stockbridge Cemetery:[55]

> ELIZABETH FREEMAN
> known by the name of MUMBET
> died Dec. 28th 1829.
> Her supposed age was 85 Years.
> She was born a slave and
> remained a slave for nearly thirty years.
> She could neither read nor write, yet in
> her own sphere she had no superior nor equal.
> She neither wasted time nor property.
> She never violated a trust, nor
> failed to perform a duty.
> In every situation of domestic trial, she was
> the most efficient helper and the tenderest friend.
> Good mother, farewell.

Elizabeth Freeman is buried beside Catharine Sedgwick and other Sedgwick family members in the "Sedgwick Pie" in Stockbridge Cemetery (graves of Elizabeth Freeman [*left*] and Catharine Maria Sedgwick, Stockbridge Cemetery, photograph by the author).

Epilogue

THE SEDGWICKS AND ELIZABETH's biological family maintained ties for decades. Shortly after her granddaughter Lydia Maria Ann's death in 1837, Betsey decided to sell the farm. Charles Sedgwick handled the sale and arranged a mortgage for the buyer.[1] Betsey moved to a small home in Lenox not far from the house Charles and his wife shared with Catharine Sedgwick. Like her mother, Betsey was long lived, dying in Lenox on April 21, 1858, at age eighty-three.[2]

Elizabeth's great-granddaughter, Mary Elizabeth Drean, and her great-great-granddaughter, Mary Jane Van Allen, worked as domestics in Charles's home during the 1830s.[3]

When Elizabeth's great-grandson, Amos Josiah Van Schaack, died in 1850 without children, Charles paid for his burial.[4]

The Sedgwicks were also determined to preserve Elizabeth's memory and, as Elizabeth would have wished, to use the example of her life as an argument against slavery.

Jane's wishes prevailed, and after a few months under the care of Dr. Eli Todd in Hartford, Connecticut, during the early part of 1830, Henry Sedgwick was brought home to Stockbridge.[5] For almost a year, Henry's condition improved. "Yet in the whole I have much to be thankful for in Harry's diminished instability & his improvement in general rationality," Jane reported to Catharine.[6]

Though nearly blind, Henry used the time to work. The project nearest to his heart during this period was a lecture entitled *The Practicability of the Abolition of Slavery*, which he prepared for presentation at the Lyceum in Stockbridge. Refuting the claims of African inferiority, Henry cited history and geography as causes of the slave trade, but the centerpiece of his argument was the life of Elizabeth Freeman: "Such has been my acquaintance with individuals of this

Epilogue

race, that I regard the pretense of original and natural superiority of whites, very much as I regard the tales of ancient fables.... But for the care of one of this calumniated race, I should not now, probably be living to give testimony."[7]

As Henry was too blind to give the lecture himself, it was read by Eliza's oldest son, Theodore Pomeroy, the baby Elizabeth and Pamela had traveled to Albany to help deliver in 1798. Given in 1831, the lecture outlined some of the major events of Elizabeth's life. Theodore II had the lecture published shortly after Henry's death. It remains one of the major sources for information about Elizabeth's life. At the time it was delivered, Jane reported to Catharine, "I presume you heard of his lecture upon the abolition of slavery written for the Lyceum & very well read by T. Pomeroy. It was very well recd by the audience & proved a source of great pleasure to Harry."[8] It would be Henry's last triumph. That fall, Henry fell into a coma and died in December at age forty-six.[9]

Two decades later, as the United States edged ever closer to war over the question of slavery, Catharine Sedgwick wrote the essay "Slavery in New England." Catharine wrote in a note to the essay, "It was said, perhaps truly, by that distinguished man, Charles Follen, that if you could establish the equality of the slave with the master in a single instance, you had answered the argument for slavery furnished by the inferiority of the African race."[10] Like her brother Henry, Catharine used vignettes from Elizabeth's life to refute the claims of racial inferiority put forth by proslavery interests. In addition to correcting inaccuracies about Elizabeth's life that had appeared in a secondhand account written by Harriet Martineau and published in London in 1838, Catharine's essay provided additional information about Elizabeth's life not mentioned in Henry's 1831 lecture, including Elizabeth's championing of the abused teen, Tamor Graham, while she herself was still a slave.[11]

Charles Sedgwick died in 1856, predeceasing Betsey Humphrey as well as his son, William Dwight Sedgwick, who would fall at the battle of Antietam in 1862, fighting for the Union cause.[12] Catharine Sedgwick lived to know the Civil War's outcome. She died in July 1867 at seventy-seven. Though she continued to struggle with the idea that Elizabeth's descendants were the victims of ongoing racism, one of her last letters, written a few months before her death to her nephew,

Henry Sedgwick, Jr., reminded him of the family's debt to Mumbet for preserving his father's life while a toddler and asked him to find Elizabeth's great-great-granddaughter, Mary Jane Van Allen Carter, a job as a cook.[13] As Catharine wished, upon her death, she was laid beside Elizabeth in the family plot at the Stockbridge cemetery.

Of course, none of these efforts by the Sedgwicks changed the harsh racial and class inequities to which Elizabeth's biological descendants were subject. In 1835, a few years after Elizabeth's death, Jonah Humphrey, Betsey's erstwhile husband, reappeared briefly in Stockbridge. Now in his early sixties, Jonah was done struggling to make his way in a country dominated by European Americans. The Pennsylvania and New York Colonization Societies were offering passage to Liberia, and Jonah wanted to go. He had two young girls with him—Rebecca, age nine, and Mary, age six—probably children from a subsequent relationship, whose mother was now dead.[14] He needed a caregiver for the children, and he wanted his adult daughter, Mary Ann Drean, to come with him.

Mary Ann's marriage to Andrew Drean had ended. It must have broken her mother Betsey's heart, but Mary Ann decided to accompany her father.[15] She left her own daughters, Mary Elizabeth and Wealthy Ann, then about twelve and eleven years old, with Betsey. Either they didn't want to go to Liberia, or their father, Andrew Drean, refused permission.

Jonah, Mary Ann, Rebecca, and Mary arrived at the Bassa Cove colony on the St. John River sometime between April and August 1835. Like many others, Jonah died shortly thereafter from the rigors of life in the new colony.[16] According to Stockbridge historian Electa Jones, Mary Ann sent word back to Stockbridge a few years later that she had "joined the colony, and made herself useful, and expressed her satisfaction with its advantages."[17] Mary Ann was about thirty-one when she arrived at Bassa Cove. If she remarried, it is possible that there are descendants of Elizabeth Freeman living in Liberia today.

Mary Ann's daughters, Mary Elizabeth and Wealthy Ann Drean, grew up in Lenox. Of all Elizabeth's descendants, it may be Wealthy Ann who lived the life closest to what Elizabeth dreamed for herself that long-ago day when her baby's father marched off for service in the American Revolution. Wealthy Ann's husband, James Prime, survived his Civil War service in the Connecticut 29th. The parents of eight children, five of whom survived to adulthood, Wealthy Ann and James lived in West Norfolk, Connecticut, after the war. James worked as a laborer and gardener. Wealthy Ann worked as a seamstress and domestic. Despite the many challenges they faced as people of color in late nineteenth-century America, they managed to build a life of modest prosperity. When Wealthy Ann died at age seventy in 1892, she left behind an estate valued at $549.75. Like Elizabeth, Wealthy Ann's grave was covered with a stone monument.[18]

Elizabeth Freeman did not get to have a long married life with many children as she once had dreamed and Wealthy Ann achieved. Instead, having already endured a quarter century subject to the heartless rule of a cruel mistress without losing her spirit or her humanity, she found herself, at the end of the Revolution, an enslaved widow and the mother of an enslaved child, with no hope of that reality ever changing. In a world that told her to give up and submit to her fate, she refused to do so.

In daring to walk into Theodore Sedgwick's law office and insist that she was no "dumb critter," so the rights of liberty and equality surely applied to her, too, she set herself on a path that brought freedom to her and her daughter, as well as thousands of other slaves in Massachusetts. That path would also empower her to vastly improve the lives of her emancipator's family and many other people she cared for in her long career as a caregiver and nurse midwife. In the alchemy of endurance and assertion that was Elizabeth Freeman's life, she proved the falsity of the racial and gender barriers that were intended to hold her back and became a glorious example of courage, self-respect, compassion, and the beauty of the human spirit at its best.

Chapter Notes

Abbreviations Used

C. Sedgwick, *LCS*: Charles Sedgwick, *Letters from Charles Sedgwick to His Family and Friends* (Boston: privately printed, 1870; repr., Whitefish, MT: Kessinger Legacy).

C.M. Sedgwick, *LLCMS*: Catharine Maria Sedgwick, *Life and Letters of Catharine M. Sedgwick*, ed. Mary E. Dewey (New York: Harper & Brothers, 1871).

C.M. Sedgwick, *PHS*: Catharine Maria Sedgwick, *The Power of Her Sympathy: The Autobiography and Journal of Catharine Maria Sedgwick*, ed. Mary Kelley (Boston: Massachusetts Historical Society, 1993).

C.M. Sedgwick, *SNE*: Catharine Maria Sedgwick, "Slavery in New England," *Bentley's Miscellany* 34 (1853): 417–24, courtesy of Stockbridge Public Library, Museum & Archives.

CMSP I: Catharine Maria Sedgwick papers I, microfilm edition, Massachusetts Historical Society, Boston.

CMSP III: Catharine Maria Sedgwick papers III, microfilm edition, Massachusetts Historical Society, Boston.

ELMH: Mark Hopkins et al., *Early Letters of Mark Hopkins and Others from His Brothers and Their Mother* (New York: John Day, 1929).

SFP: Sedgwick Family Papers, Massachusetts Historical Society, Boston.

Zilversmit, *QWM*: Arthur Zilversmit, "Quok Walker, Mumbet, and the Abolition of Slavery in Massachusetts," *William and Mary Quarterly* 25, no. 4, 3rd series (Oct. 1968): 614–24.

Zilversmit, *TFE*: Arthur Zilversmit, *The First Emancipation: The Abolition of Slavery in the North* (Chicago: University of Chicago Press, 1967).

Introduction

1. Edgar J. McManus, *Black Bondage in the North* (Syracuse: Syracuse University Press, 1973), 209, 210, 177.

Chapter 1

1. See gravestone of Elizabeth Freeman, Sedgwick Pie, Stockbridge, Massachusetts; Henry Dwight Sedgwick, *The Practicability of the Abolition of Slavery: A Lecture, Delivered at the Lyceum in Stockbridge, Massachusetts, February, 1831* (New York: J. Seymour, 1831), 14. This lecture is sometimes attributed to Theodore Sedgwick II, who facilitated its publication after his brother's death.

2. H.D. Sedgwick, *Abolition of Slavery*, 16. See also C.M. Sedgwick, SNE, 421–22. The landmark case which bears Elizabeth Freeman's pre-emancipation name spells it "Bett." The Sedgwicks sometimes spelled it "Bett" in their correspondence, but after the children coined the nickname "Mumbet," the adult Sedgwicks usually referred to her as "Bet."

3. Mary Kelley, introduction to C.M. Sedgwick, *PHS*, 4. The miniature portrait of Elizabeth Freeman painted by Susan Ridley Sedgwick is now in the holdings of the Massachusetts Historical Society, Boston, Massachusetts.

4. H.D. Sedgwick, *Abolition of Slavery*, 14.

5. For details of Pieter Hogeboom's

Notes—Chapter 1

life and the rules of the patroon system of land ownership, see Emilie Piper and David Levinson, *One Minute a Free Woman: Elizabeth Freeman and the Struggle for Freedom* (Salisbury, CT: Upper Housatonic Valley National Heritage Area, 2010), 34–35.

6. McManus, *Black Bondage*, 3.
7. *Ibid.*, 115, and appendix, 209.
8. C.M. Sedgwick, SNE, 418.
9. Piper and Levinson, *Free Woman*, 31.
10. McManus, *Black Bondage*, 20.
11. For a description of male duties, see Piper and Levinson, *Free Woman*, 33. For a detailed description of female duties, see Alice Morse Earle, *Home Life in Colonial Days* (New York: Macmillan, 1898), chapters 2–4 and 7–10.
12. Piper and Levinson, *Free Woman*, 37.
13. Will of Elizabeth Freeman, October 18, 1829, copy, courtesy of Stockbridge Public Library, Museum & Archives.
14. Piper and Levinson, *Free Woman*, 38–39.
15. Lillian Preiss, *Sheffield: Frontier Town* (North Adams, MA: Sheffield Bicentennial Committee, 1976), 11, 39.
16. *Ibid.*, 5–8, 12, 18, note 5.
17. *Ibid.*, 12.
18. Qtd. in *ibid.*, 21.
19. Piper and Levinson, *Free Woman*, 33, 35–37.
20. Arthur C. Chase and Gerard Chapman, comp., *The Ashleys: A Pioneer Berkshire Family* (Beverly, MA: Trustees of Reservations, 1982), 3.
21. Names and birthdates of the Ashley children: *Ibid.*
22. Piper and Levinson, *Free Woman*, 58.
23. Will of Pieter Hogeboom, *New York State Library History Bulletin II Early Records of the City and County of Albany and colony of Rensselaerswyck*, vol. 4 *(Mortgages 1, 1658–1660 and Wills 1–2, 1681–1765)*, translated by Jonathon Pearson, revised and edited by A.J.F. Van Laer (Albany: University of the State of New York, 1919), 182–85.
24. Some students of Freeman's life have suggested that the female slave who Elizabeth protected from Hannah Ashley's abuse in the famous shovel incident was her daughter Betsey Humphrey and that the sister "Lizzie" may not have existed (see Piper and Levinson, *Free Woman*, 63). Both Henry and Catharine Sedgwick are explicit in their description of the event, saying that it was her sister who Elizabeth defended in the attack, which left her with a permanent scar on her arm. Betsey Humphrey grew up in the Sedgwick household, and the Sedgwick siblings maintained a relationship with her throughout their lives. Betsey was a real person to them. Because they heard the story multiple times from Elizabeth, it is extremely unlikely that they would substitute in the retelling of the incident a sister who did not exist for the very real daughter with whom they had grown up.

25. C.M. Sedgwick, SNE, 418.
26. See Chase and Chapman, *Pioneer Berkshire Family*, 9; Earle, *Home Life*, 344.
27. Chase and Chapman, *Pioneer Berkshire Family*, 7, 9, 31.
28. For colony-by-colony slave population statistics and the effect of different land ownership systems, see Zilversmit, *TFE*, 4–5.
29. Chase and Chapman, *Pioneer Berkshire Family*, 3, 5.
30. Zilversmit, *TFE*, 19.
31. Piper and Levinson, *Free Woman*, 33; Earle, *Home Life*, 168.
32. Earle, *Home Life*, 56; Piper and Levinson, *Free Woman*, 33.
33. Earle, *Home Life*, 255.
34. *Ibid.*, 35, 146–47, 152–53.
35. *Ibid.*, 149–50.
36. *Ibid.*, 166, 212–13.
37. Chase and Chapman, *Pioneer Berkshire Family*, 3, 10.
38. C.M. Sedgwick, SNE, 418.
39. Chase and Chapman, *Pioneer Berkshire Family*, 10.
40. Earle, *Home Life*, 148.
41. Qtd. in Preiss, *Sheffield: Frontier Town*, 22.
42. *Ibid.*
43. Earle, *Home Life*, 371.
44. *Ibid.*, 374–76.
45. Sarah Cabot Sedgwick and Christina Sedgwick Marquand, *Stockbridge,*

1739–1974 (Stockbridge, MA: Berkshire Traveler Press, 1974), 22, note.
46. Qtd. in *ibid.*, 30.
47. For John Sergeant's language skills, see Electa F. Jones, *Stockbridge, Past and Present, or, Records of an Old Mission Station* (Springfield, MA: Samuel Bowles, 1854), 62. For John Sergeant's death and the Stockbridge Indians' love for him, see Sedgwick and Marquand, *Stockbridge, 1739–1974*, 47–49.
48. Sedgwick and Marquand, *Stockbridge, 1739–1974*, 54–55.
49. *Ibid.*, 54, 60, 69.
50. *Ibid.*, 73–74.
51. *Ibid.*, 105.
52. Chase and Chapman, *Pioneer Berkshire Family*, 12–13.
53. Richard E. Welch, Jr., *Theodore Sedgwick, Federalist: A Political Portrait* (Middleton, CT: Wesleyan University Press, 1965), 8–9.

Chapter 2

1. Chase and Chapman, *Pioneer Berkshire Family*, 12.
2. Qtd. in *ibid.*, 13. Hannah Jr.'s death nineteen days after her marriage at age twenty: Piper and Levinson, *Free Woman*, 42.
3. C.M. Sedgwick, SNE, 418.
4. *Ibid.*
5. *Ibid.*
6. Henry Sedgwick's shorter version of the story, though agreeing with his sister's in most details—that Mrs. Ashley attempted to strike Elizabeth's sister with a hot oven shovel and that Elizabeth took the blow, causing a lifelong scar—differs in that he says Elizabeth immediately left the Ashley home to seek her freedom (see H.D. Sedgwick, *Abolition of Slavery*, 15). As Catharine Sedgwick's longer version of the incident makes clear, Elizabeth continued as a slave in the Ashley home for a substantial period. Henry and Catharine apparently heard the story from Elizabeth at different times, and when telling Henry, Elizabeth apparently only told him why she had the scar, leaving him to infer many years later that it had been the cause of her freedom suit; but when talking to Catharine, she disclosed the aftermath of the incident. By the time Elizabeth instituted her lawsuit against John Ashley, her sister Lizzie was apparently dead, since she was not a party to the suit, and it is highly unlikely Elizabeth would have left her behind.
7. C.M. Sedgwick, SNE, 419.
8. *Ibid.*
9. *Ibid.*
10. *Ibid.*
11. *Ibid.*
12. *Ibid.*, 419–20.
13. *Ibid.*, 420.
14. Qtd. in *ibid.*, 420–21.
15. *Ibid.*, 419.
16. Qtd. in *ibid.*, 421.
17. McManus, *Black Bondage*, 45–49.
18. Piper and Levinson, *Free Woman*, 47.
19. Franklin Bowditch Dexter, *Biographical Sketches of the Graduates of Yale College: With Annals of the College History*, vol. 3, *1763–1778* (New York: Henry Holt, 1903), 93.
20. *Ibid.*
21. C.M. Sedgwick, PHS, 53.
22. Dexter, *Biographical Sketches*, 147.
23. *Ibid.* See also C.M. Sedgwick, PHS, 49.
24. Welch, *Theodore Sedgwick, Federalist*, 10.
25. *Ibid.*, 10–11.
26. C.M. Sedgwick, PHS, 48–49.
27. Pamela Dwight to Abigail Dwight, undated, SFP, Box 11, Folder 1.
28. Pamela Dwight to Abigail Dwight, undated, SFP, Box 11, Folder 1. While it is possible this letter refers to Theodore Sedgwick and was written to her mother while they lived together in the same house in Stockbridge as a means of sorting out her thoughts, it is more likely that it was written during her time in Boston when Theodore was married to Eliza Mason and that the subject of the letter was a Boston suitor.
29. Abigail made a business trip to Boston in 1769, during which she delighted in purchasing finery for her daughter back in Stockbridge: Abigail Dwight to Pamela Dwight, June 12, 1769, SFP, Box 11, Folder 1.

Notes—Chapter 3

30. Welch, *Theodore Sedgwick, Federalist*, 11; Piper and Levinson, *Free Woman*, 65; Dexter, *Biographical Sketches*, 148.
31. C.M. Sedgwick, *PHS*, 56; Welch, *Theodore Sedgwick, Federalist*, 11; Dexter, *Biographical Sketches*, 148.
32. Qtd. in C.M. Sedgwick, *PHS*, 56.
33. *Ibid,*. 56–57.
34. *Ibid*.
35. Dexter, *Biographical Sketches*, 93.
36. Chase and Chapman, *Pioneer Berkshire Family*, 13. See also Preiss, *Sheffield: Frontier Town*, 37.
37. Qtd. in Preiss, *Sheffield: Frontier Town*, 37.
38. Chase and Chapman, *Pioneer Berkshire Family*, 19
39. *Sheffield Declaration*, January 12, 1773, reprinted in Preiss, *Sheffield: Frontier Town*, appendix, 172.
40. Joseph A. Conforti, *Samuel Hopkins and The New Divinity Movement* (Grand Rapids: Christian University Press, 1981) 43, 75.
41. *Ibid.*, 79–82.
42. Abigail Dwight to Pamela Dwight, June 11, 1770, SFP, Box 11, Folder 1.
43. Conforti, *Samuel Hopkins*, 128.
44. Pamela Dwight to Theodore Sedgwick, June 1, 1773, SFP, Box 1, Folder 1.
45. "Sedgwick Genealogy North America," Sedgwick.org, accessed March 8, 2018, www.sedgwick.org/na/families/robert1613/B/4/B4-sedgwick-theodore.html.
46. Jones, *Stockbridge, Past and Present*, 142.
47. Pamela insisted that the child be named Eliza Mason Sedgwick: C.M. Sedgwick, *PHS*, 58. For one of many letters in which Theodore refers to Pamela as the "best of women," see Theodore Sedgwick to Pamela Sedgwick, June 14, 1786, SFP, Box 1, Folder 2.
48. Lorenzo J. Greene, *The Negro in Colonial New England: 1620–1776* (New York: Columbia University Press, 1942), 82, 337.
49. *Ibid.*, 245–47.
50. *Ibid.*, 194, 249–51, 254.
51. C.M. Sedgwick, SNE, 418.
52. Greene, *Colonial New England*, 193.
53. H.D. Sedgwick, *Abolition of Slavery*, 16.

Chapter 3

1. For a discussion of the idea that Brom is the father of Elizabeth Freeman's daughter, see Piper and Levinson, *Free Woman*, 68–69.
2. Bernard A. Drew, *If They Close the Door on You, Go in the Window* (Great Barrington, MA: Attic Revivals Press, 2004), 43–44.
3. Case No. 1, *Brom and Bett v. J. Ashley, Esq.*, Book 4A, 55, copy, Inferior Court of Common Pleas, Berkshire County, Great Barrington, MA, 1781, courtesy of Stockbridge Public Library, Museum & Archives.
4. Greene, *Colonial New England*, 138.
5. For a rare case during the colonial period of a female slave suing for her freedom, see *Jenny Slew of Ipswich v. John Whipple also of Ipswich, 1766*, described in George H. Moore, *Notes on the History of Slavery in Massachusetts* (New York: D. Appleton, 1866; repr., Bedford, MA: Applewood Books, 2008), 113.
6. Drew, *Close the Door*, 34.
7. Greene, *Colonial New England*, 192, note 10.
8. Benjamin Quarles, *The Negro in the American Revolution* (Chapel Hill: University of North Carolina Press, 1961), 9, 78. See also Greene, *Colonial New England*, 190.
9. Drew, *Close the Door*, 11.
10. Quarles, *American Revolution*, 15.
11. *Ibid.*, 16.
12. Qtd. in *ibid.*, 72.
13. *Ibid.*, 53–54.
14. Jones, *Stockbridge, Past and Present*, 240.
15. Quarles, *American Revolution*, 58–59.
16. *Ibid.*, 9–10.
17. Welch, *Theodore Sedgwick, Federalist*, 14.
18. *Ibid.*; Preiss, *Sheffield: Frontier Town*, 40.
19. Preiss, *Sheffield: Frontier Town*, 44.
20. Jones, *Stockbridge, Past and Present*, 170.

21. *Ibid.*, 171.
22. Qtd. in Quarles, *American Revolution*, 12.
23. Jones, *Stockbridge, Past and Present*, 170, 172.
24. Preiss, *Sheffield: Frontier Town*, 41.
25. Welch, *Theodore Sedgwick, Federalist*, 15.
26. Theodore Sedgwick to Pamela Sedgwick, May 25, 1776, SFP, Box 1, Folder 1.
27. Mark Hopkins is described as having died of camp fever at White Plains by David Dudley Field and Chester Dewey, *History of Berkshire County, Massachusetts*, vol. 1 (Pittsfield: SW Bush, 1829; repr., New York: Beers, 1885). Catharine Sedgwick says that he was injured in battle at White Plains and that her father had him carried from the field: C.M. Sedgwick, *PHS*, 55.
28. Jones, *Stockbridge, Past and Present*, 240; Drew, *Close the Door*, 16.
29. Welch, *Theodore Sedgwick, Federalist*, 24.
30. Timothy Kenslea, *The Sedgwicks in Love* (Boston: Northeastern University Press, 2006), 15.
31. Henry Dwight to Theodore Sedgwick, February 18, 1779, SFP, Box 3, Folder 1. Catharine Sedgwick specifically cites Pamela's postpartum depression after the birth of Frances as the first episode of Pamela's bouts with mental illness. See Catharine Sedgwick's introduction to C. Sedgwick, *LCS*, 13. For the duration of the event, see Henry Dwight to Theodore Sedgwick, April 25, 1779, SFP, Box 3, Folder 1.
32. *Ibid.*
33. *Ibid.*
34. Zilversmit, *TFE*, 103.
35. Qtd. in *ibid.*, 98.
36. *Ibid.*
37. *Ibid.*, 100–01.
38. *Ibid.*, 101.
39. Petition to General Thomas Gage, dated June 1774 in "Letters and Documents Relating to Slavery in Massachusetts," *Collections of the Massachusetts Historical Society*, 5th series, vol. 3 (1877): 434–45.
40. Zilversmit, *TFE*, 102.
41. *Ibid.*, 94, 96.
42. Drew, *Close the Door*, 30. See also Piper and Levinson, *Free Woman*, 65–66.
43. Zilversmit, *TFE*, 112.
44. Welch, *Theodore Sedgwick, Federalist*, 27.
45. 1st Article of the Massachusetts Constitution of 1780, qtd. in William O'Brien, "Did the Jennison Case Outlaw Slavery in Massachusetts?" *William and Mary Quarterly*, 17, no. 2 (April 1960): 219.
46. Electa Jones, in her history of Stockbridge written in the early 1850s, describes a public meeting in Stockbridge "at the close of the Revolutionary War" in which "the Act which abolished slavery in the Commonwealth" was discussed. Since there was no such legislation, it is probably the meaning of Article I of the 1780 Massachusetts Constitution, which was discussed at a meeting during the period when the proposed Constitution was submitted to the voters for approval. According to Jones, when the sense of the meeting proved to be in favor of abolition, Theodore Sedgwick audibly quoted scripture in affirmation: "Lord now lettest thou thy servant depart in peace, for mine eyes have seen thy salvation." Jones, *Stockbridge, Past and Present*, 239.
47. C.M. Sedgwick, *LLCMS*, 73, note.
48. McManus, *Black Bondage*, 111–12.
49. Piper and Levinson, *Free Woman*, 63, 69.
50. C.M. Sedgwick, SNE, 421.
51. Zilversmit, QWM, 618.
52. Welch, *Theodore Sedgwick, Federalist*, 20.
53. Drew, *Close the Door*, 34.
54. Piper and Levinson, *Free Woman*, 47.
55. C.M. Sedgwick, SNE, 421.
56. O'Brien, "Jennison Case," 225.
57. Qtd. in *ibid.*, 226.
58. McManus, *Black Bondage*, 161. For the view that the drafters of the 1780 Constitution had intended to outlaw slavery, see Jeremy Belknap, "Queries Respecting the Slavery and Emancipation of Negroes in Massachusetts, Proposed by the Hon. Judge Tucker of Virginia, and Answered by the Rev. Dr. Belknap," 1795, *Collections of the Massachusetts*

Notes—Chapter 4

Historical Society, 1st series, vol. 4, 203. For the view that there was no such intent, see Zilversmit, *TFE*, 112.
59. Zilversmit, *TFE*, 47.
60. Chase and Chapman, *Pioneer Berkshire Family*, 26.
61. Zilversmit, QWM, 619–20.
62. *Ibid.*, 618.
63. Qtd. in *ibid.*, 621. The Court issued a judgment confirming the verdict: *Ibid.*
64. Zilversmit, QWM, 615, 621–22.
65. Zilversmit, *TFE*, 208.

Chapter 4

1. Pamela Sedgwick to Betsey Mayhew, June 15, 1781, SFP, Box 11, Folder 4.
2. Mary Wilds, *Mumbet: The Life and Times of Elizabeth Freeman* (Greensboro, NC: Avisson Press, 1999), 20–21.
3. Pamela Sedgwick to Betsey Mayhew, June 1, 1783, SFP, Box 11, Folder 4.
4. Welch, *Theodore Sedgwick, Federalist*, 128, 130.
5. Kelley, introduction to C.M. Sedgwick, *PHS*, 8.
6. C.M. Sedgwick, *PHS*, 69.
7. *Ibid.*, 70.
8. John Sedgwick to Theodore Sedgwick, June 5, 1784, SFP, Box 3, Folder 1; Kenslea, *Sedgwicks in Love*, 16.
9. C.M. Sedgwick, introduction to C. Sedgwick, *LCS*, 11. See also Preiss, *Sheffield: Frontier Town*, 76.
10. Drew, *Close the Door*, 46–47.
11. C.M. Sedgwick, introduction to C. Sedgwick, *LCS*, 11–12; Jones, *Stockbridge, Past and Present*, 85, 101–02.
12. C.M. Sedgwick, introduction to C. Sedgwick, *LCS*, 12, note 1.
13. Welch, *Theodore Sedgwick, Federalist*, 33.
14. Piper and Levinson, *Free Woman*, 80.
15. Welch, *Theodore Sedgwick, Federalist*, 34.
16. Robert J. Taylor, *Western Massachusetts in the Revolution* (Providence: Brown University Press, 1954), 134.
17. *Ibid.*, 131–32.
18. Agrippa Hull's bond, courtesy of Stockbridge Public Library, Museum & Archives.
19. Taylor, *Western Massachusetts*, 128; Welch *Theodore Sedgwick, Federalist*, 28–29.
20. C.M. Sedgwick, SNE, 422.
21. Welch, *Theodore Sedgwick, Federalist*, 147.
22. Taylor, *Western Massachusetts*, 143, 146–47.
23. Welch, *Theodore Sedgwick, Federalist*, 47.
24. *Ibid.*, 48.
25. Taylor, *Western Massachusetts*, 146; Jones, *Stockbridge, Past and Present*, 188.
26. Qtd. in Welch, *Theodore Sedgwick, Federalist*, 48.
27. C.M. Sedgwick, SNE, 422.
28. The Jenny Gray incident is described both by Henry Sedgwick and by Catharine Sedgwick. Henry's version sets the event on the infamous night of February 27 during the Hamlin raid, but Catharine's version sets it as a separate event that occurred sometime other than during the Hamlin raid. Catharine's version is clearly correct because the horse was never returned, as it probably would have been in the aftermath of the Hamlin raid. See C.M. Sedgwick, SNE, 423, and H.D. Sedgwick, *Abolition of Slavery*, 17.
29. Taylor, *Western Massachusetts*, 144.
30. C.M. Sedgwick, SNE, 422. There is no mention of Betsey being present in the Sedgwick home in either Henry or Catharine Sedgwick's account of Elizabeth's heroics during Shays' Rebellion. It is extremely unlikely that she would have behaved the way she did on the night of the Hamlin raid, exchanging insults with the intruders and prioritizing the security of the Sedgwicks' property, if the insurgents had her child in their power.
31. Taylor, *Western Massachusetts*, 156–57.
32. Sedgwick and Marquand, *Stockbridge, 1739–1974*, 157.
33. *Ibid.*
34. Taylor, *Western Massachusetts*, 159.
35. Welch, *Theodore Sedgwick, Federalist*, 50.
36. *Ibid.*
37. *Ibid.*
38. Taylor, *Western Massachusetts*, 160–62.

Notes—Chapter 5

39. *Ibid.*, 162.
40. *Ibid.*, 160, 162–63.
41. *Ibid.*, 144.
42. Jones, *Stockbridge, Past and Present*, 191–92.
43. *Ibid.*, 192.
44. *Ibid.*, 193.
45. *Ibid.*, 192.
46. Sedgwick and Marquand, *Stockbridge, 1739–1974*, 161. See also Jones, *Stockbridge, Past and Present*, 193.
47. Sedgwick and Marquand, *Stockbridge, 1739–1974*, 161.
48. C.M. Sedgwick, SNE, 423.
49. H.D. Sedgwick, *Abolition of Slavery*, 17.
50. Qtd. in *ibid.*, 17.
51. C.M. Sedgwick, SNE, 423–424 and H.D. Sedgwick, *Abolition of Slavery*, 17.
52. Qtd. in C.M. Sedgwick, SNE, 423–424.
53. Sedgwick and Marquand, *Stockbridge, 1739–1974*, 162.
54. Welch, *Theodore Sedgwick, Federalist*, 49.
55. Sedgwick and Marquand, *Stockbridge, 1739–1974*, 162.
56. Jones, *Stockbridge, Past and Present*, 195, 193.
57. *Ibid.*, 197.
58. Welch, *Theodore Sedgwick, Federalist*, 52. See also Jones, *Stockbridge, Past and Present*, 199. (Though John Ashley, Elizabeth Freeman's former master, was known as John Ashley, Jr., well into middle age because his father, Captain John Ashley, lived to be 90, I refer to Elizabeth's master as John Ashley and his son as John Ashley, Jr., for simplicity's sake.)
59. Jones, *Stockbridge, Past and Present*, 199.
60. Sedgwick and Marquand, *Stockbridge, 1739–1974*, 165.
61. Jones, *Stockbridge, Past and Present*, 142.
62. Welch, *Theodore Sedgwick, Federalist*, 53.

Chapter 5

1. Welch, *Theodore Sedgwick, Federalist*, 138–9.
2. Taylor, *Western Massachusetts*, 203, note 107.
3. Qtd. in Welch, *Theodore Sedgwick, Federalist*, 41.
4. Welch, *Theodore Sedgwick, Federalist*, 41, 54, note.
5. Pamela Sedgwick to Theodore Sedgwick, June 17, 1787, SFP, Box 1, Folder 2.
6. *Ibid.*
7. Welch, *Theodore Sedgwick, Federalist*, 59.
8. *Ibid.*, 64.
9. Pamela Sedgwick to Theodore Sedgwick, January 1788, SFP, Box 1, Folder 2.
10. Pamela Sedgwick to Theodore Sedgwick, February 24, 1788, SFP, Box 1, Folder 2.
11. Pamela Sedgwick to Elizabeth Mayhew, July 19, 1788, SFP, Box 11, Folder 4.
12. Pamela Sedgwick to Betsy Mayhew, August 10, 1788, SFP, Box 11, Folder 4.
13. Theodore Sedgwick to Pamela Sedgwick, November 1788, SFP, Box 1, Folder 2. See also Welch, *Theodore Sedgwick, Federalist*, 66.
14. Theodore Sedgwick to Pamela Sedgwick, January 27, 1789, SFP, Box 1, Folder 3.
15. Pamela Sedgwick to Theodore Sedgwick, January 31, 1789, SFP, Box 1, Folder 3.
16. Pamela Sedgwick to Theodore Sedgwick, February 17, 1789, SFP, Box 1, Folder 3.
17. Welch, *Theodore Sedgwick, Federalist*, 66.
18. Pamela Sedgwick to Betsy Mayhew, April 1789, SFP, Box 11, Folder 5.
19. Theodore Sedgwick to Pamela Sedgwick, June 18, 1789, SFP, Box 1, Folder 3.
20. Theodore Sedgwick to Pamela Sedgwick, July 10, 1789, SFP, Box 1, Folder 4.
21. Theodore Sedgwick to Pamela Sedgwick, July 21, 1789, SFP, Box 1, Folder 4.
22. Theodore Sedgwick to Pamela Sedgwick, June 18, 1789, SFP, Box 1, Folder 3.
23. Pamela Sedgwick to Theodore

Notes—Chapter 6

Sedgwick, July 17, 1789, SFP, Box 1, Folder 4.
24. Pamela Sedgwick to Theodore Sedgwick, July 27, 1789, SFP, Box 1, Folder 4.
25. Piper and Levinson, *Free Woman*, 129; H.D. Sedgwick, *Abolition of Slavery*, 16.
26. C.M. Sedgwick, SNE, 422.
27. Pamela Sedgwick to Betsy Mayhew, August 21, 1789, SFP, Box 11, Folder 5.
28. Piper and Levinson, *Free Woman*, 99.
29. Jane Darby's story is a good illustration of the ragged end of slavery in Massachusetts. Even after Elizabeth's successful freedom suit, some masters hoped to rely on their slaves' ignorance of abolition to keep them in bondage. Some, like Jane, had to continue to escape these masters and then seek help in asserting their rights. For a detailed rendition of Jane Darby's situation, see Jones, *Stockbridge, Past and Present*, 241.
30. Piper and Levinson, *Free Woman*, 96; Jones, *Stockbridge, Past and Present*, 238.
31. C.M. Sedgwick, *PHS*, 67. Though Catharine Sedgwick says she was two months premature, it is unlikely she was that severely premature given that she was relatively healthy. Her father was home briefly in the spring, and that is probably when she was conceived.
32. Theodore Sedgwick to Pamela Sedgwick, January 30, 1790, SFP, Box, 1, Folder 6.
33. Theodore Sedgwick to Pamela Sedgwick, February 20, 1790, SFP, Box 1, Folder 6.
34. Pamela Sedgwick to Betsy Mayhew, September 27, 1789, SFP, Box 1, Folder 5.
35. C.M. Sedgwick, *PHS*, 67.
36. Theodore Sedgwick to Pamela Sedgwick, February 6, 1790, SFP, Box 1, Folder 6.
37. Pamela Sedgwick to Theodore Sedgwick, February 26, 1790, SFP, Box 1, Folder 6.
38. Pamela Sedgwick to Theodore Sedgwick, March 19, 1790, SFP, Box 1, Folder 6.

39. Pamela Sedgwick to Theodore Sedgwick, undated, SFP, Box 1, Folder 6.
40. Theodore Sedgwick to Pamela Sedgwick, February 25, 1790, SFP, Box 1, Folder 6. See also Theodore Sedgwick to Pamela Sedgwick, April 3, 1790, Box 1, Folder 7.
41. Theodore Sedgwick to Pamela Sedgwick, June 17, 1790, SFP, Box 1, Folder 8.
42. Welch, *Theodore Sedgwick, Federalist*, 98.
43. *Ibid.*, 95.
44. Theodore Sedgwick to Pamela Sedgwick, June 17, 1790, SFP, Box 1, Folder 8.
45. Pamela Sedgwick to Theodore Sedgwick, June 26, 1790, SFP, Box 1, Folder 8.
46. C.M. Sedgwick, SNE, 418.
47. C.M. Sedgwick, *LLCMS*, note, 29.
48. C.M Sedgwick, introduction to C. Sedgwick, *LCS*, 11.
49. Pamela Sedgwick to Theodore Sedgwick, June 26, 1790, SFP, Box 1, Folder 8.
50. Pamela Sedgwick to Theodore Sedgwick, June 11, 1790, SFP, Box 1, Folder 8.
51. Kenslea, *Sedgwicks in Love*, 19.

Chapter 6

1. Theodore Sedgwick to Pamela Sedgwick, December 26, 1790, SFP, Box 1, Folder 9.
2. Rufus W. Griswold, *The Republican Court; or, American Society in the Days of Washington* (New York: D. Appleton, 1867; repr., Sagwan Press, an imprint of Creative Media Partners), 326.
3. Qtd. in *ibid*.
4. Pamela Sedgwick to Theodore Sedgwick, January 10, 1791, SFP, Box 1, Folder 10.
5. *Ibid.*
6. H.D. Sedgwick, obituary of Pamela Sedgwick, qtd. in C.M. Sedgwick, *PHS*, 65.
7. C.M. Sedgwick, introduction to C. Sedgwick, *LCS*, 13.
8. Pamela Sedgwick to Theodore Sedgwick, January 10, 1791, SFP, Box 1, Folder 10.

Notes—Chapter 6

9. Welch, *Theodore Sedgwick, Federalist*, 98.
10. Theodore Sedgwick to Pamela Sedgwick, January 16, 1791, SFP, Box 1, Folder 10 and Theodore Sedgwick to Pamela Sedgwick, January 28, 1791, SFP, Box 1, Folder 10.
11. Pamela Sedgwick to Theodore Sedgwick, January 30, 1791, SFP, Box 1, Folder 10.
12. *Ibid.*
13. *Ibid.*
14. Qtd. in C.M. Sedgwick, *PHS*, 125, C.M. Sedgwick, introduction to C. Sedgwick, *LCS*, 11.
15. Theodore Sedgwick to Pamela Sedgwick, May 15, 1791, SFP, Box 1, Folder 11.
16. Pamela Sedgwick to Theodore Sedgwick, October 23, 1791, SFP, Box 1, Folder 12.
17. Welch, *Theodore Sedgwick, Federalist*, 102.
18. Pamela Sedgwick to Theodore Sedgwick, November 18, [year unnoted] SFP, Box 1, Folder 10.
19. *Ibid.*
20. Theodore Sedgwick to Pamela Sedgwick, November 9, 1791, SFP, Box 1, Folder 12; Welch, *Theodore Sedgwick, Federalist*, 105.
21. Theodore Sedgwick to Pamela Sedgwick, November 20, 1791, SFP, Box 1, Folder 12.
22. Pamela Sedgwick to Theodore Sedgwick, December 4, 1791, SFP, Box 1, Folder 13.
23. *Ibid.*
24. C.M. Sedgwick, *PHS*, 67.
25. Theodore Sedgwick to Pamela Sedgwick, December 14, 1791, SFP, Box, 1, Folder 13.
26. *Ibid.*
27. *Ibid.*
28. *Ibid.*
29. Welch, *Theodore Sedgwick, Federalist*, 111, note 9.
30. Qtd. in C.M. Sedgwick, introduction to C. Sedgwick, *LCS*, 11.
31. Qtd. in C.M. Sedgwick, introduction to C. Sedgwick, *LCS*, 12.
32. Qtd. *ibid.*, 11.
33. *Ibid.*
34. Welch, *Theodore Sedgwick, Federalist*, 102.
35. *Ibid.* Pennsylvania had passed a gradual abolition law during the Revolution, but there were some who were calling for the complete and present abolition of slavery in the state.
36. Qtd. by C.M. Sedgwick, introduction to C. Sedgwick, *LCS*, 11.
37. Will of Elizabeth Freeman, October 18, 1829, copy, courtesy of Stockbridge Public Library, Museum & Archives.
38. For an example of Charles Sedgwick's feelings about Elizabeth Freeman in her old age, see Charles Sedgwick to Elizabeth Sedgwick, October 4, 1825, C. Sedgwick, *LCS*, 46.
39. Pamela Sedgwick to Elisabeth Mayhew, undated, SFP, Box 11, Folder 5.
40. Theodore Sedgwick to Pamela Sedgwick, November 29, 1792, SFP, Box 1, Folder 14; Theodore Sedgwick to Pamela Sedgwick, February 22, 1793, SFP, Box 1, Folder 16.
41. Theodore Sedgwick to Pamela Sedgwick, November 29, 1792, SFP, Box 1, Folder 14.
42. Pamela Sedgwick to Theodore Sedgwick, December 8, 1792, SFP, Box 1, Folder 14.
43. Pamela Sedgwick to Theodore Sedgwick, December 11, 1792, SFP, Box 1, Folder 14.
44. Pamela Sedgwick to Theodore Sedgwick, December 18, 1792, SFP, Box 1, Folder 14.
45. Theodore Sedgwick to Pamela Sedgwick, January 11, 1793, SFP, Box, 1, Folder 15.
46. Pamela Sedgwick to Theodore Sedgwick, January 21, 1793, SFP, Box 1, Folder 15.
47. Theodore Sedgwick to Pamela Sedgwick, February 18, 1793, SFP, Box 1, Folder 16.
48. Pamela Sedgwick to Theodore Sedgwick, December 11, 1792, qtd. in Welch, *Theodore Sedgwick, Federalist*, 112.
49. Pamela Sedgwick to Theodore Sedgwick, January 1, 1793, SFP, Box 1, Folder 15; Pamela Sedgwick to Theodore Sedgwick, December 18, 1792, SFP, Box 1, Folder 14.
50. Pamela Sedgwick to Theodore Sedgwick, January 8, 1793, SFP, Box 1,

Folder 15; C.M. Sedgwick, *LLCMS*, 73, note; C.M. Sedgwick, *PHS*, 73.
51. C.M. Sedgwick, SNE, 423; Piper and Levinson, *Free Woman*, 103.
52. Piper and Levinson, *Free Woman*, 142.
53. *Ibid.*
54. Jones, *Stockbridge, Past and Present*, 241.
55. C.M. Sedgwick, *PHS*, 63, 74.
56. Theodore Sedgwick to Pamela Sedgwick, October 10, 1793, SFP, Box 1, Folder 16.
57. Theodore Sedgwick to Eliza and Frances Sedgwick, February 27, 1794, SFP, Box 3, Folder 2.
58. Theodore Sedgwick to Pamela Sedgwick, March 6, 1794, SFP, Box 1, Folder 17.
59. Welch, *Theodore Sedgwick, Federalist*, 136.
60. *Ibid.*, 136–37, 137.
61. Theodore Sedgwick to Henry Sedgwick, April 24, 1794, SFP, Box 2, Folder 15.
62. Pamela Sedgwick to Frances Sedgwick, June 4, 1794, SFP, Box 11, Folder 2.
63. C.M. Sedgwick, *PHS*, 69.
64. Pamela Sedgwick to Theodore Sedgwick, February 2, 1795, SFP, Box 1, Folder 20.

Chapter 7

1. Pamela Sedgwick to Theodore Sedgwick, February 4, 1795, SFP, Box 1, Folder 20; Theodore Sedgwick to Pamela Sedgwick, February 23, 1795, Box 1, Folder 20.
2. Piper and Levinson, *Free Woman*, 139.
3. *Ibid.*
4. *Ibid.*, 137, 139.
5. *Ibid.*, 139.
6. See Piper and Levinson, *Free Woman*, for the suggestion that Mrs. Harry Van Schaack's given name was Elizabeth but see a contemporaneous letter from Catharine Sedgwick to her sister Frances Watson describing the details surrounding the death of Elizabeth's granddaughter in which she refers to the deceased as Lydia: Catharine Sedgwick to Frances Watson, undated, SFP, Box 79, Folder 23. See also C.M. Sedgwick, *PHS*, 71, written several decades later stating that the name of this beloved grandchild of Elizabeth Freeman was named Lydia Maria. Given that Elizabeth's granddaughter was a frequent visitor in the Sedgwick household throughout Catharine Sedgwick's childhood and young adulthood and that Catharine was present to comfort Elizabeth when the young Mrs. Van Schaack died, it is unlikely that Catharine would misstate her given name.
7. Theodore Sedgwick to Pamela Sedgwick, February 23, 1795, SFP, Box 1, Folder 20.
8. Theodore Sedgwick to Eliza and Frances Sedgwick, December 16, 1795, SFP, Box 3, Folder 2.
9. *Ibid.*
10. C.M. Sedgwick, *PHS*, 68.
11. *Ibid.*, 63.
12. Qtd. in *ibid.*, 58–59.
13. Theodore Sedgwick to Eliza and Frances Sedgwick, January 19, 1796, SFP, Box 3, Folder 3.
14. C.M. Sedgwick, *PHS*, 59.
15. Theodore Sedgwick to Eliza Sedgwick and Frances Sedgwick, December 25, 1795, SFP, Box 3, Folder 2.
16. C.M. Sedgwick, *PHS*, 70.
17. Henry Dwight to Theodore Sedgwick, February 10, 1796, SFP, Box 3, Folder 3.
18. Welch, *Theodore Sedgwick, Federalist*, 144.
19. *Ibid.*, 145, 149.
20. Qtd. in *ibid.*, 150.
21. Theodore Sedgwick to Eliza and Frances Sedgwick, March 12, 1796, SFP, Box 3, Folder 3.
22. Theodore Sedgwick to Eliza and Frances Sedgwick, March 23, 1796, SFP, Box 3, Folder 3.
23. Welch, *Theodore Sedgwick, Federalist*, 152.
24. *Ibid.*, 159.
25. Theodore Sedgwick to Pamela Sedgwick, January 20, 1797, SFP, Box 1, Folder 21.
26. *Ibid.*
27. Pamela Sedgwick to Theodore Sedgwick, January 16, 1796 [sic], SFP, Box 1, Folder 21. This letter was probably

misdated and should actually be dated January 16, 1797. Pamela was suffering with severe depression and living separately from her family in January 1796, but she was functional and planning for Eliza's wedding in January 1797.
28. Sedgwick and Marquand, *Stockbridge, 1739–1974*, 167.
29. Theodore Sedgwick to Pamela Sedgwick, December 29, 1796, SFP, Box 1, Folder 21.
30. Pamela Sedgwick to Theodore Sedgwick, January 23, 1797, SFP, Box 1, Folder 21.
31. Pamela Sedgwick to Theodore Sedgwick, February 2, 1797, SFP, Box 1, Folder 21.
32. *Ibid.*
33. C.M. Sedgwick, *PHS*, 87.
34. *Ibid.*, 84.
35. *Ibid.*, 87.
36. *Ibid.*
37. Welch, *Theodore Sedgwick, Federalist*, 161–2.
38. *Ibid.*, 165–66.
39. *Ibid.*, 163.
40. Theodore Sedgwick to Pamela Sedgwick, June 7, 1797, SFP, Box 1, Folder 22.
41. Theodore Sedgwick to Pamela Sedgwick, June 14, 1797, SFP, Box 1, Folder 22.
42. Pamela Sedgwick to Theodore Sedgwick, January 28, 1798, SFP, Box 1, Folder 23.
43. Theodore Sedgwick to Pamela Sedgwick, December 12, 1797, SFP, Box 1, Folder 22.
44. Theodore Sedgwick to Pamela Sedgwick, January 30, 1798, SFP, Box 1, Folder 15.
45. Pamela Sedgwick to Theodore Sedgwick, February 2, 1798, SFP, Box 1, Folder 24.
46. Pamela Sedgwick to Theodore Sedgwick, February 9, 1798, SFP, Box 1, Folder 24.
47. *Ibid.*
48. Pamela Sedgwick to Theodore Sedgwick, February 12, 1798, SFP, Box 1, Folder 24.
49. Pamela Sedgwick to Theodore Sedgwick, February 17, 1798, SFP, Box 1, Folder 24.
50. Pamela Sedgwick to Theodore Sedgwick, March 3, 1798, SFP, Box 1, Folder 25.
51. Pamela Sedgwick to Theodore Sedgwick, March 12, 1798, SFP, Box 1, Folder 25.
52. Pamela Sedgwick to Theodore Sedgwick, March 29, 1798, SFP, Box 1, Folder 25.
53. Theodore Sedgwick to Pamela Sedgwick, February 13, 1798, SFP, Box 1, Folder 24; Welch, *Theodore Sedgwick, Federalist*, 173.
54. Theodore Sedgwick to Frances Sedgwick, March 31, 1798, SFP, Box 3, Folder 4.
55. Pamela Sedgwick to Theodore Sedgwick, April 20, 1798, SFP, Box 1, Folder 26.
56. Theodore Sedgwick to Pamela Sedgwick, March 7, 1798, SFP, Box 1, Folder 25.
57. Theodore Sedgwick to Pamela Sedgwick, April 20, 1798, SFP, Box 1, Folder 26. Sedgwick was also a supporter of the highly unpopular and probably unconstitutional Sedition Act, arguing that it was similar to punishment of seditious libel under English common law; see Welch, *Theodore Sedgwick, Federalist*, 196.
58. Pamela Sedgwick to Theodore Sedgwick, July 2, 1798, SFP, Box 1, Folder 26.
59. Pamela Sedgwick to Theodore Sedgwick, December 25, 1797, SFP, Box 1, Folder 22; Piper and Levinson, *Free Woman*, 44.
60. H.D. Sedgwick, 18.
61. Welch, *Theodore Sedgwick, Federalist*, 176.
62. *Ibid.*
63. *Ibid.*, 173.
64. *Ibid.*, 190, note 4.
65. Pamela Sedgwick to Theodore Sedgwick, January 14, 1799, SFP, Box 1, Folder 27.
66. Theodore Sedgwick to Pamela Sedgwick, February 3, 1799, SFP, Box 1, Folder 27.
67. *Ibid.*
68. North Callahan, *Henry Knox, General Washington's General* (New York: Rinehart, 1958), 365.
69. Qtd. in *ibid.*, 371.

Notes—Chapter 8

70. Welch, *Theodore Sedgwick, Federalist*, 174.
71. *Ibid.*, 183.
72. *Ibid.*
73. *Ibid.*, 187–190.
74. *Ibid.*, 203.
75. *Ibid.*, 206.
76. Theodore Sedgwick II to Theodore Sedgwick, December 12, 1799, SFP, Box 2, Folder 7.
77. One of Sedgwick's few substantive achievements during his speakership was to cast the tie-breaking vote in the House for America's first national bankruptcy law. See Welch, *Theodore Sedgwick, Federalist*, 209.
78. Theodore Sedgwick to Pamela Sedgwick, April 19, 1800, SFP, Box 2, Folder 2.
79. Welch, *Theodore Sedgwick, Federalist*, 205, 219, note 33.

Chapter 8

1. Charles Sedgwick to Theodore Sedgwick, January 5, 1800, SFP, Box 3, Folder 5.
2. Theodore Sedgwick II to Theodore Sedgwick, August 27, 1800, SFP, Box 2, Folder 8.
3. C.M. Sedgwick to Theodore Sedgwick, January 19, 1801, CMSP I, Reel 1, Box 1, Folder 1.
4. C.M. Sedgwick to Theodore Sedgwick, February 1, 1801, CMSP I, Reel 1, Box 1, Folder 1.
5. Theodore Sedgwick to Theodore Sedgwick II, February 16, 1801, SFP, Book 2, Folder 10.
6. Welch, *Theodore Sedgwick, Federalist*, 230.
7. Frances Sedgwick to Theodore Sedgwick, February 18, 1799, SFP, Box 1, Folder 27.
8. Theodore Sedgwick II to Theodore Sedgwick, January 26, 1800, SFP, Box 2, Folder 8.
9. Theodore Sedgwick II to Theodore Sedgwick, March 10, 1800, SFP, Box 2, Folder 8.
10. "Sedgwick Genealogy North America," Sedgwick.org, accessed March 8, 2018, www.sedgwick.org/na/families/robert1613/B/4/B4-sedgwick-theodore.html.
11. Theodore Sedgwick to Henry Sedgwick, July 20, 1801, SFP, Box 2, Folder 15.
12. Theodore Sedgwick to Theodore Sedgwick II, September 9, 1801, SFP, Box 2, Folder 10.
13. Theodore Sedgwick to Theodore Sedgwick II, March 17, 1802, SFP, Box 2, Folder 10.
14. C.M. Sedgwick to Theodore Sedgwick, February 3, 1802, CMSP l, Reel 1, Box 1, Folder 1.
15. In 1799, New York enacted a gradual abolition law that provided that female children of slaves born on or after July 4, 1799, would serve as indentured servants until age 25 and male children of slaves born on or after that date until age 28. The status of slaves born prior to July 4, 1799, remained unchanged. In 1817, a law was passed freeing all slaves in New York on July 4, 1827. See McManus, *Black Bondage*, 177.
16. Kenslea, *Sedgwicks in Love*, 47.
17. Theodore Sedgwick II to Theodore Sedgwick, March 27, 1802, SFP, Box 2, Folder 11.
18. Theodore Sedgwick to Pamela Sedgwick, May 1, 1802, SFP, Box 2, Folder 3.
19. Theodore Sedgwick to Henry and Robert Sedgwick, April 18, 1802, SFP, Box 3, Folder 6.
20. Theodore Sedgwick to Theodore Sedgwick II, March 17, 1802, SFP, Box 2, Folder 10; Theodore Sedgwick to Theodore Sedgwick II, April 18, 1802, SFP, Box 2, Folder 10.
21. Theodore Sedgwick to Theodore Sedgwick II, June 20, 1802, SFP, Box 2, Folder 11.
22. Francis Bacon Trowbridge, *The Ashley Genealogy* (New Haven: Tuttle, Morehouse & Taylor, 1896), 59; Chase and Chapman, *Pioneer Berkshire Family*, 31, 33.
23. Drew, *Close the Door*, 46–7.
24. Piper and Levinson, *Free Woman*, 143.
25. *Ibid.*, 145.
26. *Ibid.*, 143.
27. *Ibid.*, 132. The long period between the births of Betsey Humphrey's two

Notes—Chapter 8

daughters suggests that she may have suffered intervening miscarriages or given birth to infants who died very young. According to Piper and Levinson (133–34), a list of destroyed grave stones in the Stockbridge Cemetery compiled in the early 1900s mentions "Bub," "Sister to Bub," and "colored-children of Mumbet." Piper and Levinson suggest that Bub and Sister to Bub were actually the children of Mary Ann Humphrey because they were buried next to a grave that Piper and Levinson believe may be the grave of Mary Ann's husband, Andrew Drean. It is also possible that these children were the twin children of Betsey Humphrey, who were stillborn or died shortly after birth, and who were born at a time when Elizabeth would have handled the arrangements and paid for the burials, thus confusing the gravedigger. As Piper and Levinson point out, Elizabeth was over forty when she made the move to Stockbridge from Sheffield, and both Catharine Sedgwick and Electa Jones are quite specific that she had only one child, Betsey Humphrey.

28. Theodore Sedgwick II to Theodore Sedgwick, March 13, 1804, SFP, Box 2, Folder 12.

29. Catharine Sedgwick to Theodore Sedgwick, April 1, 1804, CMSP I, Reel 1, Box 1, Folder 1.

30. Pamela Sedgwick to Sarah Tucker, October 17, 1804, SFP, Box 11, Folder 5.

31. Theodore Sedgwick to Pamela Sedgwick, November 5, 1804, SFP, Box 2, Folder 4.

32. Theodore Sedgwick to Henry D. Sedgwick, December 8, 1804, SFP, Box 2, Folder 15; Theodore Sedgwick to Henry D. Sedgwick, December 31, 1804, SFP, Box 2, Folder 15; Theodore Sedgwick to Catharine M. Sedgwick, December 24, 1804, SFP, Box 2, Folder 23.

33. Theodore Sedgwick II to Theodore Sedgwick, December 8, 1804, SFP, Box 2, Folder 12.

34. Theodore Sedgwick to Catharine Sedgwick, December 24, 1804, SFP, Box 2, Folder 23.

35. Theodore Sedgwick to Theodore Sedgwick II, October 7, 1805, SFP, Box 2, Folder 12.

36. Theodore Sedgwick to Catharine Sedgwick, December 2, 1805, CMSP III, Reel 15, Box 2, Folder 1.

37. Kenslea, *Sedgwicks in Love*, 53–54.

38. Theodore Sedgwick to Catharine Sedgwick, January 2, 1806, CMSP III, Reel 15, Box 2, Folder 1; Catharine Sedgwick to Pamela Sedgwick, January 17, 1806, CMSP I, Reel 1, Box 1, Folder 1.

39. Piper and Levinson, *Free Woman*, 156.

40. Catharine Sedgwick to Pamela Sedgwick, January 17, 1806, CMSP I, Reel 1, Box 1, Folder 1.

41. Piper and Levinson, *Free Woman*, 156.

42. Jones, *Stockbridge, Past and Present*, 260–1.

43. Sedgwick and Marquand, *Stockbridge, 1739–1974*, 174–76.

44. *Ibid.*, 179.

45. Piper and Levinson, *Free Woman*, 154.

46. *Ibid.*, 156.

47. *Ibid.*, 146–49.

48. *Ibid.*, 156.

49. *Ibid.*, 146.

50. John Sedgwick to Theodore Sedgwick, July 15, 1806, SFP, Box 3, Folder 7.

51. Qtd. in Kenslea, *Sedgwicks in Love*, 25; Kenslea, *Sedgwicks in Love*, 25.

52. Catharine Sedgwick to Robert Sedgwick, July 25, 1806, CMSP III, Reel 15, Box 2, Folder 1.

53. Frances Watson to Pamela Sedgwick, November 7, 1806, SFP, Box 11, Folder 2.

54. Theodore Sedgwick to Charles Sedgwick, January 1, 1807, SFP, Box 3, Folder 7.

55. Catharine Sedgwick to Henry Sedgwick, March 17, 1807, CMSP III, Reel 15, Box 2, Folder 2.

56. Catharine Sedgwick to Henry Sedgwick, March 24, 1807, CMSP III, Reel 15, Box 2, Folder 2.

57. Catharine Sedgwick to Henry Sedgwick, March 24, 1807, CMSP III, Reel 15, Box 2, Folder 2.

58. Theodore Sedgwick to Susan Ridley, August 3, 1807, SFP, Box 3, Folder 7 and Theodore Sedgwick to Theodore Sedgwick II, July 23, 1807, SFP, Box 2, Folder 13. See also, Kenslea, *Sedgwicks in Love*, 48.

59. Henry Sedgwick to Theodore Sedgwick II, September 17, 1807, SFP, Box 11, Folder 16.
60. Qtd. in Kenslea, *Sedgwicks in Love*, 30; Kenslea, 30.
61. Qtd. in Kenslea, 30.
62. *Ibid*.
63. Qtd. in *ibid*.; Kenslea, 30.
64. Qtd. in C.M. Sedgwick, *PHS*, 71; C.M. Sedgwick, *PHS*, 71.
65. H.D. Sedgwick, obituary of Pamela Sedgwick, qtd. in C.M. Sedgwick, *PHS*, 71.

Chapter 9

1. Henry Sedgwick to Theodore Sedgwick II, October 16, 1807, SFP, Box 11, Folder 5.
2. Catharine Sedgwick to Frances Watson, December 28, 1807, CMSP I, December 28, 1807, Reel 1, Box 1, Folder 1.
3. Kenslea, *Sedgwicks in Love*, 28.
4. Catharine Sedgwick to Henry Sedgwick, April 2, 1808, CMSP III, Reel 15, Box 2, Folder 2.
5. Henry Sedgwick to Theodore Sedgwick, April 25, 1808, SFP, Box 2, Folder 17.
6. Henry Sedgwick to Catharine Sedgwick, April 26, 1808, CMSP III, Reel 15, Box 2, Folder 2.
7. Theodore Sedgwick to Theodore Sedgwick II, April 18, 1808, SFP, Box 2, Folder 14.
8. Theodore Sedgwick II to Henry Sedgwick, June 12, 1808, SFP, Box 11, Folder 17.
9. C.M. Sedgwick, *PHS*, 66–67.
10. *Ibid*., 67.
11. Theodore Sedgwick to Susan Ridley, August 27, 1808, SFP, Box 3, Folder 7.
12. Theodore Sedgwick to Catharine Russell, December 18, 1809, SFP, Box 3, Folder 8; Theodore Sedgwick to Catharine Russell, January 23, 1810, SFP, Box 3, Folder 8.
13. C.M. Sedgwick, *PHS*, 126.
14. Theodore Sedgwick to Theodore Sedgwick II, October 20, 1808, SFP, Box 2, Folder 14.
15. Theodore Sedgwick II to Theodore Sedgwick, October 18, 1808, SFP, Box 2, Folder 14.
16. Theodore Sedgwick II to Theodore Sedgwick, November 1, 1808, SFP, Box 2, Folder 14.
17. Henry Sedgwick to Theodore Sedgwick, November 7, 1808, SFP, Box 3, Folder 7.
18. Henry Sedgwick to Theodore Sedgwick II, October 30, 1808, SFP, Box 11, Folder 17.
19. Henry Sedgwick to Theodore Sedgwick, November 7, 1808, SFP, Box 3, Folder 7.
20. Theodore Sedgwick to Henry Sedgwick, November 12, 1808, SFP, Box 2, Folder 17.
21. *Ibid*.
22. Postscript of Eliza Pomeroy to letter of Charles Sedgwick to Theodore Sedgwick, November 15, 1808, SFP, Box 3, Folder 7.
23. H.D. Sedgwick, *Abolition of Slavery*, 18.
24. Piper and Levinson, *Free Woman*, 146–47.
25. Henry Sedgwick to Catharine Sedgwick, January 1, 1809, CMSP III, Reel 15, Box 2, Folder 2.
26. Kenslea, *Sedgwicks in Love*, 66–67.
27. Theodore Sedgwick to Catharine Sedgwick, January 31, 1809, CMSP III, Reel 15, Box 2, Folder 2.
28. Theodore Sedgwick to Catharine Sedgwick, January 3, 1809, CMSP III, Reel 15, Box 2, Folder 2.
29. C.M. Sedgwick, introduction to C. Sedgwick, *LCS*, 16.
30. Theodore Sedgwick to Theodore Sedgwick II, May 8, 1809, SFP, Box 2, Folder 14.
31. C.M. Sedgwick, SNE, 424.
32. Catharine Sedgwick to Frances Watson, December 17, 1809, CMSP I, Reel 1, Box 1, Folder 2.
33. Theodore Sedgwick to Henry Sedgwick, January 21, 1810, SFP, Box 1, Folder 18.
34. Piper and Levinson, *Free Woman*, 156.
35. *Ibid*., 147, 156.
36. *Ibid*., 147, 158.
37. Jones, *Stockbridge, Past and Present*, 242.
38. Theodore Sedgwick II to Henry

Notes—Chapter 9

Sedgwick, January 27, 1811, SFP, Box 11, Folder 18.

39. This painting of Elizabeth Freeman is in the collection of the Massachusetts Historical Society.

40. Theodore Sedgwick to Henry Sedgwick, December 4, 1810, SFP, Box 2, Folder 18; Theodore Sedgwick to Catharine Sedgwick, December 11, 1810, CMSP III, Reel 15, Box 2, Folder 3.

41. Theodore Sedgwick to Henry Sedgwick, October 11, 1810, SFP, Box 2, Folder 18.

42. *Ibid.*

43. Theodore Sedgwick to Theodore Sedgwick II, February 7, 1809, SFP, Box 2, Folder 14.

44. Dissent of Justice Theodore Sedgwick in Greenwood v. Curtis, 6 Mass. 358 (1810), qtd. in Richard E. Welch, Jr. "Mumbet and Judge Sedgwick," *Boston Bar Journal* 8 (January 1964): 17.

45. Theodore Sedgwick to Catharine Sedgwick, January 7, 1811, CMSP III, Reel 15, Box 2, Folder 4.

46. Catharine Sedgwick to Henry Sedgwick, January 8, 1811, CMSP III, Reel 15, Box, 2, Folder 4.

47. Theodore Sedgwick to Catharine Russell, January 23, 1810, SFP, Box 3, Folder 8.

48. Catharine Sedgwick to Henry Sedgwick, June 10, 1811, CMSP III, Reel 15, Box 4, Folder 2.

49. Theodore Sedgwick II to Henry Sedgwick, July 10, 1811, SFP, Box 11, Folder 19.

50. Charles Sedgwick to Robert Sedgwick, July 29, 1811, qtd. in Kenslea, *Sedgwicks in Love*, 57.

51. Theodore Sedgwick to Catharine Sedgwick, January 7, 1811, CMSP III, Reel 15, Box 2, Folder 4; Theodore Sedgwick to Henry Sedgwick, January 28, 1811, SFP, Box 2, Folder 19.

52. *Ibid.*

53. For the approximate marriage date of the Van Schaacks and the approximate birth dates of their children, see Piper and Levinson, *Free Woman*, 132. The author accepts Catharine Sedgwick's authority that Elizabeth's elder granddaughter was named Lydia Maria like her daughter, while Piper and Levinson suggest that Elizabeth's elder granddaughter might have been named Elizabeth like her mother and grandmother.

54. Piper and Levinson, *Free Woman*, 135–36.

55. Piper and Levinson, 136. Though W.E.B. Dubois made the statement that it was Elizabeth Freeman who had a partnership with Jack Burghardt in DuBois's two autobiographies, subsequent scholarship has concluded that it was her daughter, Betsey Humphrey, who was probably Burghardt's partner. Elizabeth Freeman was about twenty years older than Burghardt, while Betsey Humphrey was about ten years younger. One of the letters that DuBois relied on for his claim was from his cousin Lucinda, who states with respect to Burghardt, "His second wife's name was Betsey Humphrey." Qtd. in Piper and Levinson, *Free Woman*, 135. There is also no evidence in the historical record that after Elizabeth Freeman's move to Stockbridge in 1785, she ever lived anywhere other than the Sedgwick home and her own farm.

56. Catharine Sedgwick to Henry Sedgwick, October 10, 1811, CMSP III, Reel 15, Box 2, Folder 4.

57. Catharine Sedgwick to Henry Sedgwick, November 28, 1811, CMSP III, Reel 15, Box 2, Folder 4.

58. Theodore Sedgwick to Henry Sedgwick, December 5, 1811, SFP, Box 2, Folder 20.

59. Theodore Sedgwick to Henry Sedgwick, January 23, 1812, SFP, Box 2, Folder 21.

60. *Ibid.* See also www.Sedgwick.org.

61. Kenslea, *Sedgwicks in Love*, 58.

62. Charles Sedgwick to Theodore Sedgwick, April 23, 1812, SFP, Box 3, Folder 8.

63. Theodore Sedgwick to Henry Sedgwick, June 11, 1812, SFP, Box 2, Folder 21.

64. Theodore Sedgwick to Henry Sedgwick, July 3, 1812, SFP, Box 2, Folder 21.

65. Theodore Sedgwick to Henry Sedgwick, June 19, 1812, SFP, Box 2, Folder 21.

66. H.D. Sedgwick, *Abolition of Slavery*, 18.

Chapter 10

1. Theodore Sedgwick II to Henry Sedgwick, September 11, 1812, SFP, Box 11, Folder 20.
2. *Ibid.*
3. Catharine Sedgwick to Henry Sedgwick, November 2, 1812, CMSP III, Reel 15, Box 2, Folder 2.
4. Robert Sedgwick to Theodore Sedgwick, December 3, 1812, SFP, Box 3, Folder 8.
5. Welch, *Theodore Sedgwick, Federalist*, 249.
6. Theodore Sedgwick II to Henry Sedgwick, December 28, 1812, SFP, Box 11, Folder 20; Kenslea, *Sedgwicks in Love*, 60.
7. Eliza Pomeroy to Theodore Sedgwick, November 30, 1812, SFP, Box 3, Folder 8.
8. Theodore Sedgwick to Henry Sedgwick, December 2, 1805, SFP, Box 2, Folder 16.
9. Catharine Sedgwick to Frances Watson, January 5, 1813, CMSP I, Reel 1, Box 1, Folder 3. Though the term "Unitarian" was not formally proclaimed by Channing until 1819, the term was in common usage in the immediately preceding years.
10. *Ibid.*
11. Catharine Sedgwick to Eliza Pomeroy, January 15, 1813, CMSP I, Reel 1, Box 1, Folder 3.
12. Henry Sedgwick to Theodore Sedgwick II, January 17, 1813, SFP, Box 11, Folder 21.
13. *Ibid.*
14. Henry Sedgwick to Theodore Sedgwick II, January 25, 1813, SFP, Box 11, Folder 21.
15. *Ibid.*
16. Qtd. in Welch, *Theodore Sedgwick, Federalist*, 250; Welch, *Theodore Sedgwick, Federalist*, 250.
17. Kenslea, *Sedgwicks in Love*, 61.
18. Theodore Sedgwick II to Henry Sedgwick, January 29, 1813, SFP, Box 11, Folder 21.
19. Henry Sedgwick to Theodore Sedgwick II, February 3, 1813, SFP, Box 11, Folder 21.
20. Catharine Sedgwick to Frances Watson, March 12, 1813, CMSP I, Reel 1, Box 1, Folder 3.
21. Catharine Sedgwick to Robert Sedgwick, March 11, 1813, CMSP I, Reel 1, Box 1, Folder 3.
22. Henry Sedgwick to Catharine Sedgwick, March 11, 1813, CMSP III, Reel 15, Box 2, Folder 6.
23. Catharine Sedgwick to Henry Sedgwick, March 21, 1813, CMSP III, Reel 15, Box 2, Folder 6.
24. Catharine Sedgwick to Henry Sedgwick, June 7, 1813, CMSP III Reel 15, Box 2, Folder 6.
25. *Ibid.*
26. Catharine Sedgwick to Henry Sedgwick, August 18, 1813, CMSP III, Reel 15, Box 2, Folder 6.
27. H.D. Sedgwick, *Abolition of Slavery*, 18.
28. C.M. Sedgwick, SNE, 418.
29. Catharine Sedgwick to Robert Sedgwick, November 31 [*sic*], 1818, CMSP I, Reel 1, Box 1, Folder 5.
30. C.M. Sedgwick, *PHS*, 70.
31. Piper and Levinson, *Free Woman*, 166; Catharine Sedgwick to Jane Sedgwick, July 16, 1818, CMSP III, Reel 15, Box 2, Folder 12.
32. Catharine Sedgwick to Robert Sedgwick, September 8, 1814, CMSP I, Reel 1, Box 1, Folder 4.
33. The only other surviving child, Lydia Maria Ann Van Schaack, gave birth to a child in 1826, so it could not have been her. Though it is possible the baby died, Catharine describes a normal birth without complications, so it is likely the baby was Amos Josiah. See Piper and Levinson, *Free Woman*, 132, for the 1826 birth date of Lydia Maria Ann's son Gilbert Van Allen.
34. Catharine Sedgwick to Frances Watson, undated, SFP, Box 79, Folder 23.
35. C.M. Sedgwick, *PHS*, 71.
36. Catharine Sedgwick to Frances Watson, undated, SFP, Box 79, Folder 23.
37. *Ibid.*
38. See Piper and Levinson, *Free Woman*, 140 for Elizabeth Freeman's granddaughter's date of death. (Catharine Sedgwick refers to this granddaughter as Lydia or Lydia Maria. Piper and Levinson suggest her name could have

Notes—Chapter 11

been Elizabeth. Given the closeness of the Sedgwick and Freeman families and Catharine's presence at the burial preparations, the author believes Catharine Sedgwick would not have inaccurately stated Mrs. Van Schaack's given name.)

39. Kenslea, *Sedgwicks in Love*, 70.

40. Theodore Sedgwick II to Henry Sedgwick, September 21, 1815, SFP, Box 11, Folder 23; Theodore Sedgwick II to Henry Sedgwick, February 8, 1816, SFP, Box 11, Folder 23. See also Kenslea, *Sedgwicks in Love*, 73.

41. Kenslea, *Sedgwicks in Love*, 76.

42. Theodore Sedgwick II to Henry Sedgwick, July 30, 1816, SFP, Box 11, Folder 23.

43. Henry Sedgwick to Catharine Sedgwick, October 12, 1817, CMSP III, Reel 15, Box 2, Folder 11.

44. Edward Channing to Catharine Sedgwick, October 15, 1818, CMSP III, Reel 15, Box 2, Folder 13; Catharine Sedgwick to Frances Watson, March 28, 1819, CMSP I, Reel 1, Box, 1, Folder 5.

45. Kelley, introduction to C.M. Sedgwick, *PHS*, 23–24.

46. Catharine Sedgwick to Robert Sedgwick, March 24, 1819, CMSP I, reel 1, Box 1, Folder 5.

47. Kelley, introduction to C.M. Sedgwick, *PHS*, 30.

48. Ibid.

49. Ibid., 4, 33. See also Carolyn Karcher, introduction to *Hope Leslie or, Early Times in the Massachusetts*, by Catharine Maria Sedgwick (first published, 1827; repr., New York: Penguin, 1998), x.

50. Kelley, introduction to C.M. Sedgwick, *PHS*, 15–17, 40.

51. C.M. Sedgwick, *Hope Leslie*, 97.

52. Piper and Levinson, *Free Woman*, 132, 140, 182.

53. Catharine Sedgwick to Jane Sedgwick, September 15, 1820, CMSP III, Reel 15, Box 2, Folder 14.

Chapter 11

1. Catharine Sedgwick to Frances Watson, March 1820, CMSP I, Reel 1, Box 1, Folder 6. For Sarah Drean's death, see Piper and Levinson, *Free Woman*, 132, 140.

2. Catharine Sedgwick to Charles and Elizabeth Sedgwick, June 17, 1825, CMSP I, Reel 1, Box 1, Folder 9; Theodore Sedgwick II to Henry Sedgwick, May 31, 1822, SFP, Box 11, Folder 25; Theodore Sedgwick II to Henry Sedgwick, June 25, 1822, SFP, Box 11, Folder 25.

3. Charles Sedgwick to Elizabeth Sedgwick, October 4, 1825, C. Sedgwick, *LCS*, 46.

4. Jones, *Stockbridge, Past and Present*, 241.

5. Charles Sedgwick to Robert Sedgwick, August 3, 1826, C. Sedgwick, *LCS*, 48–49.

6. Qtd. in Jones, *Stockbridge, Past and Present*, 242.

7. Catharine Sedgwick to Charles Sedgwick, June 22, 1827, CMSP I, Reel 1, Box 1, Folder 11; Kenslea, *Sedgwicks in Love*, 205.

8. Catharine Sedgwick to Eliza Cabot, June 10, 1827, CMSP III, Reel 16, Box 3, Folder 6.

9. Catharine Sedgwick to Robert Sedgwick, July 8, 1827, CMSP I, Reel 1, Box 1, Folder 11.

10. Eliza Cabot to Catharine Sedgwick, October 26, 1827, CMSP III, Reel 16, Box 3, Folder 7.

11. Catharine Sedgwick to Frances Watson, January 12, 1829, CMSP I, Reel 1, Box 1, Folder 11.

12. Ibid.

13. Catharine Sedgwick to Robert Sedgwick, August 25, 1829, SFP, Box 78, Folder 23.

14. Catharine Sedgwick to Robert Sedgwick, September 2, 1829, SFP, Box 78, Folder 23.

15. Mark Hopkins, *ELMH*, 195; Albert Hopkins to Mark Hopkins, October 11, 1829, *ELMH*, 198. See also Sedgwick and Marquand, *Stockbridge, 1739–1974*, 195.

16. Albert Hopkins to Mark Hopkins, September 21, 1829, *ELMH*, 196.

17. Piper and Levinson, *Free Woman*, 11.

18. Mark Hopkins to Harry Hopkins, October 2, 1829, *ELMH*, 197.

19. Harry Hopkins to Mark Hopkins, November 29, 1829, *ELMH*, 205.

20. *Ibid.*
21. Jane Sedgwick to Catharine Maria Sedgwick, March 31, 1829, CMSP III, Reel 16, Box 3, Folder 10.
22. Will of Elizabeth Freeman, October 18, 1829, copy, courtesy of Stockbridge Public Library, Museum & Archives; Piper and Levinson, *Free Woman*, 15.
23. Will of Elizabeth Freeman, October 18, 1829, copy, courtesy of Stockbridge Public Library, Museum & Archives.
24. William Minot to R.C. Winthrop, February 2, 1884, *Proceedings of the Massachusetts Historical Society*, 2nd series vol. I (1884–85), 3. This is probably the necklace Elizabeth wore in her portrait by Susan Ridley Sedgwick.
25. C.M. Sedgwick, *PHS*, 70–71.
26. *Ibid.*, 71.
27. Catharine Sedgwick to Charles Sedgwick, December 17, 1829, CMSP I, Reel 1, Box 1, Folder 11.
28. Piper and Levinson, *Free Woman*, 92.
29. C.M. Sedgwick, *PHS*, 69, 71.
30. *Ibid.*, 71.
31. Piper and Levinson, *Free Woman*, 162.
32. Charles Sedgwick to Catharine Sedgwick, December 13, 1829, SFP, Box 79, Folder 2.
33. *Ibid.*
34. Catharine Sedgwick to Charles Sedgwick, December 17, 1729, CMSP I, Reel 1, Box 1, Folder 11.
35. Jane Sedgwick to Catharine Sedgwick, December 6, 1829, CMSP III, Reel 16, Box 3, Folder 10.
36. *Ibid.*
37. Catharine Sedgwick to Jane Sedgwick, December 8, 1829, CMSP III, Reel 16, Box 3, Folder 10.
38. Catharine Sedgwick to Charles Sedgwick, December 17, 1829, CMSP I, Reel 1, Box 1, Folder 11.
39. Charles Sedgwick to Catharine Sedgwick, December 13, 1829, SFP, Box 79, Folder 2.
40. Jane Sedgwick to Catharine Sedgwick, December 6, 1829, CMSP III, Reel 16, Box 3, Folder 10.
41. Charles Sedgwick to Catharine Sedgwick, January 1, 1830, SFP, Box 79, Folder 2.
42. *Ibid.*
43. *Ibid.*
44. Charles Sedgwick to Catharine Sedgwick, January 1, 1830, SFP, Box 79, Folder 2.
45. *Ibid.*
46. Obituary of Elizabeth Freeman, *Berkshire Journal*, January 21, 1830, qtd. in Piper and Levinson, *Free Woman*, 116.
47. Sedgwick and Marquand, *Stockbridge, 1739–1974*, 191–2.
48. Charles Sedgwick to Catharine Sedgwick, January 1, 1830, SFP, Box 79, Folder 2.
49. *Ibid.*
50. Catharine Sedgwick, *PHS*, 70.
51. *Ibid.*, 68.
52. Charles Sedgwick to Catharine Sedgwick, January 1, 1830, SFP, Box 79, Folder 2.
53. *Ibid.*
54. Draft of the epitaph for Elizabeth Freeman's gravestone, SFP, Box 79, Folder 2.
55. Piper and Levinson, *Free Woman*, 167.

Epilogue

1. Piper and Levinson, *Free Woman*, 182.
2. *Ibid.*, 183.
3. Charles Sedgwick to Catharine Sedgwick, May 12, 1838, SFP, Box 79, Folder 6; Charles Sedgwick to Katharine Sedgwick, Jr., July 1838, C. Sedgwick, *LCS*, 95; Piper and Levinson, *Free Woman*, 191.
4. Piper and Levinson, *Free Woman*, 191.
5. Charles Sedgwick to Catharine Sedgwick, January 1, 1830, SFP, Box 79, Folder 2; Dr. Eli Todd to Jane Sedgwick, CMSP III, Reel 16, Box 3, Folder 11.
6. Jane Sedgwick to Catharine Sedgwick, May 18, 1830, CMSP III, Reel 16, Box 3, Folder 11.
7. H.D. Sedgwick, *Abolition of Slavery*, 14.
8. Jane Sedgwick to Catharine Sedgwick, February 1831, CMSP III, Reel 16, Box 3, Folder 12.
9. Charles Sedgwick to Robert

Sedgwick, January 11, 1832, C. Sedgwick, *LCS*, 65.

10. C.M. Sedgwick, SNE, 418, note.

11. *Ibid.*, 420.

12. C.M. Sedgwick, introduction to C. Sedgwick, *LCS*, 356; Catharine Sedgwick to Mrs. Russell, undated, C.M. Sedgwick, *LLCMS*, 393, 396, note.

13. Catharine Sedgwick to Henry Sedgwick, Jr., January 17, 1867, CMSP III, Reel 16, Box 5, Folder 9.

14. Piper and Levinson, *Free Woman*, 157.

15. *Ibid.*, 140.

16. *Ibid.*, 157. See also Jones, *Stockbridge, Past and Present*, 243.

17. Jones, *Stockbridge, Past and Present*, 243.

18. Piper and Levinson, *Free Woman*, 202.

Bibliography

Manuscript Collections

Berkshire Historical Society
   Documents and materials related to Elizabeth Freeman.
Massachusetts Historical Society
   Catharine Maria Sedgwick Papers I, microfilm edition, Boston: Massachusetts Historical Society.
   Catharine Maria Sedgwick Papers III, microfilm edition, Boston: Massachusetts Historical Society.
   Sedgwick Family Papers, Boston: Massachusetts Historical Society.
Stockbridge Public Library, Museum & Archives, Stockbridge, MA
   Documents, newspapers, and personal papers relating to Elizabeth Freeman, Agrippa Hull, and the Sedgwick family.

Books

Benton, Josiah Henry. *Warning Out in New England*. Boston: W.B. Clarke, 1911.
Callahan, North. *Henry Knox, General Washington's General*. New York: Rinehart, 1958.
Chase, Arthur, C., and Gerard Chapman, comp. *The Ashleys: A Pioneer Berkshire Family*. Beverly, MA: The Trustees of Reservations, 1982.
Conforti, Joseph A. *Samuel Hopkins and the New Divinity Movement*. Grand Rapids: Christian University Press, 1981.
Davis, David B. *The Problem of Slavery in the Age of Revolution 1770–1823*. Ithaca: Cornell University Press, 1975.
Drew, Bernard A. *If They Close the Door on You, Go in the Window*. Great Barrington, MA: Attic Revivals Press, 2004.
Earle, Alice Morse. *Home Life in Colonial Days*. New York: Macmillan, 1898.
Ellis, Joseph J. *The Quartet: Orchestrating the Second American Revolution 1783–1789*. New York: Alfred A. Knopf, 2015.
Fenn, Elizabeth. *Pox Americana*. New York: Hill and Wang, 2001.
Field, David Dudley, and Chester Dewey. *History of Berkshire County, Massachusetts*. Vol. 1. Pittsfield, MA: S.W. Bush, 1829. Reprint, New York: Beers, 1885.
Graham, Paul F. *The Life and Times of Elizabeth Freeman*. Unpublished paper, 1981.
Greene, Lorenzo, J. *The Negro in Colonial New England: 1620–1776*. New York: Columbia University Press, 1942.
Griswold, Rufus W. *The Republican Court; or, American Society in the Days of Washington*. New York: D. Appleton, 1867. Reprint, Sagwan Press, an imprint of Creative Media Partners.

Bibliography

Hawke, David Freeman. *Everyday Life in Early America*. New York: Harper & Row, 1988.

Hopkins, Mark, et al. *Early Letters of Mark Hopkins and Others from His Brothers and Their Mother*. New York: John Day, 1929.

Jones, Electa F. *Stockbridge, Past and Present, or, Records of an Old Mission Station*. Springfield, MA: Samuel Bowles, 1854.

Kaplan, Sidney, and Emma Nogrady Kaplan. *The Black Presence in the Era of the Revolution*. Amherst: University of Massachusetts Press, 1989.

Kenslea, Timothy. *The Sedgwicks in Love*. Boston: Northeastern University Press, 2006.

Kobrin, David. *The Black Minority in Early New York*. Albany: University of the State of New York, 1975.

Larson, Edward J. *A Magnificent Catastrophe: The Tumultuous Election of 1800, America's First Presidential Campaign*. New York: Free Press, 2007.

McCullough, David. *1776*. New York: Simon & Schuster Paperbacks, 2005.

McManus, Edgar, J. *Black Bondage in the North*. Syracuse: Syracuse University Press, 1973.

Miller, Brandon Marie. *Good Women of a Well-Blessed Land: Women's Lives in Colonial America*. Minneapolis: Lerner Publications, 2003.

Moore, George H. *Notes on the History of Slavery*. New York: D. Appleton, 1866. Reprint, Bedford, MA: Applewood Books, 2008.

Nash, Gary B., and Graham Russell Gao Hodges. *Friends of Liberty: Thomas Jefferson, Tadeusz Kosciuszko, and Agrippa Hull*. New York: Basic Books, 2008

Norton, Mary Beth. *Liberty's Daughters: The Revolutionary Experience of American Women 1750–1800*. Boston: Little, Brown, 1980.

Piper, Emilie, and David Levinson. *One Minute a Free Woman: Elizabeth Freeman and the Struggle for Freedom*. Salisbury, CT: Upper Housatonic Valley National Heritage Area, 2010.

Preiss, Lillian. *Sheffield: Frontier Town*. North Adams, MA: Sheffield Bicentennial Committee, 1976.

Quarles, Benjamin. *The Negro in the American Revolution*. Chapel Hill: University of North Carolina Press, 1961.

Scott, John Anthony, ed. *The Diary of the American Revolution, 1775–1781*. New York: Washington Square Press, 1967.

Sedgwick, Catharine Maria. *Hope Leslie or, Early Times in the Massachusetts*. First published 1827. Reprint, New York: Penguin, 1998.

Sedgwick, Charles. *Letters from Charles Sedgwick to His Family and Friends*. Boston: privately printed, 1870. Reprint, Whitefish, MT: Kessinger Legacy.

Sedgwick, Henry Dwight. *The Practicability of the Abolition of Slavery: A Lecture, Delivered at the Lyceum in Stockbridge, Massachusetts, February, 1831*. New York: J. Seymour, 1831. Published postmortem by Theodore Sedgwick II. Courtesy of Stockbridge Public Library, Museum & Archives.

Sedgwick, Sarah Cabot, and Christina Sedgwick Marquand. *Stockbridge, 1739–1974*. Stockbridge, MA: Berkshire Traveler Press, 1974.

Smith, Merrill D. *Women's Roles in Eighteenth-Century America*. Santa Barbara: Greenwood Press, 2010.

Taylor, Alan. *Liberty Men and Great Proprietors: The Revolutionary Settlement on the Maine Frontier, 1760–1820*. Chapel Hill: University of North Carolina Press, 1990.

Taylor, Robert J. *Western Massachusetts in the Revolution*. Providence: Brown University Press, 1954.

Trowbridge, Francis Bacon. *The Ashley Genealogy*. New Haven: Tuttle, Morehouse & Taylor, 1896.

Volo, Dorothy Denneen, and James M. Volo. *Daily Life During the American Revolution*. Westport, CT: Greenwood Press, 2003.

Welch, Richard E., Jr. *Theodore Sedgwick, Federalist: A Political Portrait*. Middleton, CT: Wesleyan University Press, 1965.

Bibliography

Wilbur, Keith C. *Revolutionary Medicine 1700–1800.* 2nd ed. Old Saybrook, CT: Globe Pequot Press, 1997.
Wilds, Mary. *Mumbet: The Life and Times of Elizabeth Freeman.* Greensboro, NC: Avisson Press, 1999.
Wood, Gordon S. *The American Revolution: A History.* New York: Modern Library, 2003.
Zilversmit, Arthur. *The First Emancipation: The Abolition of Slavery in the North.* Chicago: University of Chicago Press, 1967.

Reference Works

Commonwealth of Massachusetts. *Massachusetts Soldiers and Sailors of the Revolutionary War,* vol. 6. Boston: Wright and Potter Printing, State Printers, 1899.
Dexter, Franklin Bowditch. *Biographical Sketches of the Graduates of Yale College: With Annals of the College History.* Vol. 3, 1763–1778. New York: Henry Holt, 1903.
"Letters and Documents Relating to Slavery in Massachusetts." In *Collections of the Massachusetts Historical Society,* 5th series, vol. 3 (1877), 373–442.
"Minutes of the Debates in the Massachusetts Convention which met in Boston in January 1788 for ratifying the Federal Constitution." In *Proceedings of the Massachusetts Historical Society* 3 (1855–1858): 296–304.
Proceedings of the Massachusetts Historical Society, 2nd series, vol. 1 (1884–85): 341–42.
"Queries Respecting the Slavery and Emancipation of Negroes in Massachusetts, Proposed by the Hon. Judge Tucker of Virginia, and Answered by the Rev. Dr. Belknap." In *Collections of the Massachusetts Historical Society,* 1st series, vol. 4 (1795): 191–211.
Washburn, Emory. "The Extinction of Slavery in Massachusetts." In *Collections of the Massachusetts Historical Society,* 4th series, vol. 4 (1858): 333–346.
Will of Pieter Hogeboom. *New York State Library History Bulletin II. Early Records of the City and County of Albany and colony of Rensselaerswyck,* vol. 4 *(Mortgages 1, 1658–1660 and Wills 1–2, 1681–1765).* Translated by Jonathon Pearson. Revised and edited by A.J.F. Van Laer. University of the State of New York, 1919.

Diaries, Journals, and Memoirs

DuBois, W.E.B. *The Autobiography of W.E.B. DuBois.* New York: International Publishers, 1968.
Sedgwick, Catharine Maria. *Life and Letters of Catharine M. Sedgwick.* Edited by Mary E. Dewey. New York: Harper & Brothers, 1871.
Sedgwick, Catharine Maria. *The Power of Her Sympathy: The Autobiography and Journal of Catharine Maria Sedgwick.* Edited and with an introduction by Mary Kelley. Boston: Massachusetts Historical Society, 1993.

Articles

Association for the Study of African American Life and History. "Eighteenth Century Slaves as Advertised by Their Masters." *Journal of Negro History* 1, no. 2 (April 1916): 163–216.
Cayton, Mary Kupiec. "Who Were the Evangelicals? Conservative and Liberal Identity in the Unitarian Controversy in Boston, 1804–1833." *Journal of Social History* 31, no. 1 (Autumn 1997): 85–107.
Cushing, John D. "The Cushing Court and the Abolition of Slavery." *American Journal of Legal History* V (1961): 118–144.

Bibliography

Karcher, Carolyn. Introduction to *Hope Leslie or, Early Times in the Massachusetts*, by Catharine Maria Sedgwick, x–xvii. New York: Penguin, 1998.

Kelley, Mary. Introduction to *The Power of Her Sympathy: The Autobiography and Journal of Catharine Maria Sedgwick*, by Catharine Maria Sedgwick, 3–41. Edited and with an introduction by Mary Kelley. Boston: Massachusetts Historical Society, 1993.

Kelley, Mary. "Vindicating the Equality of Female Intellect: Women and Authority in the Early Republic." *Prospects: An Annual Journal of American Cultural Studies* 17 (1992): 1–27.

MacEacheren, Elaine. "Emancipation of Slavery in Massachusetts: A Reexamination 1770–1790." *Journal of Negro History* 55, no. 4 (October 1970): 289–306.

Martineau, Harriet. "The Story of Mum Bett." In *Retrospect of Western Travel*, vol. 1, 245–249. London: Saunders and Otley, 1838. Courtesy of Stockbridge Public Library, Museum & Archives.

O'Brien, William. "Did the Jennison Case Outlaw Slavery in Massachusetts?" *William and Mary Quarterly* 17, no. 2 (April 1960): 219–241.

Piper, Emilie S. "The Family of Agrippa Hull." *Berkshire Genealogist* 22, no. 1 (Winter 2001): 3–6.

Sedgwick, Catharine Maria. "Letters." Introduction to *Letters of Charles Sedgwick to His Family and Friends*, by Charles Sedgwick, 5–14. Boston: privately printed, 1870. Reprint, Whitefish, MT: Kessinger Legacy.

Sedgwick, Catharine Maria. "Slavery in New England." *Bentley's Miscellany* 34 (1853): 417–24. Courtesy of Stockbridge Public Library, Museum & Archives.

Twombly, Robert C. "Black Resistance to Slavery in Massachusetts." Chap. 12 in *Insights & Parallels: Problems and Issues of American Social History*. Edited by William L. O'Neill. Minneapolis: Burgess, 1973.

Welch, Richard E., Jr. "Mumbet and Judge Sedgwick." *Boston Bar Journal* 8 (January 1964): 13–18.

Wright, Conrad. "Ministers, Churches, and the Boston Elite." In *Massachusetts and the New Nation*, edited by Conrad Wright, 118–125. Boston: Massachusetts Historical Society, 1992.

Zilversmit, Arthur. "Quok Walker, Mumbet, and the Abolition of Slavery in Massachusetts." *William and Mary Quarterly* 25, no. 4, 3rd series (October 1968): 614–624.

Zilversmit, Arthur. "Mumbet: Folklore and Fact." *Berkshire History* I, no. 1 (Spring, 1971): 2–11.

Electronic Sources

Sedgwick, Hubert Merrill. "Theodore Sedgwick." Sedgwick.org. http://www.sedgwick.org/na/library/books/sed1961/sed1961-167.html.

Sedgwick.org. "Sedgwick Genealogy North America." accessed March 8, 2018, www.sedgwick.org/na/families/robert1613/B/4/B4-sedgwick-theodore.html.

Oral Source

Hendricks, Holly. Lecture on the history of Arlington Street Church and its predecessors. Arlington Street Church, Boston, MA. Dec. 4, 2016.

Index

abolition 30, 40–47, 78, 97, 107, 139, 157–158
Abolition Society of Pennsylvania 78
Adams, Abigail 67, 72, 95
Adams, Charles 72
Adams, John 37, 90, 91, 95, 99, 100, 101, 103, 104, 105
Adams, Sam 28
Africa 9, 41, 129
African Americans 35, 41, 43, 66, 82, 90, 97, 110
Albany, New York 8, 9, 14, 15, 92, 93, 94, 96, 97, 101, 102, 106, 107, 109, 112, 116, 118, 127, 128, 132, 135, 137, 138, 157
Albany County, New York 9
Alien Acts of 1798 99
American Revolution 31, 32, 35, 46, 52, 53, 60, 70, 86, 112, 113, 129, 159, 160
Andrews, Loring 92, 93, 96, 97, 98, 105
Anti-Federalists 63; *see also* Democratic Republicans
Antigua 112
Appleton, Rev. Nathaniel 40
Article IV (of the U.S. Constitution) 77–78
Articles of Confederation 62
Ashley, Hannah ("Annetje") Hogeboom 5, 10, 11–14, 17, 18, 23, 24, 32, 39, 42, 46–48, 54, 65, 96, 109, 139
Ashley, Col. John (Elizabeth Freeman's owner) 5, 8–13, 17, 18, 20, 23, 24–26, 28, 29, 31, 32, 36, 37, 42–48, 65, 109, 110
Ashley, John, Jr. 11, 16, 33, 34, 42, 60, 65, 99
The Ashley House 12
Asylum for the Insane *see* McLean Hospital
Atlantic Ocean 108

Backus (a freed man) 57, 59
Baptista tinctoriam 148
Barbados 9
Barre, Massachusetts 45
Bassa Cove Colony 159
Battle of Bunker Hill 145
Battle of Lexington and Concord 37
Battle of Long Island 38
Battle of Saratoga 38, 39, 41
Battle of White Plains 38
Belknap family 35
Benny, Joab 66
Benny, Rose 66
Benson, Egbert 132
Berkshire County, Massachusetts 7, 20, 28, 35–37, 46, 50, 52, 55, 56, 77, 92, 106, 108, 114, 122, 145, 153
Berkshire County Court 149
Berkshire Mountains 142
Bernard, Gov. Francis 28
Bidwell, Mary Gray 115, 117, 118; *see also* Aunt Gray
Boston, Massachusetts 11, 17, 19, 27, 37, 40, 49, 57, 62, 63, 65, 67, 83, 89, 101, 111, 112, 116–119, 123, 124, 128, 130, 132, 134, 137–139, 142, 145, 147; Town Meeting 152
Bowdoin, Gov. James, II 60
Brant, Joseph 40
Bristol, Joel 114, 127
British Crown 40
Brom 33, 46, 47
Brom & Bett v. J. Ashley, Esq. 45–47
Burghardt, Jackson 131
Burr, Aaron, 74
Butler, John 40
Bryant, William Cullen 142–143

Caesar (an enslaved person) 27
Caldwell brothers 47
Calvinism 73, 145

185

Index

Cambridge, Massachusetts 37
Canaan, Connecticut 22
Canada 38
Canada Campaign 38
Canfield, John 46
Carter, Mary Jane Van Allen 157, 159
Ceaser (a freed man) 73, 74, 79
Channing, Edward 142
Channing, the Rev. William Ellery 135, 136, 142
Chenango Purchase 113
Cherry Hill Road, Stockbridge 110
Christ 26
Christianity 19
Christmas 32, 55
Civil War 158
Clap, Thomas 26
Clarke, Doctor 148–149
Claverack, New York 7, 9, 14, 22, 42, 47, 107
Claverack Landing 11
Clinton, New York 113
Coercive Acts 36, 44
Columbia County, New York 9
Committee of Seventeen 55
Concord, Massachusetts 35
Confederation Congress 51, 52, 62
Congregational Church 10, 17, 27, 30, 82, 83, 145, 146, 150, 154
Congress (U.S.) 61, 63, 64, 69, 72–77, 79, 80, 83, 84, 92, 95, 96, 100, 101, 104, 105, 108, 109, 134
Congress Water 145
Connecticut 42, 46, 115
Connecticut 29th Regiment 160
Considerations on Slavery 40
Constitution (Commonwealth of Massachusetts) *see* Massachusetts Constitution of 1780
Constitution (United States of America) 62, 63, 77, 78
Continental Army 39, 40
Continental Congress 30, 35
Continental Line 35
Cooper, James Fenimore 143
Cooper, Sam 59
Cornwall, Connecticut 20
Court of Common Pleas 20, 37, 45–47, 53, 57
Crocker (a hired man) 111

Daggett, Naphthali 26
Darby, Jane 66
Dawe, Thomas 107

Declaration of Independence 7, 43
Democratic Republicans 87, 90, 100, 108, 128; *see also* Anti-Federalists
Drean, Andrew 144, 159
Drean, Mary Ann Humphrey 110, 144, 149, 157, 159
Drean, Mary Elizabeth 144, 149, 159
Drean, Sarah 144, 145
DuBois, W.E.B. 131
Dutch Reformed Church 11, 15
Dutcher, Jane Ashley 11, 17, 20, 22, 42
Dutcher, Ruloff 20
Dwight, Abigail Wells (Aunt Dwight) 72, 90, 125, 139
Dwight, Abigail Williams Sergeant 18, 31, 57, 65, 79, 93
Dwight, Henry 39, 40, 89, 90, 136
Dwight, Joseph 19, 20

East Room 116
Edwards, the Rev. Jonathan 20, 51, 66, 74
Edwards, Timothy 51, 59
Egremont, Massachusetts 60
emancipation case *see Brom & Bett v. J. Ashley, Esq.*
Embargo Act 124
England 9, 136, 137; *see also* Great Britain
Estabrook, Benjamin 36
Estabrook, Prince 35
European Americans 40, 43, 46, 49, 50, 66, 82, 111, 146, 159

Fairman, Sally 117
Federal Street, Boston 136
Federalists 60, 64, 87, 89–91, 95, 99, 100–103, 105, 108, 132
Fellows, John 20, 29, 36–38, 41, 44
Fellows, Mary Ashley 11, 17, 42, 99
Field, the Rev. David Dudley 150, 153, 154
Field, Submit 154
Follen, Charles 158
Fort Dayton 39
Fort Edward 17
Fort Orange 8; *see also* Albany, New York
Fort William Henry 17
Fourth Congress 87
Fourth Pennsylvania Battalion 35
Framingham, Massachusetts 35
France 95, 99–103
Franklin, Connecticut 27
Frazer, Persifer 35
French and Indian War 17, 35, 36

Index

French Revolution 100
Fugitive Slave Act (first) 77–78

Gage, Gen. Thomas 37
General Sessions Court 53
George III, King of Great Britain 36
Georgia 102
German Flatts, New York 39
Gleazen, Solomon 60
God 26, 79, 91, 101, 133, 146, 150, 154
Graham, Tamor 24–25, 158
Granary Burial Ground 139
Gray, Aunt 79; *see also* Bidwell, Mary Gray
Great Barrington, Massachusetts 20, 26, 27, 29, 37, 57, 59, 131; courthouse 53; public house 59; Town Meeting 28
Greenwood v. Curtis 129–130
Great Britain 28, 29, 31, 36, 53, 95, 133

Hamlin, Perez 56, 60
Hamlin's Raid 65, 74
Hamilton, Alexander 69, 72, 87, 95, 99, 101, 102
Hamilton College 114
Hamilton Oneida Academy 114
Hampshire County, Massachusetts 20, 55, 56
Hancock, John 51
Hartford, Connecticut 14, 152, 157
Heath, General 37
Hemmings, Sally 107
Hogeboom, Pieter 5, 8, 9, 12–14, 42
Hogeboom siblings 47
Hope Leslie 144
Hopkins, Albert 148
Hopkins, Archibald 110, 113, 148
Hopkins, Electa Sergeant 18, 26, 38, 72, 110, 113, 148
Hopkins, Henry, the elder 58–60
Hopkins, Henry, the younger 148–149
Hopkins, Mark, the elder 26, 29, 38, 148
Hopkins, Mark, the younger 148–149
Hopkins, Mary Curtis 148, 150
Hopkins, the Rev. Samuel 29, 30, 41
Hopkins, Sewall 113
Housatonic Indians 10, 50, 86; *see also* Stockbridge Indians
Housatonic River 10, 11, 14, 27
Housatonic River Valley 10
House Judiciary Committee 74, 76, 77
House of Representatives (U.S.) 87, 90, 91, 99, 100, 102, 105
Hubbard, Paul 55–56

Hudson, New York 11, 107
Hudson Valley 8, 15
Hull, Agrippa 35, 38, 52, 66, 73, 74, 79, 80, 82, 85, 110, 129, 146
Humphrey, Betsey Freeman (Elizabeth Freeman's daughter) 42, 43, 54, 65, 66, 72, 80, 82, 85–87, 109, 110, 113, 114, 116, 125, 127, 131, 141, 149–151, 153, 154, 157, 159
Humphrey, Enoch, Jr. 114, 125, 128
Humphrey, Enoch, Sr. 86, 110
Humphrey, Jonah 86, 97, 110, 113, 114, 116, 125, 127, 128, 131, 159
Humphrey, La Minta Elkey 128
Humphrey, Mary 159
Humphrey, Penelope Fortune 86
Humphrey, Rebecca 159
Hutchinson, Gov. Thomas 41

immigration 8
imputed righteousness (a Congregational religious doctrine) 26
"Indians" 35, 40
Ingersoll, Mr. 66
Ironworks River 14
Irving, Washington 143

Jacob, Mr. 67
Jamaica 9
Jay Treaty 87, 90
Jefferson, Thomas 105, 107
Jennison, Mrs. 45
Jennison, Nathaniel 45, 47
Jenny Gray (a horse) 54
John (a freed man) 79
Jones, Captain 57, 59
Jones, Electa 128, 146, 159
Jones, Josiah 57, 59
Jones, William 57, 59

Katy (a freed woman) 90
King George's War 19
Kingston, New York 9, 11
Kirkland, the Rev. Samuel 113–114
Knox, Henry 69–72, 87, 101, 102, 109
Knox, Lucy 70–72, 87
Konkapot 10
Konkapot River *see* Ironworks River
Kosciusko, Taddeusz 85

Lenox, Massachusetts 37, 60, 66, 106, 134, 157, 159
Lexington, Massachusetts 35; Lexington Green 36

187

Index

Lilly (a freed woman) 125
Lincoln, Gen. Benjamin 39, 55, 56
Litchfield Law School 46
Little Bet 43; *see also* Humphrey, Betsey Freeman
Livingston, Edward 90–91
Livingston, John 117
Lizzie (an enslaved person, sister of Elizabeth Freeman) 13, 14, 18, 22, 23, 69
London, England 158
Lord's Day 17
Loyalists 44

Macon, Nathaniel 102
Magawisca 144
Main Street, Stockbridge 51; *see also* Plain Street, Stockbridge
Maine 101, 102, 109, 128
Marshall, John 99
Martineau, Harriet 158
Mason, Jeremiah 27
Massachusetts (Commonwealth of) 34, 39, 45, 52, 53, 60, 82, 97, 107, 109, 114, 128–130, 155, 160
Massachusetts Bar 129
Massachusetts Bay Colony 5, 10, 15
Massachusetts Constitution of 1778 42, 45
Massachusetts Constitution of 1780 7, 42–45, 155
Massachusetts General Court 17, 19, 40, 41, 51
Massachusetts Historical Society 150, 155
Massachusetts House of Representatives 28, 42, 45, 49, 61, 136
Massachusetts ratifying convention for U.S. Constitution 62
Massachusetts Senate 92, 136
Mayhew, Elizabeth 48, 63, 64, 79
McLean Hospital 147, 152
merchants 52
midwifery skills 25, 31, 66, 76–78, 96, 98, 108, 119, 127, 128, 135, 140, 144
militia 35, 37, 39, 61
Minot, Mrs. William 150
Mohawk Valley 8, 39, 50
Monument Mountain 110
Moses (a freed man) 96
Mullen, Zach 34, 43, 45, 46, 50, 110
Murray, William Vans 102

Negro Pond 110
"Negroes" 5, 12, 35, 37; *see also* African Americans

Netherlands 9
New England 15, 16, 21, 32, 35, 72, 133
A New England Tale 143
New Jersey 8
New Lebanon, New York 56
New York (colony) 5, 9, 15, 17
New York (state) 40, 47, 59, 60, 90, 107
New York City 8, 11, 37, 38, 51, 63, 64–68, 72, 86, 99, 105–109, 115, 116, 124–126, 134, 135, 137, 142, 145, 147, 148, 150; Port of New York 8
New York Colonization Society 159
Newburgh, New York 9
Newport, Rhode Island 30
Niagara 40, 130
Noble, David 46
Northampton, Massachusetts 82
nursing skills 25, 31, 54, 63, 69–70, 84, 91, 104, 117

Olds, Ann 27
Oneida Indians 50, 113
Otis, James, Jr. 28, 40

Paine, Thomas 41
Parker, Captain 36
Parsons, Theophilus 114
Partridge, Doctor 68
Paterson, Miss 90
Patriots 40, 41, 44, 46
patroon system 8
Patterson, Col. John 37
Penfield, Mr. 86
Pennsylvania Colonization Society 159
Peters, Thomas 109
Petersham, Massachusetts, 56
Philadelphia, Pennsylvania 56, 69, 72, 73, 76, 77, 79, 80, 89, 90, 93–95, 98, 99, 101, 102, 112, 155
Pinckney, Charles Cotesworth 99
Pinckney, Thomas 95
Pittsfield, Massachusetts 56, 81, 125
Plain Street, Stockbridge 51, 57, 59, 155; *see also* Main Street, Stockbridge
Pomeroy, Egbert 112, 155
Pomeroy, Eliza Sedgwick 41, 48, 67, 68, 72, 75, 77, 79, 80, 83, 84, 87, 89–98, 101, 106, 111–113, 115, 116, 118, 125–127, 132, 134, 136, 140–142, 147, 149, 155, 157
Pomeroy, George 111
Pomeroy, Thaddeus 92, 94, 111, 113, 115, 147, 152
Pomeroy, Theodore 157

188

Index

Potomac River 69
Poughkeepsie, New York 9
The Practicability of the Abolition of Slavery 157
Prime, James 159, 160
Prime, Wealthy Ann Drean 144, 149, 159, 160

Quakers 78
Quebec, Canada 38

The Red Lion Inn 36, 57, 59, 92
Redcoats 36
Reeve, Tapping 46
Richmond, Massachusetts 89, 90
Roxbury, Massachusetts 37, 38
"Ruffled Shirts" 52
Rush, Dr. Benjamin 41
Russell, Catharine 112, 121–123
Russell, Dr. Charles 112
Russell, Elizabeth Vassall 112

St. John River 159
Schaghticoke Indians 20
Scott, Mercy 57
Sedgwick, Betsey 82, 85
Sedgwick, Charles 8, 9, 80, 104, 105, 109, 115, 119, 123–126, 128, 130–132, 134, 136, 138, 139, 141, 142, 144, 146, 147, 149–155, 157, 158; birth and neonatal care 76–78; executor of will 149
Sedgwick, Catharine Maria 8, 9, 13, 22–28, 32, 43, 44, 49, 50, 58, 59, 65–70, 73, 74, 76, 77, 80, 82, 83, 85, 87–90, 104, 105, 107, 108, 111, 112, 115, 116, 118–121, 123–127, 130–132, 134, 135, 137–153, 155–159; birth and neonatal care 66–67; literary career 143–144
Sedgwick, Catharine the younger ("Kitty") 145, 149, 150
Sedgwick, Eliza Mason 27, 28, 31, 70
Sedgwick, Elizabeth Buckminster Dwight 142, 144
Sedgwick, Elizabeth Dana Ellery 143
Sedgwick, Henry Dwight 8, 9, 32–34, 51, 54, 63, 65, 73, 80, 81, 84, 99, 106, 115–120, 123–125, 128, 130, 132–139, 141–143, 146, 147, 152, 154, 155, 157, 158; abolition lecture *see The Practicability of the Abolition of Slavery*
Sedgwick, Henry, Jr. 159
Sedgwick, Jane Minot 142, 144, 147, 149, 152, 154, 155, 157, 158
Sedgwick, John 20, 26, 106

Sedgwick, Maria 138
Sedgwick, Pamela Dwight 7, 20, 26, 29, 33, 38–42, 44, 47–51, 54 58, 61, 62, 64, 65, 67, 68–76, 78–84, 86–101, 103, 104, 106, 109, 111–118, 120–122, 139, 146, 147, 149, 155; birth 18; death 117–118; marriage 30–31; post-partum depression 39, 66–67, 75–77
Sedgwick, Penelope Russell 112, 120–127, 130, 132, 134–139
Sedgwick, Robert 8, 62, 68, 80, 81, 91, 106, 107, 115–118, 128, 134–136, 139, 140, 143, 147, 148
Sedgwick, Susan Ridley 8, 117, 120, 124, 127, 128, 135, 138, 142, 152, 154, 155
Sedgwick, Theodore 20, 25–30, 33, 34, 36, 38, 39, 41, 42, 44–81, 83, 84, 86–108, 110–137, 139, 146, 149, 155, 160; abolition case 45–47; birth 20; death 134–136; education 20, 25–26; first marriage 27–28; *Greenwood v. Curtis* 129–130; military service 38–39, 54–56; second marriage 30–31; Speaker of the House 102–103; third marriage 120–124
Sedgwick, Theodore II 8, 48, 80, 101, 105, 106, 108, 111, 112, 115–121, 123, 124, 127, 128, 130, 132, 134, 136, 137, 141, 153–155, 158
Sedgwick, Theodore III 138
Sedgwick, William Dwight 158
Sedgwick Pie 156
Senate (U.S.) 92, 99, 100, 102
Sergeant, Doctor 148–149
Sergeant, Doctor Erastus 18, 27, 57, 66, 68
Sergeant, the Rev. John 18, 20
Sergeant, John, Jr. 18
Shays, Daniel 55, 56
Shays' Rebellion 60–62, 88, 100
Sheffield, Massachusetts 10, 11, 14, 17, 22, 26, 39, 42, 44, 50, 53, 60, 66, 109; Sheffield Green 56; Town meeting 29
Sheffield Declaration 29, 44
Sheffield Resolves *see* Sheffield Declaration
Shepard, General 56
Six Nations 40
Slavery in New England 158
smallpox 27, 38
Speaker of Massachusetts House of Representatives 63
Speaker of U.S. House of Representatives 102, 104

Index

Springfield, Massachusetts 55, 56, 134
Stamp Act 28, 40
Stockbridge, Massachusetts 20, 27, 30, 50, 51–53, 55–57, 59, 60, 63–66, 72–74, 80–84, 86, 87, 91, 92, 95–97, 99, 101, 104, 106, 107, 109, 113–116, 121, 125–129, 132, 134, 136–139, 142, 144, 147–149, 154, 157, 15; lyceum 157–158; public school 33
Stockbridge Cemetery 156, 159
Stockbridge Indians 10, 18, 19, 57; *see also* Housatonic Indians
Stowe, Harriet Beecher 8
Strong, Caleb 91
Supreme Court (Massachusetts) 53
Supreme Court (U.S.) 100
Supreme Judicial Court (Massachusetts) 47, 107, 108, 128

Taming of the Shrew 73
Thomas, General John 38
Ticonderoga 35
Todd, Dr. Eli 152, 157
Ton (an enslaved woman) 41
Townshend Act 28, 46
Training Day 32
The Trustees of Reservations 12, 19
Tucker, John 111, 119, 134
Tucker, Sarah 111, 119, 134
typhoid fever 44

Ulster County, New York 9
Uncle Tom's Cabin 8
Unitarians 135, 146, 153
United States of America 61, 66, 71, 99, 100, 158, 160

Van Allen, George Cato 144
Van Allen, Gilbert 144
Van Allen, Lydia Maria Ann Van Schaack 131, 144, 149–151, 157
Van Rensselaer, Cornelius 69
Van Rensselaer family 8
Van Schaack, Amos Josiah 131, 140, 149, 157
Van Schaack, Harry 131
Van Schaack, Lydia Maria Humphrey ("Mrs. Harry Van Schaack") 87, 131, 140, 144
Van Schaack, Mister 76

Vermont 56
veterans 48, 86
Vosburgh, Hannah Ashley 11, 17, 22
Vosburgh, Martin 20

Waldo, Doctor 89–90
Walker, Quok 45, 47, 155
war debt 75
War of 1812 124, 139, 141
Washington, Bushrod 100
Washington, George 38, 64, 69–71, 87, 90, 91, 100–102, 108, 109, 150
Washington, Martha 72, 91
Washington, D.C. 100, 104, 105, 112
Watson, Catharine 113
Watson, Eben 105–108, , 117, 131, 141, 142
Watson, Eben, Jr. 115
Watson, Frances Sedgwick 39, 48, 75–77, 84, 85, 88, 91, 92, 96–98, 105–108, 112, 113, 115, 117, 125, 127, 132, 134–138, 140–142, 147, 148
Watson, Theodore Sedgwick 108, 145
Webster, Daniel 145
West, Elizabeth Williams 31
West, Dr. Stephen 30, 59, 94, 150
West Indies 9, 97
West Stockbridge, Massachusetts 55
The Western Star 92
Whiskey Rebellion 101
Whiting, Mr. 131
widow 7, 32
Williams, Abigail Jones 18
Williams, Elisha 76
Williams, Ephraim 18, 58, 60, 92
Williams College 148
Williamstown, Massachusetts 106
Wilson, James 100
Wisconsin 50
Wolcott, Mr. 131
Woodbridge, Jahleel 59
Woodbridge, the Rev. Timothy 57
Worcester, Massachusetts 132
Worcester County, Massachusetts 56
Worcester Town Meeting 41
Wyman, Dr. Rufus 147, 152, 153

XYZ Affair 99

Yale University 10, 16, 20, 25, 26, 28, 135

www.ingramcontent.com/pod-product-compliance
Lightning Source LLC
Chambersburg PA
CBHW032046300426
44117CB00009B/1205